children of the DAY

1 & 2 Thessalonians

BETH MOORE

LifeWay Press®
Nashville, Tennessee

Published by LifeWay Press®. © 2014 Beth Moore

ISBN 978-1-4300-2860-4 • Item 005600950

Dewey Decimal Classification: 227.1
Subject Headings: BIBLE. N.T. THESSALONIANS—STUDY \ CHRISTIAN LIFE \SPIRITUAL LIFE—GROWTH

To order additional copies of this resource, write to LifeWay Church Resources Customer Service; One LifeWay Plaza; Nashville, TN 37234-0113; fax 615.251.5933; phone toll free 800.458.2772; email *customerservice@lifeway.com;* order online at *www.lifeway.com;* or visit the LifeWay Christian Store serving you.

Printed in the United States of America

Adult Ministry Publishing, LifeWay Church Resources, One LifeWay Plaza, Nashville, TN 37234-0152

Dedication

To the church in Thessaloniki:
Alive.
Awake.
And beautiful.
Every step of this journey bears sand from your shores.
May the fresh breezes of the Holy Spirit among you
stir into gales of great revival in Greece.
You were marked on the map for faith
the day a man named Paul
swept through your gates with the gospel of Jesus Christ.
Rise up from the ruins, resurrected and radiant.

You marked my heart forever,
Beth

Ἰωάννης 1:4 Μέσα του ήταν ζωή και η ζωή αυτή ήταν το φως των ανθρώπων

Contents

WEEK FIVE

Children of Light

114

WEEK SIX

Mobilized Ministry

140

WEEK SEVEN

To Love the Truth

164

WEEK EIGHT

The Lord of Peace

190

About the Author

BETH MOORE has written best-selling Bible studies on the patriarchs, Esther, Moses, Paul, Isaiah, Daniel, John, David, Jesus, and James. *Breaking Free, Praying God's Word,* and *When Godly People Do Ungodly Things* have all focused on the battle Satan is waging against Christians. *Believing God, Loving Well,* and *Living Beyond Yourself* have focused on how Christians can live triumphantly in today's world. *Stepping Up* explores worship and invites us to reach a new level of relationship and intimacy with God.

Beth and her husband, Keith, are devoted to the local church and have the privilege of attending Bayou City Fellowship in Houston, Texas, where their son-in-law Curtis Jones pastors. Beth believes that her calling is Bible literacy: guiding believers to love and live God's Word. Beth has a passion for Christ, a passion for Bible study, and a passion to see Christians living the lives Christ intended.

Beth loves the Lord, loves to laugh, and loves to be with His people. Her life is full of activity, but one commitment remains constant: counting all things but loss for the excellence of knowing Christ Jesus, the Lord (see Phil. 3:8).

About the Study

CHILDREN OF THE DAY is designed for both interactive personal study and group discussion. Here are a few suggestions for making your time with the study more meaningful.

First, to enhance your learning and application of Scripture, the study is written in an interactive format. I encourage you to complete all of the written work in your workbook. This isn't just fill-in-the-blanks. The interactive questions represent the very places where we'd look together in Scripture as we shared a cup of French roast coffee together. Please don't let the word "homework" scare you. The Holy Spirit uses your efforts as you respond to the activities in your own words.

Second, to enhance your group time together, you'll find five Principal Questions and five Personal Discussion Questions each week. The Principal Questions alert you to look for information as you study and prepare for group discussion. They are marked with a solid dot like this:

● This is a Principal Question. "Principal" means "of chief importance."

Your small group will likely discuss the Principal Questions when you meet each week. In addition to the Principal Questions, you will find Personal Discussion segments identified by a circle like this:

○ This is a Personal Discussion Question designed for personal sharing.

These learning activities help you personally apply the material by relating the events to your own life. They give your group a core of shared items to discuss. Your small group will allow time for you to share your personal discussion responses, but you will not be required to share unless you so desire.

As an aid to group discussion the Principal and Personal Discussion Questions appear on the viewer guide pages along with the page numbers of the questions in the text. For the sake of space, the questions on the viewer guide pages may be less detailed. They are intended to remind you of the questions you completed during the previous week.

Oh, how I wish I could be personally present with you each week in your personal study time and in your group time. This interactive format provides the most personal contact possible until the time we can share that cup of coffee. Then I'll look forward to listening to you as you have graciously listened to me through all these studies. I pray that you will gain as much from this journey as I have. Thank you for the privilege to serve you.

This may be our first series together and, if so, I pray with all of my heart that this in-depth study and others like it will fan a lifelong flame in your heart for God's Word. Perhaps we've studied together before and, if so, I'm thrilled to tell you that this one earned its own place in my heart. Each series from *A Woman's Heart: God's Dwelling*

Place to this one has been used by God to accomplish a distinctive and lasting work in me. The mention of each name stirs up the remembrance of that prevailing revelation.

I won't tell you in advance what God worked in my life through this journey, because the fun of it for me is to process the material along the way with you. When I penned week 1, day 1, for instance, I had no clearer idea where we were headed than you do now. When you get to difficult material, you will see that I am struggling through it too. When you're convicted, you can know that my stomach is turning upside down as well. I love the uncertainty of what's ahead as long as I'm in the security of God's hands. It's like driving a winding highway in a convertible for the very first time. I want to feel the wind in my face. If you do too, we're going to make good traveling partners.

This time God placed on my heart the idea of offering you options. Goodness knows we need a few of those amid frantic schedules and demanding roles.

You get to choose your own level of participation.

LEVEL 1: *Participate in the video sessions only.*

Through the years I've watched women drop out of weekly Bible study because they couldn't keep up with the homework. Don't think for a moment that if you can't do all of it, you're better off doing none of it. A shorter time in Scripture is far better than none at all. Watch the video sessions even if you can't get your homework assignments accomplished. You have LifeWay's blessing to copy the viewer guides for this purpose.

LEVEL 2: Participate in the video sessions *+ do the weekly homework assignments.*

Moving up to level 2 in which you meet with God on the pages of Scripture numerous times each week exponentially increases your experience. When you turn the last page, you will truly know the Letters to the Thessalonians and the important circumstances surrounding these first books of the New Testament. If you've got the stamina to do the homework (and you do!), you've got it in you to view the sessions. Keep in mind that many of the larger themes are addressed in the sessions, so try your hardest to view the coinciding ones at the end of each week of homework.

LEVEL 3: Participate in the video sessions + do the weekly homework assignments *+ handwrite the two books to the Thessalonians.*

I'm really excited about this level! For only the second time in my nearly 20 years of writing Bible studies, we've arrived at books of the Bible short enough to invite this exercise. During the first session of this series, we'll get acquainted with the circumstances that inspired the writing. Then in sessions 2 through 9, and the corresponding weeks of homework, we'll study one chapter per week. Each time we come to a new segment of the letters, I will ask you to read it then handwrite it in the back of your member book on pages designed for this exercise. If you don't choose level 3, you'll simply read the portion—without a hint of self-condemnation, I pray. This option is simply available for those who want to take the next step to retain what they're learning.

LEVEL 4: Participate in the video sessions
+ do the weekly homework assignments
+ handwrite the two books to the Thessalonians
+ *memorize the books.*

Trying to picture some of your faces almost has me tickled. But don't blame me. Remember all those women who kept asking for more? Blame them. Beloved, if you commit to all four of these levels, the Letters to the Thessalonians will live in the marrow of your bones—probably for the rest of your life. You'll find a short tutorial in the DVD bonus material that may help you if you're interested in this level.

Needless to say, we're not recommending that anyone try to memorize both books in the nine short weeks of this series. In the tutorial, I suggest a chapter a month for a total of eight months, but the best recommendation is whatever works. Since this time we're studying two short books, you might even memorize just the first. If you do, I think you'll be so hooked you'll have to go on to the second.

Because God led me to take this challenge, in the process of writing this study I've recited the eight chapters aloud more times than I can count. The exercise continues to bless me beyond what I could have imagined. Think about it! Pray about it! Then, some of you, do it!

OK, Sister, which level seems the most doable for you right now?

1 2 3 4

I'm asking you up front because I'd like to challenge you to go one level above what seems reasonably attainable. If you're willing, stretch yourself one more level! If you're pretty sure you can reach level 1, try stretching yourself into level 2 and see what happens. All you overachievers, keep in mind that higher levels and harder work won't make God love you any more than He already does. Nor will memorizing the two whole books make us superior to someone else who can barely manage a few sessions. We are secure in Christ and acceptable to God through Him.

We have nothing to lose here but much Scripture to gain if we're game for a challenge. Do only what blesses and not what burdens.

I'd like to say one last thing to you. I believe in experiences like this. I believe in Bible studies and God-centered books. I believe He can use them to change your life. A subject doesn't have to be new; it just has to speak to the predicament you're in right now.

Introduction

May I pull back the curtain about publishing here for a minute? You've heard of the little boy who was an excellent archer and always hit his target. But his mother watched as he first shot his arrow, then drew a target around where the arrow landed. Publishing is a bit like that. First you write the book. Then you write the introduction telling where the book is headed. It just works better that way. Makes it look like you knew it all along.

Well, in this case I've reversed the order. Here is a note I wrote expressing my heart on the way to Greece at the very beginning of this journey. It matches my reality just a bit. You and I are in this together, so come along and let's get this journey off the ground.

greetings to you, my friend,
in the name of our Lord Jesus Christ!

I write you with an inkjet full of joy at an altitude of 25,000 feet on Aegean Air flight 530 from my layover in Frankfurt on the way to our destination. Under the plane a solid floor of bleached white cumulus clouds reflect the sun so brilliantly that I can only hold a glance out the window for a moment without my eyes watering. My youngest daughter, Melissa, is sitting two seats to my right, reading the Scriptural text in Greek that will take on such life for us in English.

What you may not realize is that you too are on this flight with me and will not leave my thoughts on this trek for a single waking moment. For whatever reason—probably the ailing economy—the plane is sparsely populated and most of the seats around us are empty. I smile as I fill them with you in my imagination. Your eyes are a little bloodshot from your previous nine-hour flight. The hands on the world clock sped so rapidly that night lasted a total of three hours. You were then spilled out of the plane abruptly at your body's own 1:30 a.m. But let's try not to think about that.

Let's also give one another grace for the way our hair looks right now. Plane-head can be decidedly worse than bed-head simply because you have no bed. Instead, you lash around with gnashing of teeth in a seat that won't go flat. You get restless leg syndrome even in your arms and neck, and you long for a world of friendly skies in which men either have had their adenoids removed or are forced to remain awake.

Through the years, I've met enough of you face-to-face to know how different you look—all so beautiful to me—and what diverse stories you have. Along the Bible-study way, God has done what we yearned and begged for. He has enlisted us from every conceivable background to study together. We've discovered that we don't always have to see a sight the exact same way to be thankful to God that we beheld it together. Let somebody else search the world over for the handful of people who line up with them 100 percent on every point of Bible interpretation. I'll gladly choose the larger community drawn together by these unbreakable bonds: the life, death, and glorious resurrection of Jesus Christ, the holy Son of God.

Did you hear that over the loud speaker? The pilot just announced our final descent to our destination.

Thessaloniki.

Welcome!
Beth Moore

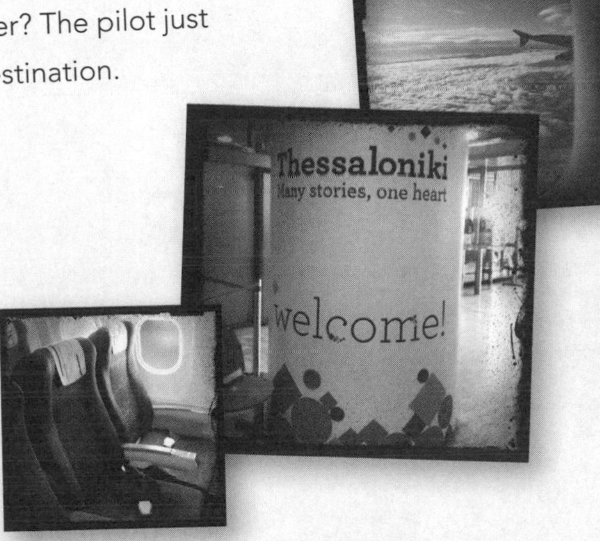

Group Session One

VIEW THE VIDEO

Introduction

In today's opening session, we'll turn to the first of two letters we're studying, and we'll give ourselves completely to the first four words. Read 1 Thessalonians 1:1 and record them here:

______________, ______________, and ______________

Luke supplies the backstory of their braiding paths in Acts 15:36–16:5. Consider Acts 15:36-41 first. Keep in mind throughout our journey that Silas in the Book of Acts is called by a more formal "Latinized" name in both 1 and 2 Thessalonians.

1. Silas (Silvanus) entered a __________ __________ __________ by a __________ __________. (Compare Acts 9:26-28.)

   In preparation for the next point, compare specific wording in Acts 15:39 to Hebrews 10:24. The Greek lexical term used in both verses is *paroxusmós* (English "paroxysm").

2. The __________ __________ that can __________ can also __________ (Prov. 27:17).

   Now let's see the third member of this party of three added to the mix. Read Acts 16:1-5.

3. The __________ __________ we __________ could become one of the __________ people in our lives.

Fast-forward to Acts 17:1. Follow it up with verses 2-10.

4. A journey __________ __________ could lead to the exact __________ of __________ God is looking to use.

As we dedicate ourselves to the task ahead, we're going to reach ahead long enough to snatch a phrase out of 1 Thessalonians 4:9: "For you yourselves have been __________ by __________." This English phrase is drawn from one rare compound word in the Greek: *theodidaktoi.*

➤ **Look inside the back cover for the map you can use throughout this study.**

Week One

The Lord's Message Rang Out

Day One

The Church of the Thessalonians

FLASH-FORWARD: Paul, Silvanus, and Timothy: To the church of the Thessalonians in God the Father and the Lord Jesus Christ. Grace to you and peace. ***1 Thessalonians 1:1***

A week ago I met the church of the Thessalonians, at least a sliver of it. Not the heaped-up relics of the one addressed by Paul centuries ago—though I did see a disturbing number of skulls in one ancient house of worship. The church I met was made up of the spiritual descendants of that small band of believers birthed with great travail in Acts 17.

You see, the lungs of Scripture did not deflate with the dying gasps of the original recipients. Paul may not have envisioned the church I saw recently, but the Holy Spirit speaking through him certainly did. Though my daughter Melissa and I had traveled to the other side of the globe to serve this gathering of Thessalonians, we were ill-prepared for the impact they'd have on us. When the doors swung open to the auditorium, women poured into the room like a waterfall coursing through the fingers of God. The clock struck seven, the lights went down, and the first slide in our opening worship showed a pair of wide-eyed Dorothys that we were a long way from Kansas.

Ο Χριστός Θεμελιο
Канара е Христос
Christ Alone Cornerstone

The spotlight of three languages washed away my nearsighted vision and sprung my heart wide open to a warm ray of divine splendor. I've ridden wings of planes to multiple foreign fields and have listened with piqued curiosity to the sounds of distinctive languages, but never so many at once. The voices bringing the words to life animated the atmosphere with an indescribable beauty. All five hundred of us in that lovely theater were singing the same praises to the same musical score, but with confessions of faith flowing from three native tongues interwoven into one victor's wreath cast like a crown at Jesus' feet. From the sense of His presence, He seemed as pleased to be enthroned among us as we were to have Him there.

Instead of creating an atmosphere of confusion, the languages fused like long lost friends who'd searched the world over to find one another. A foretaste of glory tipped our tongues—a deposit toward that day when we, "a vast multitude from every nation, tribe, people, and language, which no one [can] number," will stand "before the throne and before the Lamb" (Rev. 7:9).

The Greek over the Bulgarian and English seemed fitting. Throughout our week in Greece, the modern variety of the language surrounded us, but the words resembled the ancient tongue of the New Testament enough to stir in us a feeling of continuity. We sensed that the original plan remains underway, and a thousand years is as a day to our God. He had foreseen our gathering in 21st-century Thessaloniki through those who had first professed Christ on that same beach.

Note how Jesus referred to this continuum in John 17:20: "I pray not only for these, but also ______________________

On the eve of His passion, Jesus lifted that first band of Thessalonians before heaven in the cupped hands of His intercession. God knew the exact number of those saved in the initial gospel tide on that eastern Greek shore. He has written each name one by one in the Lamb's book of life.

The opening video session recalls how the message of Christ first came to the Thessalonians, but let's make sure we all begin our written work on the same page. Even if you participated in the session, please read Acts 17:1-4 and respond to the following.

To what location did Paul and Silas first go in Thessalonica?

● How many Sabbaths did they serve in Thessalonica—2, 3, or 6?

Carefully read Acts 17:2-3. What method did Paul use in his approach to the Thessalonians?

Compare the relative number of Jews who were persuaded in Thessalonica to the number of devout Greeks (Acts 17:4).

The original covey of believing Thessalonians was largely Gentile.

The comparison doesn't indicate that the church in Thessalonica was more or less than it might have been had the tables been turned. It simply informs us that the original covey of believing Thessalonians was largely Gentile—a statistic that will color the pages of both Bible books before us. Trying to decide which is more beautiful, Jew or Gentile, is a waste of ink. The shades are equally bold but rightfully distinct.

If you've studied the Book of James, perhaps you recall the Jewish texture of the body of believers James served. We now behold the flip side of a Christian movement still wet behind the ears. One last question from the segment:

How many leading women joined Paul and Silas? ______________

I am a woman called to serve women, so statements like "a number of the leading women" jump out at me. You may be the last person on earth looking for a spotlight, but if you're a woman who pursues God and serves people in this carnal culture, squint your eyes in the spotlight's brightness. You are "among the number of the leading women," and you count, Sister. All it takes to lead is for people to see you following Jesus.

Remember our earlier reference to Christ's prayer in John 17:20? That He prayed for those who would believe in Him 20 years later in Acts 17 is not the astonishing part. What most amazes me is that He also prayed with fervent intention for those who would believe in Him today.

Jesus also prayed for those who would believe in Him today.

I stared into the faces of those Thessalonian women, seeking to memorize each like someone drawing a mural with colored chalk. Nameless, faceless people don't set my heart ablaze to share the Scriptures. Real, warm-blooded, distinct-looking, God-seeking, problem-ridden women do.

As I write, I try to imagine you and the place you call home. I wonder whether you're right- or left-handed, whether you draw your eyebrows down when you study or raise them up. We're not colorful clay that God has rolled into a ball of gray. We are thousands of ones, each present and accounted for on the cross. When we gather in Jesus' name, we are exquisite in our distinctiveness to Him.

Name three specific characteristics that make you different from your family or friends (tastes, learning style, personality). As you do, try to appreciate your distinctiveness as a child of God instead of resisting it.

organist - church music.
tennis lover
chess player.

At the close of our first session in Thessaloniki, my friend Chris offered a Scripture-engraved invitation for women to receive Christ as Savior. Our hearts exploded as a crowd 60 people long and several people thick pressed to the platform's edge. Before my very eyes "the church of the Thessalonians in God the Father and the Lord Jesus Christ" (v. 2) multiplied. The thought was almost more than I could bear.

Would you believe that you rolled into my mind the very next moment? My thoughts did somersaults from Christ's reference to those first disciples in John 17 to those original Thessalonians fewer than 20 years later and on to those newborn Christians gathered right before my eyes. I thought of the wonder of God's Word: the marvel of Scripture etched by the breath of God on the page with every earnest reader in all of human history in mind.

In the address, printed in the first verse of 1 Thessalonians, Paul pictured the faces of those original Thessalonians: some Jews, "a great number of God-fearing Greeks, as well as a number of the leading women" (Acts 17:4). But what about the Holy Spirit pouring words through that quill of a man? Ah, now: He pictured us all.

- ○ How are you impacted by the knowledge that the Holy Spirit had you in mind as Scripture was penned?

praise God for his grace

So let's gather around the letters postmarked Thessalonica. Lean in like the throng at the altar. Don't let pride or timidity come between you and the presence of God. Press in tightly, professing Christ. You'll be in the company of others but also known intimately by name, circumstance, and condition.

You have a place here—a purpose unique and substantial, not merely some spiritual reality, floating like a fleck in the air.

This is your journey to the shore of Thessalonica, so write your personal signature (use your whole name) and a slice of your biography as you'd introduce yourself here in this sand.

Marietta Botts - trying to follow Christ to the glory of God.

If you know what your given name means, share it here. If you don't know what it means, consider doing some research and adding it.

Little Mary

How would you describe your present circumstances (in the margin)?

Blessed.

This is where we begin. Your circumstances are not coincidental in your journey. God's timing is impeccable. We have before us real words for real crises, real medical diagnoses, real afflictions, real relationships, real doubts, real concerns, and real fears.

For those willing to participate, we're adopting the discipline of writing 1 and 2 Thessalonians in the back of our workbook as we go. The brevity of the books makes it feasible. I commit to you with a grin that, if we ever study the Book of Jeremiah together, we'll forgo this discipline.

Please turn to page 214 and write 1 Thessalonians 1:1 in the Bible translation of your choice.

I'm ecstatic that we've landed together on these Thessalonian shores. Let's not brush the sand off quickly. Let's sit awhile and let the tide come in and wash our eyes with fresh vision for eight beautiful weeks.

We don't always have to see eye to eye to be glad we're side by side. Let's pat the sand beside us and welcome each other along.

Day Two

We Recalled

FLASH-FORWARD: We recall, in the presence of our God and Father, your work of faith, labor of love, and endurance of hope in our Lord Jesus Christ. *1 Thessalonians 1:3*

"We" is an amazing, empowering word. We are so much stronger than I am. We study so much harder than I would. We believe God for so much more than I could. This tiny, two-letter word is the driving force the Holy Spirit used to push the pen across the scroll and roll it all the way to Thessalonica. Let's flip some pages of contrast so we can fully embrace the word "we" during the next eight weeks. Glance at the very first verse of the following letters and note each of the names of the writers/senders.

WE

pronoun, plural in construction. 1: I and the rest of a group that includes me: you and I: you and I and another or others: I and another or others not including you—used as pronoun of the first person plural.[1]

Abbreviate below using the first letter of each name. I'll get you started by answering the first two:

Romans *P*
1 Corinthians *P & S*
2 Corinthians
Galatians
Ephesians
Philippians
Colossians
1 Timothy
2 Timothy
Titus
Philemon

Star the epistles attributed to one person. Circle the ones attributed to two people. How many of the letters are attributed to three people?

- Now look at the first verse of each letter to the Thessalonians. Who were the writers/senders?

An intriguing anomaly appears in the introduction to Galatians. Additional senders are listed but unnamed (see 1:2). Who are they?

First Thessalonians and Galatians are widely accepted as Paul's earliest letters. One characteristic, however, sets 1 and 2 Thessalonians apart from Galatians—Paul retains the plural touch almost throughout. He makes several detours into "I," but "we" predominates. In Galatians, Paul refers to the brothers with him but thereafter addresses the recipients personally.

So, what's the big deal? We are, that's what! Over and over in 1 and 2 Thessalonians, Silvanus and Timothy are tied up together with Paul by the leathery ribbon of that little inclusive word. Don't lose sight of that for a moment.

As you copy 1 Thessalonians 1:2-3 in the back of your workbook, write the word "we" in capital letters.

Notice that the word appears first in reference to prayer and recollection. "We always thank God … We recall." We can have no intimacy with God without our individual pursuit of Him, but we also possess an intrinsic need to be part of a team. Our fellow God-chasers challenge our stale prayer lives and loosen the latch on our locked-down thanks. When we're tempted to claim that God has not been good, their very presence begs to differ. They are mercies of God stuffed in crude human form imprinting decent memories on a difficult time.

Ecclesiastes 4:10 says to "pity the one who falls without another to lift him up." It's easy to fall alone but, Girl, it's hard to get back up.

- ○ Think back on a harsh season of your life and record a good memory —perhaps even a funny one—you carried out of it because of the company of others.

Now look carefully at 1 Thessalonians 1:3 and document three specific things Paul, Silvanus, and Timothy recalled in the presence of God.

Work of Faith

Labor of Love

Steadfastness of Hope

In the Greek, Paul gave it a drumbeat. Say these phrases in the margin several times aloud, and you'll hear the rhythm for yourself.

When I'm in a particularly negative mood, three thoughts come to me with those phrases: *Faith can be work. Love can be labor. Hope can get long.*

We hear much hairsplitting over faith and works, but does anybody else occasionally think that faith *is* the work? Believing what we cannot see can sometimes be the highest high in the human experience, but at other times it's like inhaling fire. And just try to convince me that love is never a labor.

The NIV translates the phrase as "your labor prompted by love," but multiple translations cast love as part of the labor. One scholar translates the Greek as "toil of love."[2] That's even better. Sometimes loving comes easy. Other times, it nearly kills us. Does your heart feel like a nail to a hammer right now?

Without using anyone's name, how has loving been difficult in your experience?

disappointment when someone does not live up to expectations

The toil of love climbs to its Everest peak when it is unreturned. Since God has promised to make us like Jesus and because rejection was Christ's relentless companion, we likely won't run low on opportunities for unrequited love.

Trying to love a spouse who doesn't love you is torturous. Trying to love a stepchild who wishes you didn't exist is demoralizing. Trying to love a friend through a baffling fiasco is exhausting. Human affection can't bear up. We need a Romans 5:5 kind of work.

What does Romans 5:5 describe?

We have access to the Holy Spirit welling up in us like a spring. Tapping into Him requires deliberation and cooperation so God can love through us. Like me, you've probably asked Him to love through you, then fizzled out within the hour. Here's the catch: we cannot love when we perceive ourselves as unloved. We cannot offer to others what we don't possess.

Jude 21 says, "Keep yourselves in the love of God, expecting the mercy of our Lord Jesus Christ." That means practicing the mindset of being profusely loved by God. We must invite our souls to plunge into His love like a dolphin romping in the sea. Actively engaging in His unending, extravagant, no-strings-attached affection for you is not narcissism. It's necessity. It can mean our survival when we're faced with loving the loveless.

Glance back at today's "Flash-Forward" and fill in the blanks: your work of ______________, labor of ______________, and endurance of ______________.

Anything God emphasizes, the Devil seeks to exterminate.

Consider also 1 Corinthians 13:13, penned by the same apostle, Paul: "Now these three remain: faith, hope, and love." Those comprise the three abiding priorities and enduring virtues of time and eternity. These facts alone earn each of them a distinct spot on the Enemy's target. Anything God emphasizes, the Devil seeks to exterminate.

Let's examine a short checklist:

Are you in a season where faith feels like hard work? Yes/No

Is loving laborious? Yes/No

Is hope circling the drain as you keep longing and waiting? Yes/No

If you answered yes to all three questions, you're under a triple threat. Satan can't snatch faith, hope, and love from you. You have to hand them over.

When spiritual people are down to the dregs, we often grip tighter to what we have left: our legalism. We fill up the loss with the law. Don't go there. Keep believing, hoping, and loving. All else is just existing.

I recently headed 90 miles west with my oldest daughter's family to spend the afternoon with a large group of friends. The folklore began 25 years ago when six families from the same church decided to spend Thanksgiving together and, to my knowledge, a core group hasn't missed a year yet. Each time we get to go, we pick up right where we left off and laugh like there's no tomorrow. We have to live like that, you know. Tomorrow isn't promised.

What is your current, ongoing reminder that life here is temporal?

I'll tell you one of mine. The ringleader of that gregarious pack of thankful friends is battling brain cancer. Overlooking the severity of his illness would be easier without a six-inch scar on one side of his shaved head. He also happens to be hilarious enough to play the cancer card to get his way: "Hey, Beth, can you cut me a bigger piece of that cake? You know I have cancer."

At times we've talked about his illness with unembarrassed sadness, but we kept it short that recent day. Too much glad chaos was occurring around us. We sat in rocking chairs on the front porch, surrounded by our adult children and watching a flurry of their little ones play tag and chase balls.

As I looked from face to familiar face, my thoughts drew loops around the past and present. A small encyclopedia of life experience tucked in my heart told me that some of those young couples had troubles and doubts. I knew most of their stories, and few escaped the scarring licks of a blazing fire growing up. My daughters didn't escape them, and in no small part, due to their parents. But this wasn't a time for guilt or blame. It was a time for beholding. There before me were the young and the old, the living and the dying, the surviving and the thriving. What a slice of life, I thought, and I whispered under my breath, *Such is common to man.*

Such is common to man.

But I was wrong. It hit me later that such is common to *redeemed* man. Had we been a large group of unbelievers still bound by legitimate friendship, yes, we would have comprised a fair composite of human life, but our condition in its midst would have been worlds apart.

Faith is a game changer. Know that to your bones.

That night alone in my house, a spring of tears erupted and rushed over me like a levee had broken. A sense of sadness over my friend's illness collided with inexpressible elation and gratitude. Grief and grace rose up within me like two giant wrestlers stopping long enough to shake hands. Pain and beauty tangled in a big knot called hope.

I'm not talking about the theoretical kind of hope. I'm talking about the kind that gets you to your next anniversary when it would be easier to give up now. The kind that gets you through your long season of loneliness so you don't jump into a disastrous marriage on lame legs. The kind that counts on a future whether or not the treatment takes. The kind that gets you through a move when you really want to stay. The kind that grants you something gained after a terrible loss. The kind that … well, you fill in the blank.

We are not just like everybody else breathing the world's toxic air. Our flight has been hijacked by hope.

Day Three

But Also in Power

FLASH-FORWARD: **For our gospel did not come to you in word only, but also in power, in the Holy Spirit, and with much assurance.** ***1 Thessalonians 1:5***

Have you ever been in an environment where the Holy Spirit fell with such unexplainable force that He felt almost palpable? Maybe you've experienced such exhilaration in Him that your skin felt too tight for your soul. Perhaps you've known the merest whisper of the exposure the prophet Isaiah expressed when, after a full-blown revelation of God, he exclaimed, "Woe is me! for I am undone" (Isa. 6:5, KJV). These moments may be rare for us, but their roots are deeply embedded in Scripture. They can be startlingly real.

Many of us are new to environments of faith, but some of us who have been around awhile could describe extraordinary times when the sense of God's invading presence was almost our undoing. It unraveled our pretense and left our cover in tatters. As we stood before a God we thought we knew, we suddenly realized that, whoever this God is, He is greater than we thought.

Mark 4 records such a moment in the lives of Christ's disciples when He wrecked their limited notions of Him on a storm-pitched boat. Hear their minds scurrying for divine redefinition in their exclamation.

Read Mark 4:41. What question did they ask in their great fear?

Who is this? Even the wind & the waves obey him!

Trying to wrap human language around holy exposure is like trying to cover a big-screen TV with six inches of Christmas paper. At times, the presence of the resurrected Christ penetrates the usual walls, and the One whom "no one has seen or can see" (1 Tim. 6:16) is, for a moment, felt. The conditions can dramatically differ. No location or mood assures it. No singular messenger always carries it. No worship center, event, group, singer, or evangelist always has it. No formula suffices to get it. Nothing common about it. God's presence can be sought, but it can't be planned, because it's not of man.

What on earth is it? Whatever it is, Paul, Silvanus, and Timothy experienced it right there in Thessalonica. Let's pray voraciously to encounter it on our journey along with them.

Please handwrite 1 Thessalonians 1:4-5 in the back of this book.

Do you ever wish someone would risk a little subjectivity to suggest a few things that could fall within the norm for someone in Christ? I do! Call it an overdeveloped sense of you-too-me-too, but I'm thinking many believers long to know what others experience in this gorgeous and mysterious relationship we have with an invisible God. If you're not one of them, please pole-vault over the next few paragraphs. But if you want to stick around on some slippery ground to catch another view, anchor tight to your Bible and we'll try not to break any bones. We can't build doctrines out of personal experiences, but we can share what we've encountered firsthand if it doesn't contradict Scripture and helps another believer.

Sometimes I feel very little in my praying, Scripture reading, or fellowshipping with believers. I'm consciously blessed, but nothing measurably reactive is going on inside. You too? That's normal.

Sometimes physical exhaustion can make us feel spiritually dull, but that passes with some rest. During dry times we trust the God-promised values of prayer, worship, and Scripture reading, knowing they each bear fruit even when we can't see it. God is ever-present no matter how sluggish our souls feel toward Him. However, if I remain unmoved by God and the revelation of His Word for days, I start squirming. I begin asking God to pinpoint what's amiss.

In my week-to-week experience, the Holy Spirit dwelling within me will to some degree bear witness (Rom. 8:16; Heb. 10:15) to what I am hearing, reading in Scripture, experiencing, or praying. My inner response may not be big, but it's discernible: maybe an assent of some kind—a nod in my heart, so to speak—toward something God seems to be saying, doing, or revealing. Maybe I'll feel conviction or alarm or a spurt of joy or a splash of grace. Maybe my heart will leap over the exact news I wanted from His Word or will sink temporarily because I'll realize He's saying no to something I crave.

○ Do you understand from experience what I'm talking about? If so, how would you describe the way the Holy Spirit within you bears witness?

The H.S. is my comforter.

Even questions can be discernible responses to His Spirit. I often say aloud in my Bible reading, "What does this mean?" Or, "Lord, how does that work?" One of my favorite ways the Spirit identifies His work within me is by teaching me something new or shedding fresh truth on a familiar concept. Whether in my private study or in a crowded congregation, six of my favorite words are *I have never seen that before!* That's sheer delight to this curious soul. The genius of God glimpsed by the human eye is slap-the-table stunning to me.

Sometimes we experience God in a corporate setting beyond what a transcription of the event could convey. Last Sunday, God moved my son-in-law Curtis with such unusual potency in his preaching that the Holy Spirit was almost electrifying. The room shifted from pin-drop silence to eruptions of applause and praise. When a message comes like that, we might feel the compulsion to cry even when nothing about the subject matter is heart-wrenching.

Have you ever wept during a sermon not out of sadness but out of the pure sense of God's presence and power? If so, when?

That some of these moments are fixed in our memories tells us how far from routine they are. In all the dissimilarities, one common denominator prevails: God evidences Himself in such a way that many people remarkably respond. A bona fide demonstration of the Spirit occurs. It can't be staged. It can't be explained away. It is God alone. Acts records a time when the intercessions of a group of Christ followers for Peter and John elicited a larger dose of divine response than they sought.

What happened in Acts 4:29-31?

What if you were praying for God's power and boldness to fall on somebody else and He also fell upon you? What if divine authority to proclaim God's Word gushed on thousands at a gathering instead of a few?

Our fear and timidity might say, "But that was then. This is now." Is He not the same God? Has He not said that He'd pour out His Spirit on His sons and daughters (Joel 2:28)? Must we hunker down in the cramped limits of the status quo? Or will we welcome Him to do the exceptional when He pleases, to wreck our small notions and loosen our tongues with "Who then is this who does such things?"

Will we welcome Him to do the exceptional when He pleases?

● Back to 1 Thessalonians 1:5. How did the apostle Paul say their gospel came to the Thessalonians? In the margin list every description.

In a 1 Thessalonians 1:5 moment, let's shift our thoughts from the listener to the communicator. You could share a message that you've given on numerous occasions (perhaps your own story of Christ's saving grace), but this time, His Spirit falls on you so strongly that you can feel the power of the words yourself. It surges straight through your soul like mercury in a hot thermometer, more electrifying to you than the very first time. Wouldn't we know it wasn't us?

Any human messenger paying attention knows that a demonstration of God through the gospel of Christ is not her own doing. If she's confused, God will make the reality of it hair-raisingly clear in the future. He is committed to protecting His glory even from a dearly loved, powerfully used child.

Reflecting on this beautiful phenomenon, you've got to love how Jesus described the way of the Holy Spirit. What does John 3:8 say about the Spirit?

Now slide your pen over to the margin and take down as many parallels as possible between the properties of wind and how the Holy Spirit might work. Think beyond the most obvious.

Carefully compare Acts 2:1-4. The "divided tongues ... of fire" (ESV) captivate so much attention that the role of the wind blows right out of view.

List every effect of the wind in this four-verse segment.

Wild, isn't it? But in some respects, we bump the side of the same marvel in a 1 Thessalonians 1:5 moment. Something God is doing around us begins happening to us. We're not talking about something mystical. We're talking about something spiritual. Let's not get so paranoid about the mystical that we shut ourselves off from the biblical. God can do what He wants. That's the long and short of it. He never works contrary to His Word, but He gives Himself plenty of room in the white-water river flowing from Genesis to Revelation.

Circle the last two words of 1 Thessalonians 1:5. "Because our gospel came to you not only in word, but also in power and in the Holy Spirit and with full conviction" (ESV).

I long to be keenly conscious of God's power and presence.

Some commentators think the term refers to how the message was received, but most in my library aligned it with the preceding phrases in the same verse—"in word ... in power ... in the Holy Spirit"—describing how the message was given. The surrounding verses demonstrate that the listeners had a titanic response as well. Both sides got wet with the work of the Spirit when the wave of the gospel flooded Thessalonica.

I want to get wet in that wave too. Don't you? I long to be keenly conscious of God's power and presence when He makes Himself known. I want to sense the life in God's oxygenated Word when someone preaches it. If we're the messengers, we don't want the truth to bypass our hearts on the sign-sparse highway of our tongues. We want to be shaken with the full conviction of it.

Nothing is more exhausting than trying to get people worked up over something that doesn't work on us. Authentic anointing: there is no substitute.

"He is your praise and He is your God, who has done for you these great and awesome works your eyes have seen."

DEUTERONOMY 10:21

Day Four

Reading Lives and Letters

FLASH-FORWARD: And you became imitators of us and of the Lord when, in spite of severe persecution, you welcomed the message with joy from the Holy Spirit. ***1 Thessalonians 1:6***

My siblings and I often converse in the Technicolor idioms our grandmother spray-painted all over us. Because she lived with us, we had a running editorial on every subject that arose within our walls from morning till midnight. If I could bottle her sayings like vanilla extract, you'd want to pour a teaspoon of Minnie Ola flavoring into every conversational mix just to keep it frothy.

You know the type of person who keeps to herself and is so little trouble you hardly know she's there? Well, that was not my grandmother. The woman was a handful. For 11 months a year she lived with us in Arkansas, but she spent 30 days each summer in Florida with her eldest son's family. Sometimes we'd talk to her long-distance on the wall phone and insist that we missed her, because we did. Who could help it? She always responded with the same exact words: "Well, I bet it's a happy miss."

In between Bible studies, I miss the intensity of this process, and it's not a happy miss. With no hiatus, however, I'd have no life from which to write.

Scripture isn't meant to stay thumbtacked to a delicate page. God made it hardy for tossing around and testing. We're all called to "be doers of the word and not [students] only" (Jas. 1:22). As much as I miss the process, every time I get ready to launch a new journey, I take a deep breath and think, "Well, here we go again. Let the madness begin." My desk looks like a counter at a second-hand bookstore, and I have the bedside table of an insomniac.

Please don't leave me here alone. The more you handwrite your Scriptures, the more you'll enter in, so write 1 Thessalonians 1:6-7 in the back of the book.

Joy in hardship is weird. "Weird," according to *Merriam-Webster's Collegiate Dictionary,* means "of strange or extraordinary character."[3] People who retain delight while walking through demoralizing circumstances are not normal. They are either delusional, detached, or, in the case of the new Thessalonian believers, engulfed by the Holy Spirit. My pastor, Curtis Jones, rolled out a definition of "joy" that skidded all over the tarmac of my mind: "Joy is happiness without the moodiness."[4] Does Curtis's definition resonate with you?

What do you think my pastor's statement means?

not irrational, unpredictable, fluctuating

If we want our "happiness" to outlast a caffeine buzz, we're probably referring to joy. One glorious day we'll hear Jesus say, "Come and share your master's happiness!" (Matt. 25:21, NIV) but I could use considerably less moodiness on the way. Couldn't you? We need something with a little shelf life to it—something the buzzards aren't circling over by noon. We need a sustainable quality that shows who we really are and to whom we belong. This side of heaven, happiness doesn't qualify. Biblical joy does.

First Thessalonians 1:6 wipes from the face of God all the ire and angst we paint onto Him. The Thessalonians possessed "joy from the Holy Spirit."

○ Do you embrace or struggle with the fact that our God is filled with joy? Why? Respond in the margin.

We think of joy as a by-product but, in John 15:11, Christ described it more like the point: "I have spoken these things to you so that My joy may be in you and your joy may be complete." Absorb the wonder. The very joy of Christ Jesus can fill our souls right here in these flawed, afflicted bodies. His is a completing joy—a glad satisfaction that says, "He is all I was created for."

● According to 1 Thessalonians 1:6-7, the Thessalonian believers "became" what two things?

1) imitators of us & of the Lord

2) a model

Those two "became's" make a great pair, but the parts they play are beautifully distinct. Can you think of a tie between an "imitator" and an "example" (NIV, "model")?

imitator follows an example & v.v.

The Greek for "imitators" is *mimētēs.*[5] See our word "mime" in it? *Mimētēs* is often translated positively in the New Testament for people intentionally patterning their lives after another.

Who exactly did the Thessalonians imitate? P, S & T God and the Lord

Paul hung the safety net securely under the precarious prospect of following any mortal man. What did he say about following him in 1 Corinthians 11:1?

remembering him & holding on to his teachings.

Paul, Silvanus, and Timothy wrote to the Thessalonians long before the New Testament canon was complete. Those early converts had to study lives until they could study letters. Centuries have passed since the conclusion of the New Testament, but many people still resist God's Word because they are repelled by some people pushing it.

Fair or not, people tend to judge the quality of what's being handed to them by the hand. Imitators of Christ are still crucial to spreading the gospel.

What kind of people does Hebrews 6:11-12 exhort us to imitate?

People experience the activated promises of God through much faith and perseverance. It's never been easy. When life feels like a steep climb on sharp rocks with bare feet and no rope, we can squint up toward those who have gone before. They help us remember that this is the way of earth-etched faith.

If we decide not to opt out in fear or cave to constant self-comfort, others following below us may see how we imitate lives of great faith. They may muster the strength to reach a little higher. Now that's a legacy worth leaving.

Grab hold of the second term to describe the Thessalonians. Fill in the blank according to 1 Thessalonians 1:7. "You became an ____________ to all the believers in Macedonia and Achaia."

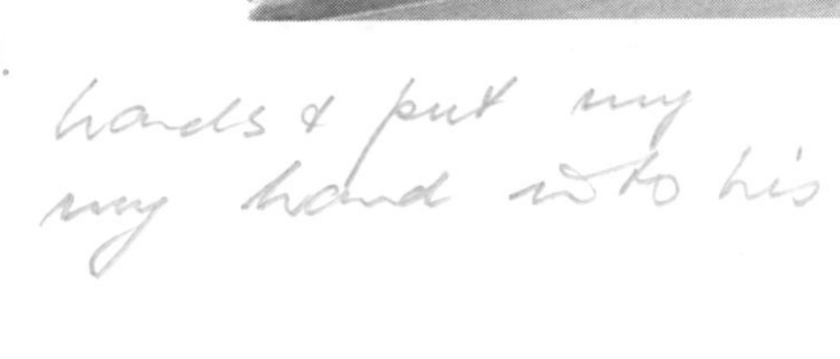

The Greek word for "example" is *túpos*, an ancient word meaning "to strike." The source of our word "type," it depicts "the mark of a blow."[6] Not long ago, I surprised Melissa with an antique Underwood typewriter. Every old typewriter is granddaddy to your laptop and touch screen, so embrace the ancestry. A typewriter like this one pecked a perfect example of *túpos* on the page with every bang of a metal letter through an ink ribbon.

One of the most fascinating occurrences of the word appears in John 20:25. What did Thomas claim? Please copy it word for word.

Now circle each appearance of the word "mark." Both are forms of the word *túpos*. To be an "example" is to have a visible mark left on you by an identifiable, original source. The Thessalonians were obviously "marked" by Jesus enough to give observers a glimpse of Him, but here's the astonishing counterpart: rewind a couple of decades to a dark afternoon when the Thessalonians unknowingly left their mark on Jesus.

My mark was left on Him that day too, and so was yours, with every pounding of a nail. We have indelibly marked one another.

We might dig up some significance in the order of the two words "imitators" and "example." To become an example before we've begun to imitate the ways of faith is hazardous. A film celebrity or sports star, for instance, might have an authentic, saving encounter with Jesus Christ. But suppose he gets thrown hastily into the Christian limelight and placed on multiple platforms as an example before he's learned an iota about how to imitate the life of Christ.

In the margin note several repercussions of such exposure.

Many of us get out there too soon with our volume exceeding our character.

God alone knows the perfect moment for an imperfect person to emerge as an example of Christlikeness. Humanly speaking, many of us get out there too soon with the result that our volume exceeds our character. This was painfully true of me. But the other hazard is shrinking back because we never know if we've attained enough integrity to sustain long-term exposure. If we'll walk in His shadow instead of showing off, we'll still be a long shot from perfect, but God will get His glory.

Note an interesting twist in the two terms in 1 Thessalonians 1:6-7. The word "imitators" is plural. The word "example" is singular. Isn't that fascinating? We are each meant to imitate the steadfast walk of faith, but maybe only together do we become a reliable example. No one but Jesus can carry that much responsibility indefinitely.

Recently I pulled out an old Betty Crocker cookbook that I got for high school graduation, searching for a recipe I'd scribbled on an index card. It flipped open to a sauce-splattered page I hadn't seen in decades. There in my 18-year-old cursive I discovered a recipe for squash pickles.

Squash Pickles

8 cups sliced sweet pickles - not too thin
2 cups sliced white onion
1 tb. salt
½ cup diced green pepper
1 cup cider vinegar
1¾ cup sugar
½ tp celery seed
½ tp. mustard

Jewell Rountree
June 9, 1976

What on earth was I thinking? I cannot recall ever dreaming of canning a squash pickle. But I've dreamed of being a woman like my Aunt Jewell. She was the wife of Minnie Ola's eldest son in Florida, the one Minnie Ola spent a month with every year. Aunt Jewell had some things that an 18-year-old already knew to want. I was just confused about fitting them into a jar.

My Aunt Jewell went to Jesus having loved one man for more than 50 years, raised fine, adventurous kids, and served God with a strength that didn't boast in itself. I couldn't have cared less about imitating Aunt Jewell's squash pickles. It's so clear to me all these years later: she was the recipe I wanted.

This could be the perfect wrap-up to today's lesson: describe somebody's recipe you want and why.

Day Five

Hear It

FLASH-FORWARD: For the Lord's message rang out from you, not only in Macedonia and Achaia, but in every place that your faith in God has gone out. Therefore, we don't need to say anything. ***1 Thessalonians 1:8***

Are we officially warmed up yet? In the in-depth Bible study groove? I'm hoping for a yes because today's Scripture segment carries extravagant significance we don't want to miss.

Go ahead and write 1 Thessalonians 1:8-10 in the back of the book.

After doing so, please look up the precise wording of verse 8 in either the NASB, KJV, or the ESV. According to one of those three versions, exactly what sounded out or sounded forth from them?

the Lord's message

You'd be hard-pressed to find a phrase in the entire Old Testament that carries more weight than the "word of the Lord." In 2 Timothy 3:16, the apostle Paul testifies that "all Scripture is inspired by God." Within the inspired Scriptures are declarations and dictations given by God that seem to peal from the heavens with a lightening-crack of clarity through the loudest possible megaphone: "Behold, the word of the LORD came to him" (Gen. 15:4, ESV).

In virtually every formal translation, you could track down the phrase "the word of the LORD came to" significantly more than 200 times in the Old Testament.[7] Sometimes the direct recipient of a "word of the LORD" was a priest or king, but the phrase was used far more often when God chose to speak through one of His prophets. Take Jeremiah—a prophet whose book offers the phrase a stunning 48 times in the ESV.

The exact placement of the first appearance of "the word of the LORD" is profoundly telling. You'd find it in Genesis 15:1, where it serves as the deliberately sky-heightened preamble to one of the most pivotal points in the history of God's people. The Lord comes to Abram in a vision. Through an elaborate ceremony of sacrifices, a smoking fire pot, and a flaming torch, God cuts a covenant with Abram and his descendants and discloses the perimeters of the promised land. His word is His bond; the blood is His path.

After these events, the word of the LORD came to Abram in a vision:
"Do not be afraid, Abram. I am your shield; your reward will be very great."
GENESIS 15:1

The following verses offer a broad-spectrum view of the power of the phrase. What does each say about the "word of the LORD"?

Psalm 18:30

Psalm 33:6

Ezekiel 37:4—Let's get specific on this one. What were the dry bones told to do?

Peruse the context. What happened as a result in verse 7?

God speaks and slings stars into orbit without lifting a finger. God speaks and the scattered bones of the dead clack and rattle back together. That's the power of the word of the Lord and precisely our point in 1 Thessalonians 1:8. Let's read it again with appreciation.

- What sounded forth from the Thessalonians after their conversion? Write it again with the volume turned up.

The time was right. Before "In the beginning" was etched on a scroll, the moment we're studying was already scheduled. Additionally, Amos prophesied a crucial precursor to the New Testament era in Amos 8:11-12.

What did Amos say about the word of the Lord?

The prophecy was fulfilled with four hundred years of divine silence. Who but God would think to break the haunting, hollow quiet with the cry of a baby in the "fullness of time" (Gal. 4:4, ESV)? Then "the Word became flesh and took up residence among us" (John 1:14). The reference to Jesus as the Word was explicitly intentional after the intolerable silence.

For centuries people searched high and low for the fresh speech of God. Then came *the* Word.

Circle that definite article.

Christ came as *the* perfect and *the* complete earthbound communication of God to man—the very embodiment of "Love divine, all loves excelling."[8]

After Jesus Christ completed His earthly mission, offering His sinless life on the cross and overcoming the grave, He ascended into the heavens and took His seat at the right hand of God. As promised, He then sent the Holy Spirit to infuse His disciples to spread the saving message of the gospel throughout the world. And suddenly, the phraseology "the word of the Lord" popped back onto the page with impressive frequency through the Book of Acts (see Acts 8:25; 13:44,48; 15:35,36; 19:10, ESV).

So why is that a big deal to us? Because the word of the Lord heralded by the early New Testament church was no less prophetic or divinely intentional than all its two hundred-plus preceding Old Testament occasions. Whatever you do, don't take that lightly. Our gospel was not an afterthought but the driving culmination of all divine declaration.

According to 1 Thessalonians 1:8, exactly what did the "word of the Lord" do?

rang out

The Greek term *exēcheō*—translated "rang out" in the HCSB and "sounded forth" in the ESV—is derived from the Greek *ēchos* and makes its one-time-only appearance in the New Testament right here.[9] In Paul's day, the word might be used to describe a clap of thunder or the blast of a trumpet. The word emphasized reverberation like that of an echo. The term could also describe a rumor running rampant.[10]

This inspired letter is believed to be Paul's first.

Keep in mind how early the visit to the Thessalonians came in the New Testament era and how this inspired letter is believed to be Paul's first. Tremendous divine intention is in play here. Why was Thessalonica so strategic? You'll remember it best if you see it for yourself.

Turn to the inside back cover and study your map. On that page, jot down a few descriptions of the city's placement.

Long quotations from commentaries can get tedious, but to understand the importance of the message ringing out specifically from Thessalonica, this one earns a careful read.

Circle each place name in the following paragraph. Then glance at them all on the map inside the back cover.

> The influence of the capital city of Thessalonica over the province of Macedonia was enormous ... It was a powerful metropolis with easy access to the interior and the northern frontier by means of good roads, and it lay not far from Asia and other Roman provinces by way of the sea. The Via Egnatia would take a person up to Byzantium

or east to the region of Illyricum and from there on to Rome across the Adriatic. The Thessalonians looked outward. These were not a rustic people who were occupied only with local concerns but a city of great influence in all spheres, not only the political and economic but also the religious. Therefore it comes as no surprise to hear that when the Thessalonians turned from their idols to the true and living God, they themselves became the ones who brought the gospel to Macedonia, Achaia, and everywhere (v. 8).[11]

Note the four-word sentence right in the middle of the excerpt and complete this sentence accordingly:

"The Thessalonians ______________ ______________."

Their faith had "gone forth everywhere."

Tie those four words to your memory. They'll pop up again in our next session.

Only one accreditation could have rivaled the word of the Lord ringing out through the Thessalonians. Amazingly, they'd earned it as well: their faith had "gone forth everywhere," so that Paul, Silvanus, and Timothy "need not say anything" (v. 8, ESV).

The Thessalonians received the messengers, then became the messengers. In the words of John Stott, we could "call it holy gossip ... the excited transmission from mouth to mouth."[12] The gospel is the treasure that we're never surer we've received than when we keep trying to give it away.

The Spirit bears witness in our churches by turning us inside out. The Thessalonians teemed with life-bearing evidence of their newborn faith.

Fill in the remainder of verse 9: "for they themselves report what kind of reception we had from you: how you turned ______________ ______________ to serve the living and true God."

○ Describe a situation in which you witnessed or participated in "the excited transmission" of the gospel.

According to Dr. Gene L. Green, "Atheists were a very rare breed during this era. Religion was part of the warp and woof of society."[13] As your perception of the Thessalonians takes shape, keep in mind that these were not "godless" people. They had more gods than they knew what to do with. They just didn't know the one true God and His Son, Jesus Christ.

Zeus was proclaimed as the highest god. Aphrodite, the "patroness of the prostitutes," was their female superstar (the soil of that ancient city has turned up all sorts of clay figurines bearing her image). Add other false gods like Heracles, Nike, and Apollo—whose symbols were minted into coins in Thessalonica—and you've got yourself one religious city.[14]

We've all had false gods. We've all given place to people and things that only God can wear and bear. We also tend to keep our gods a good bit numerous so that we don't have to steer all our worship in one direction.

We crave freedom to navigate and negotiate, but many of us arrive at a shocking revelation: spreading the love around to a host of worldly gods just adds link after link to a strangling chain of bondage. Idolatry is a python of misfit parts, squeezing the life out of us.

Fill in these two blanks:

"How you turned __to__ God __from__ idols" (v. 9).

Every turning *to* automatically involves an inherent turning *from*. That's the nature of a turn. With our deliberate turn to God comes a deliberate turning away from our old life and our previous attempts to remedy the restlessness of our souls (2 Tim. 2:19).

As you glance into your past to your own turn to God, what was the hardest part of the old you that you had to leave behind?

selfishness, self-importance

Has the turn thus far been worth the trouble? Be candid in your response and explain it briefly.

to experience & accept God's grace gives peace beyond understanding.

In Romans 8:18 Paul wrote words we can each confidently claim: "For I consider that the sufferings of this present time are not worth comparing with the glory that is going to be revealed to us." Nothing we've left behind us can compare to what we have ahead. That, Sister, is a promise.

Dry bones? "Hear the word of the LORD!" (Ezek. 37:4).

Group Session Two

REVIEW THE WEEK

Use these questions to guide your discussion of last week's homework.

● Principal Questions

DAY 1: Over how many Sabbaths did they serve in Thessalonica? (p. 16)
DAY 2: Who wrote each letter to the Thessalonians? (p. 19)
DAY 3: How, according to Paul, did the gospel come to the Thessalonians? (p. 25)
DAY 4: The Thessalonian believers "became" what two things (1 Thess. 1:6-7)? (p. 28)
DAY 5: What sounded forth from the Thessalonians after their conversion? (p. 32)

○ Personal Discussion Questions

DAY 1: How are you impacted by the knowledge that the Holy Spirit had you in mind as Scripture was penned? (p. 18)
DAY 2: What good memory do you have from a harsh season of your life? (p. 20)
DAY 3: How would you describe the Holy Spirit within you bearing witness? (p. 24)
DAY 4: Do you embrace or struggle with the fact that our God is filled with joy? (p. 28)
DAY 5: Describe a situation in which you witnessed or participated in "the excited transmission" of the gospel. (p. 34)

VIEW THE VIDEO

Introduction

Today we return to 1 Thessalonians 1:1 and do not forget the added significance: It is highly probable that we are reading the __________ __________ of __________ from the __________ of the apostle Paul.

From the opening verses of this five-chapter letter, we can draw the following applications:

1. Three groups are in operation at all times in a thriving body of believers: __________, __________, and __________.
   - __________: The __________
   - __________: The __________
   - __________: The __________

"In Acts and the letters bearing Paul's name about '________ ________, often coupled with a score of assorted titles, are associated with the Apostle.'"[1]

2. ________ get the privilege of telling ________ that ________ are ________ by God and ________ (1 Thess. 1:4).

3. Often we hope ________ is at ________, but sometimes we ________ to ________ it (1 Thess. 1:5).

4. In a world of ________ and ________, we better be ready to ________ ________. "You know what kind of men we ________ to be among you for your sake" (1 Thess. 1:5, ESV).

5. A geographical lesson from Thessalonica: Each circle of believers faces outward so that THEY ________ ________ ________ and we ________ ________ ________.

6. Until ________ ________ back, we ________ ________ back (1 Thess. 1:10).

1. D. Michael Martin, *1, 2 Thessalonians,* The New American Commentary, vol. 33 (Nashville, TN: Broadman & Holman Publishers, 2001), 48.

Week Two

Entrusted with the Gospel

Day One

On the Contrary

FLASH-FORWARD: On the contrary, after we had previously suffered, and we were treated outrageously in Philippi, as you know, we were emboldened by our God to speak the gospel of God to you in spite of great opposition. ***1 Thessalonians 2:2***

I'd never been afraid of flying. I count it an occupational grace from God since I'm on a plane enough to go platinum with United Airlines. All those miles represent scads more than distance. They detail countless delays and cancellations and late nights spent watching conveyor belts go round and round till stopping short one suitcase. Several years ago, however, I came down with a sudden case of selective aviophobia. I'm not afraid of flying in general; I'm scared of flying with my grandchildren.

Amanda's entire young family and I were on a small plane bound for a conference in North Carolina when the pilot informed us that the hydraulics had gone out. We were turning around, he explained, and would be emergency-landing in a large airport half an hour away. It was hands down the longest 30 minutes of my life.

Shifting my eyes back and forth between two darling, plump-faced children and their young parents and playing out in my mind all that could happen with that tank of gas when we touched down was so traumatizing that acid is churning in my stomach at the memory. We adults did our best to tease and occupy the children and, all the while, I studied the dimples in their hands and the thick lashes around their big, blue eyes. When we got close enough to see the runway, the lights of the emergency vehicles were flashing on the pavement. Landing on the palm of God's hand, we got out of that silver tube unscratched, the emergency personnel staring bug-eyed like they'd watched the curtain rise on a freak show. Profuse praise to God finally overtook me but, until then, I made a beeline with dry heaves straight to the ladies' room.

My aviophobia began with a case of once bitten, twice shy. The condition is perfectly understandable. Who on earth does something a second time with boldness when they were nearly broken in two the first time? Well, Paul, that's who.

Please read 1 Thessalonians 2:1-4 and write it in the back of your workbook.

In our opening session, we looked at Paul's visit to Thessalonica with his co-laborers. We briefly mentioned where they'd been previously and what had happened. Today we'll lock the spotlight on those events. Please read Acts 16:16-24.

- What happened to Paul and Silas (called Silvanus in Thessalonians) after they were dragged into the marketplace before the authorities (vv. 22-24)?

Falsely accused of advocating unlawful customs
garments torn off, beaten w. rods.
Jailed.

Imagine yourself and a close associate in place of Paul and Silas. You've both been pounded with "many blows" by rods. Not reeds. Rods. Maybe we've heard biblical accounts of beatings so often, we've ceased to squirm. We're talking about repeated impacts on our backs with only a thin layer of muscle to shield our ribs and spine. When we flippantly say, "I'd rather take a beating," we don't mean it. A beating hurts.

Then, instead of taking something for the pain and rolling up in the fetal position, imagine you and your friend locked up in a cell with your feet bound by chains. This is what Paul and Silvanus had just endured when they entered the gates of Thessalonica. They were scarred, bruised, and overly qualified for post–traumatic stress disorder.

Now read 1 Thessalonians 2:2 again. Yep, that's Paul and his crew. Instead of once bitten, twice shy; they were once beaten, twice bold. In the next verse, you can taste the iron in their blood that kept getting them up and back out there: this was real to them. The gospel of God had the incomparable power to change lives, destinies, and destinations. They didn't just think it; they knew it. They were living it and willing to die for it and, to them, nothing in the visible realm was remotely as tangible.

Instead of once bitten, twice shy; they were once beaten, twice bold.

Fill in the following contrasting columns concerning Paul and his fellow travelers according to 1 Thessalonians 2:3-4.

They were not driven by ...	They were driven by ...

Now complete verse 4: "God, who ____________________."

The verb translated "tests" (NIV/ESV) or "examines" (HCSB/NASB) is present and continuous, conveying that these are not pop tests designed by a teacher to catch his students unprepared. God is ever testing hearts. His love for us is also present and continuous, so none of this divine cardiology is detached from His own heart.

We say, "Trust God," yet we agonize privately over whether He can be trusted. The Bible repeatedly suggests, however, that God tests us to see whether or not *we* can be trusted.

Maybe His point of view is something like this: "Child, you can trust Me; I cannot do you wrong. The question is can I trust you? I have work to accomplish on this planet during your time here. I have riches of the Spirit to be stewarded. I'm testing your heart, and my desire is to find it trustworthy."

Let the words of Romans 8:27 drench you with wonder. Write them in the margin. While He searches hearts, what is the Holy Spirit doing?

God's fingertips strung our DNA. He is not naïve about us. He knows in advance what He'll find when searching the hearts of flawed human beings.

In Romans 8:26, you see that the same God who searches our hearts also "intercedes for us" according to the will of God. Aren't we infinitely more willing to show our hearts to Someone whose love doesn't budge no matter what He finds and whose reaction is divine intercession? Perfection is obviously not required for passing the ongoing testing referenced in 1 Thessalonians 2:4 or Paul, Silvanus, and Timothy wouldn't have been approved.

○ What are a few things you think He's searching out and testing our hearts to find?

God's testing of our hearts is to our benefit even when we dread what He'll find. Our freedom comes with the head-on collision between the truth of Christ and God's truth about us. There beauty meets ugly, and authenticity is born, yowling like an injured cat freed from a mousetrap.

The NIV throws a word into 1 Thessalonians 2:1 that strikes a nerve: "You know, brothers, that our visit to you was not a failure."[1]

Circle that last word. Don't you hate it? When did you last feel it?

Satan loves to fuel our feelings of failure. Just when we finally muster the courage to act or take a stand for the gospel, he prompts us to believe we blew it. Our feelings of failure can start an ongoing cycle of inadequacy: if we feel like failures, we'll act like failures and, if we let that condemnation go unchecked, we'll make our next decision out of the same perceived defeat. And the wheels on the bus go round and round.

Reflect on those first four verses of 1 Thessalonians 2 again. Ask yourself: *Did we do the will of God as best we perceived it? Were we authentic before God and man?*

The visit of Paul and Silas to Thessalonica turned into public mayhem, and they were forced to flee from town in the dark of night. Yet Paul had the perspective to say, "You know that our visit to you was not a failure." It produced fruit. Not fun, but fruit. Give it time. See what God does with it. And if He doesn't appear to have done something with *it,* did He do something with *you?* Christ's economy completely redefines failure.

This lesson is about imitating Paul and his crew and getting back out there after we get beat up. Few of us actually get physically beaten up for serving Christ. But each of us have been "treated outrageously," and the prospect of putting ourselves at risk again can be terrifying.

A wonder can occur: our God can embolden us.

We can't let Satan shut us in or he wins that battle. He's trying to make wound-lickers out of warriors. When God opens the door again, let's stand back up, brush ourselves off, and step through it.

In that wild place of getting back up, a wonder can occur: our God can embolden us. If you belong to Christ, something is in you that God wants to show you. He knows it's there because He's already searched for it, found it, and prayed His own will over it. No one is more floored than we are over what we, in the Spirit, are capable of doing. Dr. G. K. Beale adds the following:

> If we have boldness before God in what we do for him, it is a small thing to be brave toward mere humans in carrying on God's work. It was this kind of confidence before God that was the foundation upon which Martin Luther refused to deny his understanding of the gospel before his antagonistic inquisitors: "Here I stand, I cannot do otherwise."[2]

Philippians 4:13 insists that we can do all things through Christ who strengthens us. It's all the more stunning when we cannot do otherwise. So, have you been once bitten? Then, child of God, go out twice bold.

**Please note that enduring boldly for Christ does not mean allowing someone to abuse you. If you are being beaten, I implore you to get help immediately and refuse to rationalize an abuser's actions. Paul and Silas didn't sit quietly after their beating even though they'd been persecuted for the cause of Christ. They called out the wrongdoing and voiced the violation of their rights. Look for yourself in Acts 16:37. The Bible's idea of submission is for the sake of order, and those in positions of authority are charged by God to protect the people entrusted to them. An abusive authority figure is flagrantly outside the will of God and should and must be courageously reported. Otherwise, it is highly unlikely that you will be the last victim. Call the National Domestic Violence hotline at 1-800-799-7233.*

Day Two

Dear to Us

FLASH-FORWARD: **We cared so much for you that we were pleased to share with you not only the gospel of God but also our own lives, because you had become dear to us.** ***1 Thessalonians 2:8***

I keep wondering where 1 and 2 Thessalonians have been all my life. These two books encase themes so broad, you have to stretch just to pull them off the shelves. They burn with the prophetic, pound the flesh with personal holiness, and drip with the delicate honey of deep family affection. I'm in love.

Read 1 Thessalonians 2:5-8 and write these four verses in the back.

See what I'm talking about? Let's land first on the concept of Christians exploiting people, because that—in a nutshell—is what Paul, Silvanus, and Timothy are addressing in verses 4-5.

List every area of exploitation they'd tried to avoid.

Using people. It's the default mechanism of our sinful nature. If we're not fighting it, we're doing it. And the key to how well we're doing it is how well we're hiding it. "For we never used flattering speech." Flattery seeks favor by wearing a mask that mirrors the other person in the best possible light. It's a bet played on their narcissism from the hand of our own. To flatter is to fatten up an ego at the expense of the soul.

Just so we're not confused, what is the difference between flattering people and complimenting them?

Many lopsided believers are earnestly convinced that withholding every shred of affirmation is the safest way to protect people from pride. They reason that the risk of fueling a person's pride is too great and, ultimately, they'd have to take responsibility for the person's downfall (Prov. 16:18). Other reasons for withholding affirmation are far less noble—such as meanness, manipulation, pride, and desire for power. Meanwhile, the grapes of fruitful lives dry up into raisins for want of godly encouragement.

On the other side of the coin are Paul, Silas, and Timothy. I'm not sure we could get more complimentary toward people than these three men toward the Thessalonians. Yet they never flattered them. To affirm or compliment someone is not flattery unless it's insincere, self-serving, or excessive. To misunderstand the concept would be a crying shame.

"For we never … had greedy motives—God is our witness" (1 Thess. 2:5). Yes, He is and He'd have to be, because avarice and the exploitation of people can be woefully hard to prove. God alone has 20/20 vision into the heart of man's motives (Prov. 16:2).

Because money is inevitably involved in helping the poor, enslaved, and oppressed, asking for it on their behalf is an invitation to scamming and top-skimming. We want to believe that people fraudulently asking for money can't just cry on cue, but then we'd be naïve, wouldn't we? Paul's instructions in 1 Timothy 5:17-18 could also be distorted and abused.

How do you think Paul's instruction could be abused?

We don't want to get cynical and quit giving. We certainly don't want to get caught withholding a hard-worker's wages. Thank God He is witness to right motives and wrong, able in due time to vindicate where honor is due and to expose where exploitation runs mad.

"We didn't seek glory from people."

"We didn't seek glory from people, either from you or from others" (v. 6). The fight over glory is the cosmic struggle. In the terminology of *The Lord of the Rings,* glory is "the precious." Satan clamored for it before time began. Never mind that he knows he can't have it.

The heart of man has been a nest for narcissism since the day Adam and Eve decided to be in it for themselves. We may not be bigger glory-hogs than our great-grandparents, but inarguably we have more opportunities. Every social network can be a stage on which we bow for applause. We often even strut our humility for approbation. Without God's grace, where would we be?

The tender words of 1 Thessalonians 2:8 have swamped my heart and washed up on the banks of my keyboard. I love it in the ESV: "So, being affectionately desirous of you, we were ready to share with you not only the gospel of God but also our own selves, because you had become very dear to us."

- According to Paul, what are two gifts that believers might share with those to whom they minister?

With your patience, I'd like to tell you a story that very much involves you. Twenty years ago I got a call from an employee of a Christian publishing house. The caller said he'd heard about our midweek women's Bible study, and he wondered if I'd hear him out on a vision God had placed on his heart. He described what he called video-driven Bible study with multiple themes and teachers and its potential to increase obedience to Christ's commission to "go therefore and make disciples of all nations" (Matt. 28:19, ESV).

"I can't picture just standing at a lectern, teaching to a camera," I confessed.

"You wouldn't be teaching to a camera," he replied. "You'd have a class."

"Right there with me?"

"Absolutely. The class would be part of the video," he clarified.

"Like in a school room?"

"No. I was thinking more in terms of a warm, more welcoming set."

Several months later, we rolled tape. It was the scariest thing I had ever done and, for the most part, it still is. I was glad to survive 11 whopping sessions and was deeply indebted to the class of women who persevered through the grueling process. We finished the project and that was that. Nothing was said about another one. *A Woman's Heart* hit the shelves some months later, and Keith and I both cried when we first held the workbook in our hands. Then we all got on with life.

A few months later, I got the first letter from a woman who'd finished it. Since I'd told her about my life in the video series, she wanted to tell me a little bit about hers. Then other letters came. As the women shared what had made them think or laugh or cry, I'd think and laugh and cry. Soon I ran into women here and there who'd taken the course, and we'd hug each other purple.

I ran into women who'd taken the course, and we'd hug each other purple.

Amanda and Melissa were in middle school and we had a boy in elementary school the day Lee Sizemore called from that publisher. Over the 14 Bible studies that followed, my girls played innumerable ball games, started dating, got their driver's licenses, battled mean girls and acne, went to proms, had wrecks, graduated from high school, went to college, got married, and entered the full-time work world. Then one went for her master's degree and the other had my first grandbaby. Then one got a seminary degree and the other, my second grandbaby. All the while, Keith and I rode that roller coaster called marriage from our 14th wedding anniversary to our 34th, while our hair nearly blew off at the roots.

Between the second Bible study series and the third, the boy we'd had in our home for seven years went back to his birth mother, Keith's cousin. The situation was messy and complicated. The time arrived to roll tape on the third series and I conveyed my dread to Dale McCleskey, my editor and friend of many years. "I've talked about the boy so much that I don't know what to do now. I can't explain the whole thing. It's so complex even to us and we're raw. I wish I'd never told them anything."

Dale's response was something along the lines of "You don't really wish that, Beth. You invited these women into a very personal place. If you want to leave it that way, you'll have to tell them sooner or later. Otherwise, you'll need to figure out a whole new approach."

So I told them. And I cried. And they cried. And I knew from that point on that any warm and loving story I told about my family could be followed up by a messy, ugly one, so I'd better keep it real. Engagements could get broken. Marriages could fall apart. Siblings could fall out. Not every fight is followed by a kiss-and-make-up moment.

Though my heart's been broken, it has not grown cold

I don't have it in me to do the last 20 years over again, but if I did, I'd do many things differently ... but not this. I stuck my heart out there and, though it's been broken, it has not grown cold. I feel a semblance of Paul's words because I was pleased to share with you not only the gospel of God but also my own life, because you had become dear to me.

I don't know how all of this hits you. I wish we could talk about it face to face. This I do know: we're all called by Christ to serve people. We each get to decide how vulnerable we're going to be in the process.

Some believers rarely cross that line of familiarity. They still serve faithfully and effectively. Paul didn't impose a rule on the Thessalonians or on any of us. He simply shared his own approach.

- ○ Does 1 Thessalonians 2:8 stir up a story of your own? Write it out. You'll be so glad you did. Consider sharing it with your group.

I don't want to mislead you into thinking I've made my life an open book for the last 20 years—think of it more like a cracked book. I've shared many things, but a long shot from everything. Some things are too personal or hurtful to people. Other things could embarrass my loved ones.

Oversharing is foolish and costly. A line crossed publicly is impossible to erase. Ministering is messy, but is it any wonder why? The gospel gets splashed on our lives, and our lives backwash on the gospel.

There, in the sand and the saltwater, the miracle of ministry takes place.

Day Three
A Theology of Walking

FLASH-FORWARD: We encouraged, comforted, and implored each one of you to walk worthy of God, who calls you into His own kingdom and glory.
1 Thessalonians 2:12

I asked for a baby elephant to ride to school.

On the cusp of my sixth birthday, I asked my godmother for a baby elephant to ride to elementary school. I'd been picturing it for some time. In my mind's eye, it was draped with the most ornate multicolored saddle and topped with a headdress of copious beads and large pink plumes. My mid-June birthday would give me two months to train it before school started. And we'd just moved from the outskirts of town to a house only a few blocks from the school. Imagine the impressive arrival, especially for those behind me.

Lo these many years later, I have yet to climb atop an elephant, but I have a pair of size 7 soles that have carried me to places both delightful and terrible, soles callous with miles but still tender to a sharp pebble. Today's Scripture segment has a key word tucked into it that will occupy us for our entire lesson.

Please write 1 Thessalonians 2:9-12 in the back of your book.

Our next session together spotlights Paul's maternal and paternal approach in 1 Thessalonians 2:7-12, but first we'll lock down on a word that might have slipped past us. It's a word you'll find in today's Flash-Forward as well as in this quick glimpse ahead to 1 Thessalonians 4:1—"Finally then, brothers, we ask and encourage you in the Lord Jesus, that as you have received from us how you must walk and please God—as you are doing—do so even more."

- What action verb is used in 1 Thessalonians 2:12 and 4:1 to describe how we journey with God?

walk

The NIV translates the lexical Greek *peripatéō* in both places as "live" rather than "walk," but you can feel the traction in the feet of this definition: "To tread or walk about, generally to walk."[3] Why all this attention to an everyday action? In the Bible, walking is often not just an activity, but a theology.

I hope to prove that to you today, but the process will take a fair amount of page-flipping. Are you game for it? Let's start with the first and arguably the most important mention of the word "walk" in the entire Bible.

Look up Genesis 3:8 and record the context.

the Lord God was walking in the Garden of Eden, searching for A + E.

Look up each of the following and record who is walking and where.

Leviticus 26:12

Deuteronomy 23:14

Now go back to the first book of the Bible, look up the following verses, and record who did the walking and, this time, how.

Genesis 5:22,24

Genesis 6:9

Genesis 48:15

Walking "before" God isn't about who is in front. Why do you think the Bible uses the term "walk"?

Hold that thought tightly and glance again at 1 Thessalonians 2:12. Does the charge to "walk worthy of God" raise the hair on the back of your neck like it does mine? I've struggled with persistent feelings of unworthiness all my adult life. When life is rough, I feel unworthy because I'm invariably not handling it perfectly. When life is terrific, I feel unworthy because I know I don't deserve it. It's a maddening form of spiritual neurosis.

Do you happen to share my neurosis? If so, how does it play out in you? Respond in the margin.

Our titanic consolation is that, whatever it takes to "walk and please God," the young church in Thessalonica was doing it, though they were flawed and imperfect believers too. Glance ahead at 1 Thessalonians 4:1 again.

What words indicate the Thessalonians were somehow getting it right?

The Thessalonians did it and we can too.

Those beautiful words "as you are doing" are a gloriously refreshing sight, aren't they? Phrases like those keep us from throwing up our hands and saying, "Forget it! Nobody can do this!" The Thessalonians did it and we can too. We're about to get a panoramic, Word-wide glimpse into how.

Let's restate our premise to make sure we're on the same page. At times in Scripture, forms of the word "walk" mean nothing more than how individuals move physically from one spot to another, but at other times "walking" is a theology of sorts. We flipped no further than the Book of Genesis to stumble across the concept.

Fill in the blanks: Genesis 5:22—Enoch walked with God.

I'm afraid we sometimes get sidetracked into a negative theology, thinking that if we could just stop sinning, then we would be what God wants us to be. But biblical holiness is a positive rather than negative term. In spiritual terms, to walk well is to walk with God. To walk worthy of Him is to put feet to the conviction than no one is worthier than He.

You and I can't walk worthy of God when we're walking alone, no matter how much sin we're dodging. The theology of walking happens in His presence. To know God and not walk with Him is to do exactly what our original parents did in Genesis 3:10. Hide.

That you and I are working through this lesson to fellowship with God is a fair indication that our hiding—however long—was unsuccessful, praise His merciful name. In Philippians 3:9, Paul speaks of being "found in Him." To be found in Him is to have been sought by Him. Jesus carries a torch through a black forest for us. He who said "seek, and you will find" (Matt. 7:7, ESV) created us in His own image. "He who searches the hearts" (Rom. 8:27) knows their shadows and seeks our fellowship.

Pay careful attention, then, to how you walk—not as unwise people but as wise.
EPHESIANS 5:15

Savor something beautiful with me. Do you remember that the first mention of anyone walking in Scripture was God Himself? He didn't walk the garden of Eden to stretch His legs; He wanted to be near the man and the woman He'd created. So if this theology of walking unfolds as early as Genesis, how far does it reach in Scripture? Turn all the way to Revelation 2:1 and find out. Connect the interpretational dots with Revelation 1:20.

With Revelation 2:1 and 1:20 side by side, where does Christ Jesus currently "walk"? walks among the 7 golden lampstands - churches.

○ How does the knowledge that Christ walks among the churches encourage you?

The Bible unfolds with an image of God walking among His people and draws to a close with Jesus, His risen Son, doing the same. Between those corresponding divine footprints, hundreds of times and in multiple ways, He bids man "come walk with Me." To walk "before" Him, as so many verses word the concept, is to live continually God-aware. It means knowing that God is as close as His unwavering gaze, as present and pertinent as the air around us, and His Spirit is as surely within us as the blood surging through our veins.

To walk before God is to travel down the highway with your spiritual sunroof wide open. Even when you're looking straight ahead, hands on the wheel, you know those rays are bathing you in warmth and that wind is cleansing the air. If the clouds are thick and heavy overhead, you know what's above them. You relish hearing from God, talking to God, and also dwelling in contented, secure silence before God, confident that He never budges.

That "secure silence" part is crucial. If misinterpreted, silence can become a one-grave cemetery for intimacy with God. We all have seasons when we don't feel like God is near. They are temporary if we don't break fellowship and walk off in a huff. Day in, day out, we take Him at His Word.

Come walk with Me. Even with a limp. That's what Jacob did (Gen. 32:31). Even in the fire. That's what Shadrach, Meshach, and Abednego did (Dan. 3:25). Even when we feel like all hope is gone and no one came through. That's what the two on the road to Emmaus did (Luke 24:15).

Come walk with Me, whatever shape you're in, no matter how wounded or bruised. Just bring Me your whole heart—even in ten thousand shards—and let's walk the rest of this thing out together (2 Chron. 6:14). "This is the way; walk in it" (Isa. 30:21). He will never lead you into the path of a freight train, but He'll meet you in the carnage should you choose that route. He will never veer you from your destiny but, should another path seduce you, He can turn a long, ugly road back home. When you find yourself unwelcome where you thought you'd been sent, He'll help you move on. If you walk life out with Him day to day and season to season, even what seems like the most futile detour will end up taking you to a spot where a piece of your puzzle hides.

"I walk along slowly all my years because of the bitterness of my soul."
ISAIAH 38:15

Maybe all of this theology sounds OK on paper, but you feel a little like Hezekiah in Isaiah 38:15. Bitterness makes a soul so heavy that our feet drag like lead anchors, snagging on every stone, daring us to get too far from that place we need desperately to leave behind. Bitterness stoops our shoulders, makes the ground our only vision, and ages us far beyond our years.

Bitterness has gone on long enough. Let's let Him pick up the pace and walk us on out. As a friend of mine says, God can do in two weeks what we turn into years. There's some brightness out there, Child of the Light. Let's get to it.

Today is somebody's day for a fresh resolve. Would you draw this lesson to a close by writing Psalm 116:9 in the margin?

Just as Scripture testified that Enoch and Noah walked with God, may huddled angels whisper behind your back when the chronicles of history are complete, "See that woman right there? She walked with God."

For you delivered me from death, even my feet from stumbling, to walk before God in the light of life.
PSALM 56:13

Day Four

The Solidarity of Suffering

FLASH-FORWARD: For you, brothers, became imitators of God's churches in Christ Jesus that are in Judea, since you have also suffered the same things from people of your own country, just as they did from the Jews. ***1 Thessalonians 2:14***

Do you ever use a figure of speech that has never made a whit of sense to you? I'm tempted to say that we are about to open a can of worms; however, I've never once actually opened a can of worms nor seen someone do it. The saying has been around since the early 1950s when fisherman baited their hooks with live worms that were sold to them in (you guessed it) cans—like creamed corn but with considerably shorter shelf life.

Flip the lid off the can and write 1 Thessalonians 2:13-16 in the back.

● Focus on 1 Thessalonians 2:14. How had the Thessalonians become "imitators of God's churches in Christ Jesus that are in Judea"?

Suffered the same things.

Solidarity. That's the main point of the verse. Certain sufferings, as personal as they may feel, are common to many believers.

○ Share about a time when you experienced some form of persecution because of your belief in Jesus.

Paul made sure the young church knew that their afflictions mirrored the ones experienced in the very birthplace of the gospel. Though immensely challenging, these difficulties were nothing new under the Son. In both Jerusalem and Thessalonica, believers had been harassed by their compatriots.

Keep in mind that the phrase "people of your own country" refers to fellow citizens in their respective homelands. In Judea, those were Jews, but, in Thessalonica, they could have been Jew or Gentile and were probably some of each.

Those referenced by Paul in verses 15-16 were definitely Jewish, however, and there the can flips open. What he wrote was factual, but what deranged people have rationalized with similar texts through the centuries is a long shot from what Paul would've approved.

Have you ever personally witnessed an incident of anti-Semitism? If so, what was it?

Have you heard Scripture used in a way that would denigrate Jewish people? If so, how do you respond?

Paul suffered acutely at the hands of some of his countrymen.

The words of Romans 9:3 came from a pen dripping with tormented affection: "For I could almost wish to be cursed and cut off from the Messiah for the benefit of my brothers, my own flesh and blood." At the hands of some of Paul's countrymen, he had suffered acutely and, worse in his estimation, been silenced. The affliction he'd endured through them wouldn't have felt like simple persecution; it would have burned like betrayal. That's what you call a wrong wielded by your own people.

Scriptures assigning blame and wrath are like razorblades in the waving hands of those who slice them away from the rest of the canon. The Bible you are currently using may be on your computer but, if you have a bound version of the Scriptures, pick it up for a moment. Feel the weight of it. Flip through the feather-thin pages. Glance at some of the titles of the 66 books sailing past your gaze. That's a lot of Bible between those covers, isn't it?

In the study of Scripture, words have to stay in sentences, sentences have to stay in paragraphs, paragraphs have to stay in chapters, and chapters have to stay in books. This is one reason why we spend our lives studying Scripture. Entire people groups can come under horrific attack from those who misappropriate a portion of sacred text. Take a look at this exerpt:

> However we interpret the last two sentences of verse 16, they are extremely solemn words. Yet anti-Semitism cannot find any possible justification in them. No Christian can read the long history of anti-Judaism in the church without feeling profoundly ashamed. The worst example among the Fathers was Chrysostom, who in AD 386–88 in Antioch preached eight virulent sermons against the Jews. He likened them to animals, and made wild accusations against them, ranging from gluttony, drunkenness and immorality to infanticide and even cannibalism ... More embarrassing still is Luther's intemperate treatise *On the Jew and Their Lies* (1543). It is true that his health was declining, not long before his death, and that he was disillusioned over his earlier hopes for the conversion of the Jews. Yet these things do not exonerate him for his

diatribe against them, or for his call to set fire to their synagogues, destroy their homes, confiscate their Talmudic books and silence their Rabbis.[4]

The great works of the giants of the Christian faith endure, but they remind us that we, of equal fallibility, may be right about many things, but that doesn't make us right about everything. Scripture is dangerous in the itchy palms of the prejudiced.

What an observer could call a blind spot, a possessor could claim as divine insight. To walk on the balance beam of 1 Thessalonians 2:15-16 without falling, keep in mind that the Christians persecuted by the Jews in Judea were Jews as well. Paul himself was Jewish, as were scads of the people he served alongside.

Compare Matthew 23:29-39 and 1 Thessalonians 2:14-16. Make a list of every similar theme threaded between Christ's words and Paul's.

Matthew 23:29-39 themes	1 Thessalonians 2:14-16 themes

After making your list, glance back at Matthew 23:37. Why had Jesus not gathered Jerusalem's "children together, as a hen gathers her chicks under her wings"?

What fate had now befallen them according to Matthew 23:38?

Their house is left desolate.

In all likelihood, the wrath of God referenced in 1 Thessalonians 2:16 wrapped around the same idea. By this wrath that had "overtaken them at last," Paul may have had in mind a very recent event (see Acts 18:2) or an end-time event so certain that the wheels were already set in motion. Mind you, no earthly fate for Jerusalem would have been worse to them than their "house" being left to them "desolate." It was the sum of their defeat and the golden trophy to their foe. The coming destruction of their holy city and Herod's temple just around the corner in A.D. 70 would be for them the ultimate earth-tethered loss.

We know that God is just, so what was Christ's basis for saying that "all the righteous blood shed on the earth will be charged" to the generation of scribes and Pharisees standing in front of Him in Matthew 23? God in His great sovereignty chose exactly that time, place, and people in all of human history to drive a cross into the ground like a holy stake and to crack open earth like an egg to the clash of heaven and hell.

Every charge of God against humanity for all of time—past, present, and future—was issued that very day on that very soil and to that very generation. The one depicted us all. By the time the soldiers pounded the final nail through flesh and lifted that cross from the ground, it bore infinitely more than an accused man's beaten body. It bore the sins of the world. Like a crimson fountain, blood from the ultimate battle shot straight into the skies and fell to the earth in a mighty flood, its tide ever rolling to redemption's appointed finish.

Jesus' body bore the sins of the world.

Prophets, priests, commoners, and kings—all who lived before and all who'd live after—were represented in that crowd. The unrepentant, hypocritical hearts of those Jesus called out in Matthew 23 beat to the rhythm of all killers of the religious kind throughout history. They were "full of dead men's bones and every impurity ... full of hypocrisy and lawlessness" (Matt. 23:27-28). Only a short time after Jesus pronounced these searing declarations, as He predicted, He was arrested, tried, beaten, and crucified by Jews. But another band of Jews would follow Him, proclaiming His death and resurrection till their own dying breaths. In Acts 2 the church was born not among thousands of Gentiles. It was birthed among many Jews and a handful of proselytes (Acts 2:10).

Israel, as a nation, refused Christ and the ramifications would be perilous. But individuals within that nation offered up their lives in His name and changed the entire course of human history.

Paul wrote 1 Thessalonians approximately two decades after the birth of the church at Pentecost (Acts 2). The Book of Acts documents how some of his fellow Jews furiously harassed Paul during this time period (see Acts 13:45-50; 14:2,19; 17:5-9,13; 18:12). The most telling insight, however, into Paul's passion regarding the Jews may be found in the archives of his own story. Rewind his story to a former time when he was called by the name Saul.

Read the following segments and document Saul's actions:

Acts 7:58–8:3

Acts 9:1-2

It takes one to know one. As I researched these Scriptures and tried to put myself in Paul's position, I thought how much harder I tend to be on those in whom I recognize my old self. I'm on to their game because I played their game. I don't love them less; I'm just on to them more.

Paul blatantly testified to having been "one who was formerly a blasphemer, a persecutor, and an arrogant man" (1 Tim. 1:13). Maybe here in 1 Thessalonians, the Holy Spirit maximized Paul's past to raise the temperature of the ink in his pen. Perhaps it was an insider's charge: *I've been you. I get you. I couldn't get away with being you, and you won't either.*

Does that resonate with you? If so, explain how.

The gospel of Jesus Christ is meant to be the best thing that ever happened to people and to nations. To stifle the gospel does not just oppose God; it opposes all mankind.

> *"For God did not send His Son into the world that He might condemn the world, but that the world might be saved through Him."*
> JOHN 3:17

Day Five

Torn Away

FLASH-FORWARD: For who is our hope or joy or crown of boasting in the presence of our Lord Jesus at His coming? Is it not you? For you are our glory and joy! ***1 Thessalonians 2:19-20***

You're trying desperately to get to someone you love. Someone who could really use your encouragement. She needs to see you face to face before she feels abandoned. The trip is overdue because your plans keep falling through. You fear that you're beginning to look like more talk than walk. The flash flood forecast yesterday will make tonight's network news. Your flight cancels so you decide to tackle driving it. Now you're sitting on the highway, gripping the steering wheel, leaning all the way forward, trying to catch a glimpse of the taillights in front of you in the split-second swipes of the windshield wipers. Suddenly you realize that the cars passing you in the opposite lane are the ones in front of you turning around. The road is closed.

Has anything like this has happened to you? Please tell me about it.

That recollection will put you a mile ahead in today's lesson. Now with those feelings stirred up, please read 1 Thessalonians 2:17-20 and write it in the back.

How do we attempt to prove to someone that we tried our hardest to come through? Most of the time we're left to passionate language like Paul in today's text. Since the breath of God pumped air into his words, perhaps they fell on the hearers with the kind of full conviction described in 1 Thessalonians 1:5. On the other hand, maybe Paul wondered if they'd believe how hard he'd tried. Haven't we wondered the same about those we fear we've let down?

Let's take the temperature of Paul's inspired words and see if we can catch the high fever. The Greek verb translated "forced to leave" (v. 17) in the HCSB and "torn away" in the ESV is *aporphanizomai.*[5]

Hunt down the English word hidden in that Greek term and write it.

The word was "frequently used either of children who had been orphaned or of parents bereaved of their children."[6] Paul's choice of words sketched an image of the act and effect of orphaning. Particularly embrace the ESV translation, "we were torn away from you." The word leaves you not only to picture it, but also to hear the soundtrack playing behind it. Lean in and listen to the sound of something ripping.

Paul's choice of words conjures up a tender 30-year-old memory for me. Just as she had after the birth of my first daughter (Amanda), my mom came for a week after my second daughter (Melissa) was born. Amanda was nearly 3 years old and, by that time, completely obsessed with her grandmother.

Maybe Amanda was afraid that little seven-pound mini-human who'd come kicking and screaming into our lives was going to consume all hope of attention. Whatever Amanda was thinking, when the time came for my mom to get in her car and go home, we had to peel Amanda off of her like a layer of skin. That child screamed bloody murder, "No! No! Don't go, Nanny! No!" My mom cried. I cried. And Amanda wailed. Melissa probably did too, but who on earth could hear her?

Amid the city riot in Acts 17, Paul and Silvanus were forced to leave Thessalonica with such abruptness that it practically ripped their hearts out. That's the force of Paul's language in 1 Thessalonians 2:17. I love that he carefully pointed out that their separation was "in person, not in heart." Interestingly, the Greek phrase translates "literally, 'in face, not in heart.'"[7] F. F. Bruce expresses that "they felt like parents who had lost their children, but happily (they hoped) only for the time being ... and only as regards bodily presence, not as regards abiding inward affection."[8]

Their separation was "in person, not in heart."

In the margin, list the names of a handful of people outside your family to whom your heart is sewn with a similar "abiding inward affection," even if you live in different cities.

If you've never had children, maybe all Paul's family terminology is causing an unwelcome ache. Relish this beautiful excerpt: "There is nothing merely rhetorical about this language: Paul in particular, having no children of his own, found his unbounded capacity for paternal affection amply employed in his relationship with his converts."[9]

Do those words stir up any particular response in you? If so, please tell me about it.

"We greatly desired ... made every effort ... wanted to come to you ... time and again." Every phrase of verses 17-18 pumps warm through coronary arteries. They didn't just need to see this band of brothers and sisters who'd stolen their hearts; they wanted to see them. This wasn't obligation but a dominating desire. I was captivated by Jane Austen-like drama in F. F. Bruce's translation of the passage: "As for us, brothers, when we were bereft of you for the time being, in presence but not in heart, we bestirred ourselves the more abundantly, with great longing, to see you face to face again."[10]

How long has it been since you've said the word "bereft"? And I ask you, have you ever in your life told someone that you had "bestirred yourself the more abundantly" over her? Bereft and bestirred. Imagine the opportunities we've missed for using those two words, but let's not be too hasty. We can't waste bereft and bestirred over something like missing a sale at Macy's.

Bereft pictures something that leaves a huge empty bowl in your soul. Bestirred is when a big spoon drops into that basin and starts circling around, bustling up a whirlpool of determination. Together they describe a time when the settling sediment of loneliness whips up into the activation of healthy longing. Shifting from bereft to bestirred is when you cease settling for just feeling something; you actually start doing something.

Our surface relationships are leaving us increasingly lonely.

We "made every effort to return and see you face to face." The phrase "face to face" has a distant ring to it, almost like a dinner bell calling us home to a faraway place where people once lived in community.

Our surface relationships are leaving us increasingly lonely. They're so demanding that they leave us emotionally depleted for our relationships with skin on them. We ache for deeper connections as we're blinded by the spotlight of superficial public relationships. We leave someone sitting before us, waiting while we "finish one more thing" on our phone screen. But that's just it; we never seem to finish. A heart without a face looks like any other heart. It's the face-to-face that tells us if a heart-to-heart is real.

- In 1 Thessalonians 2:19-20, what words did Paul use to describe the Thessalonian Christians?

hope, joy, crown

How are these verses similar in tone to Philippians 4:1?

whom I love & long for, my joy & crown

If you'll allow me a little latitude, I'd like to throw some words in Paul's mouth. Could he be saying something like this?

> I need no other reward. Serving you in the name of Christ and serving by your side has been such joy and fulfillment to me that boasting about you at His throne is all I could ever want. The labor of my soul is paid in full and overflowing by your steadfastness and faith in Christ. To know you are well in Him would be my win. To have sought and found Him with you is my shameless gain. Whatever crowns may come my way out of the bounty of Christ's grace

> at the end of my days will be cast at His feet. Having known you, served you, and loved you here on this cold and broken earth is reward enough to carry me through all of eternity. My arms will forever be full because you were once in them.

I'm a far cry from an apostle Paul, but a lump wells up in my throat while writing those words, because I've felt them. My soul has been so moved at times by the evidence of Him in people I've known and loved that I could hardly bear it. Now and then I've whispered something like: "Take me home right now, Lord, and this moment will be all the crown I could ever want. Let me lay this at Your feet and applaud Your majesty till I bring You the merest fraction of the joy You've brought me."

"Take me home right now, Lord, and this moment will be all the crown I could ever want."

If you've had a similar feeling about an individual or group you've served or served alongside, please share who and why.

We were created for community. We thrive in healthy intimacy. We have to give fully to create the space to receive fully. Had Paul and Silvanus waved at the Thessalonians from the Via Egnatia, think what angst they'd been spared. After their last go-round in Philippi (Acts 16:22-23), who could have blamed them for not getting involved at least until their wounds turned to scars?

○ Have you ever avoided relationships to avoid pain? If so, explain.

If you're like me, you have wounds that are years old, because you pick at them so much they never heal. We're still using those same old excuses for staying back from people. No time. No energy. It's all been spent elsewhere. Here's the rub: had Paul and Silvanus forfeited the emotional pain of being torn away from the Thessalonians, they'd have forfeited their joy and a glorious crown of boasting before the Lord Jesus.

If it's all fun, it's probably all games. We were meant to put ourselves out there for people. An earthly cause is nothing without a people it affects.

We greatly desired ... made every effort ... wanted to come to you ... time and again.

Even so, therefore go.

Group Session Three

REVIEW THE WEEK

Use these questions to guide your discussion of last week's homework.

● Principal Questions

DAY 1: What happened to Paul and Silas after they were dragged into the marketplace before the authorities (Acts 16:22-24)? (p. 39)

DAY 2: What two gifts might believers share with those to whom they minister? (p. 44)

DAY 3: What action verb describes how we journey with God? (p. 47)

DAY 4: Focus on 1 Thessalonians 2:14. How had the Thessalonians become "imitators of God's churches in Christ Jesus that are in Judea"? (p. 51)

DAY 5: In 1 Thessalonians 2:19-20, what words did Paul use to describe the Thessalonian Christians? (p. 58)

○ Personal Discussion Questions

DAY 1: What do you think He's searching out and testing our hearts to find? (p. 41)

DAY 2: Does 1 Thessalonians 2:8 stir up a story of your own? (p. 46)

DAY 3: How does Christ walking among the churches encourage you? (p. 49)

DAY 4: Share a time when you experienced some form of persecution because of your belief in Jesus. (p. 51)

DAY 5: Have you ever avoided relationships to avoid pain? (p. 59)

VIEW THE VIDEO

Introduction

Today we will revisit 1 Thessalonians 2:7-12 and draw a diagram depicting the makings of a healthy child in the family of God. These questions will help drive our pens:

According to 1 Thessalonians 2, what would whole parenting look like?

Or, to put it another way: How would we diagram no-holes parenting?

2. ____________ ____________

1. ____________

3. ____________ Parent's

____________ ____________

5. ____________

Greek *paramuthéomai*

4. ____________

Greek *parakaléo*

6. ____________ to ____________ ____________

See Beth live! Visit *www.lifeway.com/livingproof* for her event schedule.

Week Three

Destined for This

Day One

We Wanted To

FLASH-FORWARD: So we wanted to come to you—even I, Paul, time and again—but Satan hindered us. *1 Thessalonians 2:18*

Today and tomorrow we're going to break our usual protocol. Instead of moving on into 1 Thessalonians 3, we're going to glance behind us and grab a concept tucked in the last chapter that, if applied, could be pivotal. We'll catch up later in the week by taking a few more Scriptures than we normally do. To keep from being overwhelmed with long portions to write, we'll still jot segments of our coming chapter each day.

Knowing that we won't discuss these passages until day 3, please handwrite 1 Thessalonians 3:1-3 in the back.

Now return to a portion of Scripture I purposely dodged on day 5 of last week. What specific reason did the apostle Paul give in 1 Thessalonians 2:18 for not coming to the Thessalonians despite his deep desires to the contrary?

but Satan hindered us.

Glance even further back to 1 Thessalonians 2:14-16. How had Paul's own countrymen done something very similar?

displease God, oppose all mankind, hindering from speaking

If you're looking at the HCSB, the ESV, or the NASB translations, you see forms of the word "hinder" used twice (verses 16 and 18).

Without peeking ahead at the dictionary definition, take a shot at defining the word "hindrance" on your own.

obstacle

Circle any of the words in *Merriam-Webster's* definition of "hinder" that you used in yours: "to make slow or difficult the progress of … to hold back … to delay, impede, or prevent action … to interfere with the activity or progress of … causing harmful or annoying delay or interference with progress."[1]

The Greek words translated "hindered" or "hindering" in the New Testament overlap our current meanings and give them a splash of color. The word in 1 Thessalonians 2:18

adds the nuance of a military context, sketching the image of a road or pathway so torn up by the opposition that it was virtually impassable.[2]

Two negative hindrances for Christians pop up in 2:14-18. Verse 16 pitches the spotlight on other people. Verse 18 puts it on Satan himself. I have a feeling you could have identified both those sources from your own experiences.

During the past year, which—others or Satan—has seemed the bigger hindrance to you and how?

Some hindrances are good and God-imposed.

I qualified the hindrance as negative in the previous paragraph because some hindrances are good and God-imposed. Recently I ran into all sorts of obstacles, trying to get to work. I had to grab something from the store on the way, but in the frozen-food section, I ran into a little sister in Christ who needed some encouragement and warfare prayer in the worst way. God undoubtedly hindered me that morning so I'd be in exactly the right place at the right time to hug her and reassure her of His calling on her priceless life. Two other women walked next to us, and I'm pretty sure they wished we could all have a group hug.

You've had some positive hindrances too. Share one.

Keep those things close to your heart while we explore the topic of negative hindrances today and tomorrow, moving steadily to a victorious stance. Let's shine the spotlight first on hindrances other people bring into our path. Scripture gives a couple of examples that illustrate how broad the spectrum can be. Viewed side by side, they provide an almost perfect contrast.

Circle any form of our keyword "hindrance" in the following two Scripture segments.

- Luke 11:52 falls straight from the tongue of our Lord Jesus Christ: "Woe to you experts in the law! You have taken away the key of knowledge! You didn't go in yourselves, and you hindered those who were going in."

- In Romans 14:13-15a consider the ESV because it employs our keyword. "Therefore let us not pass judgment on one another any longer, but rather decide never to put a stumbling block or hindrance in the way of a brother. I know and am persuaded in the Lord Jesus that nothing is unclean in itself, but it is unclean for anyone who thinks it unclean. For if your brother is grieved by what you eat, you are no longer walking in love."

What fascinates me about those two examples is they illustrate equal but opposing brands of hindrances people can place on each other. The first hindrance is legalism. Legalistic people like the experts in the law in Luke 11:52 heap burdens on others that they themselves can't carry. They hold people to standards they themselves can't keep.

Legalism's socialite sister is perfectionism. Scratch this one down in permanent marker: you will never find a perfectionist who is, as it turns out, perfect. Now swing on a thick vine all the way from the first hindrance—legalism—to the second hindrance—license.

You will never find a perfect perfectionist.

Romans 14:13-15 blots the ink on how we could harm a brother or sister in Christ by an undiscerning practice of our liberty. For example, a person may be free in Christ to have a glass of wine, but if she orders it at dinner with a recovering alcoholic, she could hinder her progress or cause her to stumble.

- To nail down the concepts, write the terms "legalism" and "license" on the ends of this continuum. Under each one, jot an example of that type of hindrance.

Human Hindrance Spectrum

legalism ——————————— licence.

- Now let's zero in for a moment on 1 Thessalonians 2:18 with Satan as the hinderer. What do verses 19-20 suggest as a reason why Satan hindered them from getting back to the Thessalonians? What do you think Satan was seeking to prevent by keeping them apart?

Satan did not want Paul to share the hope, joy + crown (victory) of Jesus any further w. the Thessalonians.
Did not want Jesus to be glorified.

If Satan had a motivational poster in his staff workroom, picture this right up there in his top 10 rallying points:

Keep people who together great kingdom apart would serve purposes.

The apostle charged Satan with keeping Paul and Silvanus from the Thessalonians because of all they could mean to each other in Christ. Satan throws his head back and howls when he can use small things to keep believers from uniting in great things for the fame of Jesus Christ. He not only works hard to see that wrong people unite; he runs the chainsaw until it smokes black so that good people divide.

Satan likes to plant hedges and build roadblocks between people who would bless, encourage, and edify one another in Christ. He simply does not want people to be a joy to you. They would put your discouragement at risk. He doesn't want to give you people to boast in the Lord about, because it might put a dent in your pessimism. Satan forbid that we have a little hope in this hurting world and glimpses of good among the gore.

Two sources of hindrances: fellow humans and Satan himself.

So far we've established two sources of negative hindrances for followers of Christ: fellow humans and Satan himself. But you and I both know that we battle a third source. We looked her square in the face this morning when we glanced in the mirror and brushed her teeth.

> With that person in mind, read Hebrews 12:1 in the NIV to see our keyword used blatantly. Circle it, please:
>
> "Therefore, since we are surrounded by such a great cloud of witnesses, let us throw off everything that hinders and the sin that so easily entangles. And let us run with perseverance the race marked out for us."

If you're like me, what you've personally refused to lay or cast down along the way has been the biggest hindrance of all in how you've run the race.

- I've held on to guilt long after repentance and God's forgiveness.
- I've clutched the past when He's commanded me to run free into my future.
- I've held on to bitterness when He's given me grace to offset former damages.
- I've held on to relationships long after He's told me to let go.
- I've held on to offenses when He wanted my hands pried open to reconcile.
- I've continued practices that weren't evil in themselves but became increasingly erosive and heart-numbing.

A hindrance is not always something sinful. Even something wholesome can become less and less consistent with the path God is opening to you. Its season has passed and it's time to lay it down. These can often be the hardest hindrances to let go of because they're more subjective and easier to rationalize. They're not wrong; they're just wrong right now.

The Greek lexical term translated "hindrance" in Hebrews 12:1 is *ógkos* (pronounced OG-kahs), meaning "a tumor, mass, magnitude, weight, burden, impediment."[3]

Does anything about that definition spark recognition in you regarding a present hindrance? If so, explain how.

Be careful not to conclude that every minute of free time or recreation is automatically a hindrance to your spiritual fruitfulness. God commanded rest, and many of us are dying for lack of it. If we're not sure whether something in our lives qualifies as a hindrance, let's ask Him! Let's listen over the next few weeks as He speaks through His Word and through our circumstances. Let's also be sensitive to a churning in our souls or a growing unrest or discomfort toward that particular thing. We'll know. And when we do, let's ask God for the strength to pitch it. One way we'll know it was His will is that, even while we miss it, we'll feel relieved.

As I searched the earlier definition for the Greek term *ógkos* ("hindrance" in Heb. 12:1), I saw a similar word listed among the synonyms: *hupérogkos.* It is used twice in the New Testament in reference to people.

Compare 2 Peter 2:18 and Jude 16 in the ESV. What description do these two verses have in common?

loud-mouthed boasters.

Now check definition from a Greek dictionary: "*Hupérogkos*—from *hupér,* over, and *ógkos,* a mass. Oversized, swollen, boastful. In the NT used only figuratively to refer to a bigheaded or boastful person."

The antonym for *hupérogkos?* "Humble."[4]

Sometimes the mass that needs throwing down is my own big head. We'll never have a bigger hindrance than our own ego. The good thing about throwing down our head is that our bodies have to follow. All we have to do is go facedown. It's up from there.

Day Two

Without Hindrance

FLASH-FORWARD: Then he stayed two whole years in his own rented house. And he welcomed all who visited him, proclaiming the kingdom of God and teaching the things concerning the Lord Jesus Christ with full boldness and without hindrance. *Acts 28:30-31*

Today we will continue our tight focus on the concept of negative hindrances. Our topic will take us off-road from Thessalonians today, but we will keep up in our handwritten portions.

Please write 1 Thessalonians 3:4-5 in the back of your workbook and push "pause" on it until our next lesson.

If at all possible from memory, please list the three sources of negative hindrances we discussed in our previous lesson.

1. other people
2. satan
3. myself.

If you've bathed three children, balanced your bank statement, watched a presidential debate, or sworn off caffeine since then, you may need a hint. We found one of the sources in Hebrews 12 and we took it personally. Paul recorded the other two—one right after the other—toward the end of 1 Thessalonians 2.

I don't know about you, but I'm twice as inclined to pay attention when somebody talking to me about an issue has the street cred to back it up. No one in the entire New Testament canon listed a greater number of hindrances to what he'd been called to accomplish than the apostle Paul. We could go to a couple of places to see his rapid-fire documentations of obstacles, but we'll pick 2 Corinthians 11:23-28 for our purposes today.

Read the kinds of things Paul had endured in this segment and record the ones you're pretty sure could qualify as Goliath-level hindrances.

V23 imprisonments, beatings, often near death
24 5Y 39 lashes, 3Y w. rods, 1Y stoned, 3Y shipwrecked
danger, labor, anxiety

Only against the backdrop of that segment can we truly appreciate where we are about to turn in Scripture. Please jump ahead in the adventures of the apostle Paul just for today's lesson and look at the end of the Book of Acts. Read Acts 28:30-31 and, after you've read your translation of choice, please read the HCSB in today's "Flash-Forward."

● Exactly how did Paul go about proclaiming the kingdom of God and teaching the things concerning the Lord Jesus Christ?

When Luke penned the closing words of Acts, maybe he had in mind that we wouldn't just sigh; say something like, "That's a great book of the Bible" (and it is!); and flip to the first page of Romans like we're checking off chapters in our annual read-through-the-Bible. Maybe he meant for that wrap-up to read like a lit bundle of bottle rockets on the Fourth of July. I think maybe we were supposed to slap the table or something.

Luke's words make us want to call a Bible study friend and ask if she's ever seen that verse sitting there. Just one chapter earlier in Acts, Paul was stuffed like a sardine on a boat as a prisoner to escape an assassination attempt. The vessel got lost at sea in a 14-day winter storm. After that, they were shipwrecked then washed ashore on the wild island of Malta. And if that weren't enough, a snake with a mind to hang on bit Paul.

Even if the last blow doesn't kill you, at what point do you say to yourself, *I think I made this calling up*? When do you presume God couldn't possibly have called you to this place where so many things go wrong? *Au contraire, ma soeur.* The final destination of our calling could very well take the last drop of our lifeblood. That's entirely God's call.

Nevertheless, by the time we travelers get to Acts 28:31 and find ourselves smack in the middle of Rome with the apostle Paul, we're meant to lean forward and stare at that ending with a little enthusiasm. In fact, I might just get up and do a cartwheel.

> "with full boldness and without hindrance"

Glance at the final words of the Book of Acts again. The HCSB brings the recorded journeys of Paul to a close "with full boldness and without hindrance." The ESV has "with all boldness and without hindrance." The NASB may be the most beautiful of all: "with all openness, unhindered." No matter how our English versions translate or arrange the sentence, the entire Greek manuscript of the Book of Acts comes to a strategic and deliberate end with one word: *akōlytōs.*

"Minus hindrance."

Luke's 28-chapter narrative of the early church winds through crises, kings, chains, jail cells, successes, and failures until it seems at times that the entire future of the gospel of Christ is at risk. It then draws to a dark-defying close with that one marvelous word: *akōlytōs*.

With that final drop of inspired ink that left the master narrator's pen dry, a dam broke. The same word that drew the curtain tore the curtain. The very term that tied it up loosed it forever. With Luke's choice of that one-word closing, the Book of Acts, in effect, does not end. It explodes. *Akōlytōs* was the blast of a gospel cannon with an earsplitting sound still reverberating all over this God-chosen globe.

All this got me thinking: what made him so astonishing is that Paul wasn't hindered by his hindrances. Like us, he had a few hindrances that couldn't just be thrown down like the ones implied in Hebrews 12:1.

According to 1 Thessalonians 2:14-20, both people and Satan had authentically been successful at hindering Paul. But that's just it. He kept pressing forward and refused to let the hindrance itself become a hindrance. He kept his squinting eyes on the goal. He didn't get furious with God over all that had been permitted in his path or demand to know why God would make His will so utterly impossible to fulfill. He just stayed at it. He believed. He persevered. And he made it to Rome in one scarred-up piece.

Get a load of this: Paul didn't even consider that ministering at his own expense was a hindrance (see Acts 28:30). We might argue that Paul was special and the same can't be expected of us. After all, he received several divine reassurances from God that would have made a monumental difference. But, Sister, we also have His Word.

Is it possible that many of our addictions are attempts to take the hurt out of our hindrances? Think that possibility through and, if you see merit in the connection, give an example of how it happens.

This world is too broken for us to make our goal not getting hurt.

Life can't be sustained here on earth without a certain amount of exposure and pain. This world is too broken for us to make our goal not getting hurt. What if, instead of fixating on taking the hurt out of our hindrance, we prayed for God to take the hindrance out of our hurt?

I let myself just go with this concept in prayer and felt like God began bringing all sorts of possible equations to my mind, involving the math for living life *akōlytōs* or "minus hindrance." Certainly not all of these will resonate with you or even be agreeable perhaps, but would you read them nevertheless, just to get your own thoughts stirred? Consider the possibilities.

Heartbreak - hindrance = depth

Breakup - hindrance = breakthrough

Childhood trauma - hindrance = testimony

Singleness - hindrance = a gospel globetrotter

Celibacy - hindrance = sexual purity

Childlessness - hindrance = mother of many (Isa. 54:1-2)

Disappointment - hindrance = faith

Devastation - hindrance = trust

Injustice - hindrance = room for God's wrath

Handicap - hindrance = hero

My pain - hindrance = my passion

What happened - what hindered = an overcomer

And the sum total of all the equations: My life - the hindrance of all my hindrances = my God-ordained destiny

My prayer about removing hindrances from my hurts:

Get the idea? If so, can you think of any additions? Write them here:

anxiety - hindrance = trust

injustice - " = forgiveness.

○ Which two of all the above equations (including your own additions) speak to you most personally and specifically?

________ - ________ = ________

________ - ________ = ________

Explain why.

Is there any connection between the two? (There may not be, so don't force it, but don't dismiss it too quickly either.) If so, point out the tie.

Use the margin to record an earnest prayer to your gracious and faithful God, asking Him to begin forthrightly taking the hindrances out of these hurts. Ask Him to give you courage. Voice to Him how much He loves you and how committed He is to you. Cherished child of God, you may not be able to lay down the hurt right away. Some things ache for years while God slowly mends us and shapes us into the image of His Son. But, in Jesus' wonder-working name, you can indeed demand that the hindrance be moved from that hurt like a mountain moved into the sea. Just a little bit of faith could change everything.

Day Three

Not So Fragile

FLASH-FORWARD: Therefore, when we could no longer stand it, we thought it was better to be left alone in Athens. ***1 Thessalonians 3:1***

My 5-year-old border collie, Queen Esther, is so eaten alive by the instincts of her genius breed that she's about two wags of a dog's tail from crazy. I say that with earnest love and due respect. We Moores tend to keep our stones tucked deep in our pockets concerning obsessive-compulsive types.

Star (as we call her for short) is a dyed-in-the-wool herder. She can't help herself. She herds me. She herds Keith. She herds squirrels. She herds birds. Day before yesterday, she tried to herd a possum. Her most exasperating habit is herding other dogs, of which our family has many. Since we live in the country and have ample romping space, family get-togethers double as canine reunions. Everyone but the Queen has a good time. She darts frenetically from Amanda's golden retriever to Keith's German shorthaired to Paw Paw's humble hybrid, nipping at their haunches and trying to round them up like she's Bossy Flossy.

Being Star isn't all that easy. We will feel some of her pain as we try our best to circle up Paul, Silvanus, and Timothy today and get them each placed. Trying to pinpoint Paul as he moved all over the map is hard enough. It's like Star herding a bird dog during a quail migration.

Our third chapter of 1 Thessalonians calls for some mapping, however, so that is what we're going to do. Try not to bite anybody.

Try not to bite anybody.

Please read 1 Thessalonians 3:1-8 and write verses 6-8 in the back.

Looking no further than 1 Thessalonians 3:1, what were Paul and Silvanus/Silas willing to do when they "could no longer stand it"?

to be left behind in Athens

Review 1 Thessalonians 3:2 and answer each of these questions based on this verse alone.

Who did they send? Timothy

By what two titles did they call him? our brother &
/ Gods coworker.

● What was Timothy sent to Thessalonica to do?

to establish + exhort them in their faith

Timothy's return to Paul and Silas (Silvanus) referenced in verse 6 provides the catalyst for the first letter to the Thessalonians. That puts it high on our radar. The timing matters because God used what surely felt like complete disorganization and detouring to stick a pen in their hands. The occasion is all the more notable since this is probably Paul's first inspired epistle.

We're going to momentarily return to the Book of Acts and document every stop Paul, Silas, and Timothy made leading up to the first Thessalonian letter. Please keep in mind that we will only occasionally find all three men in the same place. To get the best grasp on their expedition, please refer to your map in the back at each stop. Be prepared for me to ask you which direction on a compass the traveler or travelers headed to reach that stop. Did they go south, for instance? Or southwest? North? Get the idea? I'll fill in the first direction so the exercise will be clearer. To help you follow the ministry maze where it's most confusing, I've added comments in italics.

Read each verse and fill in the blanks.
Acts 17:1—They (Paul and Silas) came to Thessalonica.
Direction traveled: *west*

Timothy might have accompanied them but, if so, he remained unmentioned. In greater likelihood, "Timothy had been left in Philippi with Luke when Paul and Silas moved on from there."[5]

Acts 17:10—Paul and Silas were sent to Berea.
Direction traveled: west

Acts 17:13-14—Paul was sent to the sea, but Silas and Timothy remained in Berea.
(Paul's) Direction traveled: south-east

Timothy joined them in Berea or, less likely, he was with them throughout their journey to and from Thessalonica, though unmentioned.

Acts 17:15—Paul went as far as Athens and sent word for Silas and Timothy to join him.
Direction traveled: South

Silas and Timothy departed soon after they received Paul's instructions and presumably united with him in Athens. Note this part carefully: While in Athens, they all agreed that Timothy should return to Thessalonica. This is our intersection with 1 Thessalonians. Review 1 Thessalonians 3:1-2 again so that you can connect these dots. They are crucial!

Acts 18:1—__________ left __________ and went to __________.
Direction traveled: __________

Acts 18:5—__________ and __________ arrived (in Corinth) from __________ and the three of them were reunited.
Direction traveled: __________

If you're really on top of it, you're wondering when Silas went back to Macedonia, the region where Philippi, Thessalonica, and Berea were located. We don't have a definitive answer. Since Silas arrived with Timothy according to Acts 18:5, Paul may have sent him to check on the young disciple en route and accompany him to Corinth. Silas's trip may have also doubled as a ministry visit somewhere in Macedonia to check on the new converts.

All of these travel details are strategic, particularly in view of today's lesson. Why? Because right there in Corinth where the three of them were united, Paul wrote the first letter to the Thessalonians. If you write in the margins of your Bible, Acts 18:5 is the perfect spot to jot, "1 Thessalonians penned." First Thessalonians 3:6 offers it in real time for us: "But now Timothy has come to us from you and brought us good news about your faith and love."

Circle the word "now" in the previous sentence.

Herding is hard work, isn't it?

The "now" was the occasion for the letter. Whew! Herding is hard work, isn't it? I told you it's not easy being Star. The details get tedious, but they are vital if we're to wrap our minds around what these early church pioneers endured—the miles they covered and the inconveniences and dangers they met.

Underline this sentence for emphasis: This trip to Thessalonica (referenced in 1 Thess. 3:6) would have been the virgin voyage of Timothy's solo ministry. He'd been with Paul and Silas a few months and was in his early twenties. "A round trip from Athens to Macedonia would have taken three or four weeks, not to mention the time that Timothy spent with the church. This event was a momentous step in Timothy's experience ... here he is carrying out a solo mission to dangerous Thessalonica."[6]

We may shrug our shoulders because we know the trip was successful. But when they decided to put a pack on young Timothy's back, they had no clue how it would go. Please enter into the tenuousness as you compare 1 Thessalonians 3:1 and 3:5.

What kind of angst do you think went into the decision for Timothy to make the trip to Thessalonica?

What pros and cons do you picture playing into the decision to send Timothy on this trek? Try to picture yourself as part of the decision-making process.

Pros

Cons:

A gradually increasing awareness has overtaken me since I was a wreck of an 18-year-old shaking awake to a calling. We somehow expect the turns on the highway to our destinies to be well marked and definitive. "Exit here. Turn right at the four-way stop and drive 16.7 miles."

For me, the direction or the next decision often seemed so vague. A handful of times I felt iron in my soul and made decisions with unshakable resolve. But more times than I could count, determining God's will seemed like guessing.

I'd stand at a fork in the road and feel all the certainty of a second grader saying, "Eeny, meeny, miny, moe." Other times were like standing on a diving board, wearing a blindfold. I didn't know what else to do but jump.

For years I wrestled terribly with insecurity over my calling. I panicked, fretted, and prayed as if God's call was as fragile as a glass Christmas ornament—as fragile as I felt. I believed God made the decision to use me reluctantly, against His better judgment—like I was on trial and given probation.

More than three and a half decades later, I still struggle with some of those feelings. I remain convinced that disobedience or pride can derail usefulness. But something has dramatically changed in my perspective.

Decisions that felt like stabs in the dark at the time were as determined by God as the ones that burned with conviction.

I now believe those decisions that felt like stabs in the dark at the time were as determined by God as the ones that burned with conviction. Every turn was imperative to God's plan for me and led in the direction I needed to go. Even poor decisions that seemed like disastrous detours wound themselves around until even they became crucial to the process.

I've come to believe that very little of this is as fragile as it feels. When we throw up our hands and say, "Who knows?" the answer is, "God does."

Maybe right now that's no big revelation. Maybe it sounds cliché, but the next time a detour comes and God dovetails it into your destiny, you'll drop to your face with fresh awe. God can shove us with His mighty hand wherever He wants us to go, or He can gently blow us there with an almost imperceptible breath. God is ever at the helm, patient and foreknowing. He is the furthest thing from fragile.

Mull over the wonder of it as we close. Since the day our protagonists were forced out of Thessalonica by a mob, they must have felt like the ideal plan was blown, and that all they had left was reaction mode.

○ Do you ever feel like all the planning has flown the coop and you're just reacting? Describe a time you felt that way.

Our protagonists knew the feeling. By Acts 17:10, they seemed to be responding to derailment. Lean into this with me: the letter we're studying became necessary only as an inferior replacement to the visit Paul yearned to make. But as it turned out, that very letter was blown on the page by the breath of God.

What visit could have rivaled the etching of eternal words on parchment? The consequential turned into the providential. While they were reacting, God was enacting. The result would be nothing less than preplanned, perfectly timed revelation.

While they were reacting, God was enacting.

Today here we sit, clutching that same letter tucked confidently and permanently by God into the suit pocket of the sacred canon. Now that's some kind of divine herding.

Day Four

Immovable

FLASH-FORWARD: **For when we were with you, we kept telling you beforehand that we were to suffer affliction, just as it has come to pass, and just as you know.** ***1 Thessalonians 3:4, ESV***

I'm so glad you're back today. This would be a far lonelier trip if I didn't know you were on the other side of the page. I don't take for granted a single day that we get to meet together. I consider it a privilege to serve you.

Read 1 Thessalonians 3:1-10 and write verses 9 and 10 in the back.

Today we stare in the contorted face of a word the English Standard Version uses in 1 Thessalonians 3:1-4.

Therefore when we could bear it no longer, we were willing to be left behind at Athens alone, and we sent Timothy, our brother and God's coworker in the gospel of Christ, to establish and exhort you in your faith, that no one be moved by these afflictions. For you yourselves know that we are destined for this. For when we were with you, we kept telling you beforehand that we were to suffer affliction, just as it has come to pass, and just as you know.

- By what do Paul and his cohorts not want the Thessalonians to be moved? Circle both times you find that key word in the Scripture segment above.

In the original language, the root word is *thlíbō* (pronounced THLEE-bo with a long "o"). The noun form *thlípsis* appears in verse 3, and the word is used as an infinitive in verse 4. It means "to press together, compress, afflict ... to press as a person in a crowd ... in the sense of to press together, compress ... figuratively, to oppress with evil, afflict, distress."[7] Mark this spot in today's lesson because I'll direct you back to this definition several times.

The HCSB translates *thlípsis* as "persecutions" in 3:3-4. That is a powerful word too, and one that presumes considerable hardship. But it doesn't make my skin crawl as much as the word "affliction." I hate the word "affliction." Maybe it's the middle syllable. It sounds like something awful got flicked on you. "Affliction" makes me think of boils or something equally pleasant.

- What maladies come to mind at the mention of the word "affliction"? Respond in the margin.

The word has been on the tip of my tongue for the better part of a year because it appears in two completely different segments of my Scripture memory work. Just prior to committing this portion of 1 Thessalonians to memory, I memorized the eloquent, emotional words of Psalm 25. If you have time, read all 22 verses, but if you don't have that luxury, read Psalm 25:16-20 and see where it overlaps today's lesson.

16 Turn to me and be
gracious to me, for I am
lonely and afflicted.
17 The troubles of my heart
are enlarged; bring me
out of my distresses.
18 Consider my affliction
and my trouble, and
forgive all my sins.
PSALM 25:16-18, ESV

How does the psalmist David describe himself in Psalm 25:16?

lonely & afflicted

In Psalm 25:18, what does David ask God to consider?

his affliction & trouble, forgive all his sins.

Most of the major translations employ forms of the word "affliction" in verses 16 and 18. In the margin, circle each form of our keyword.

So here's today's million dollar question: which would you rather have—an affliction or a trouble? The question has no wrong answer. We're simply discussing preferences.

Your choice: affliction or trouble? Why?

Affliction seems more intense.

Like some of you, I'm an obsessive thinker. I think the way a dog gnaws a bone, turning it over and rolling it around in the dirt. If something hurtful happens to me, my mind gets stuck on replay. If I don't do something to stop it, I could still be stuck in the same spot 3 years later ... or 30.

Some people just tell themselves not to think about certain things and they don't. I'm not one of them. Are you? Can you think up an entire torturous scenario in such detail that your body reacts as though it really happened? Me too. Can you conjure up an entire conflict with someone, then, the next time you're with him you have to remind yourself it isn't real? If you're nodding, clearly, we have an affliction. Think of it like brain boils.

Give me troubles over afflictions any day. We can have troubles without even being troubled by them. Most of us have experienced times when something is going wrong, yet we felt a strange sense of peace, even joy. For me the word "affliction" stirs up a whole different stew. In the English, a malady qualifies as an affliction precisely because we're afflicted by it. Troubles don't always trouble, but afflictions always afflict.

Afflictions have another particularly hazardous side from the Bible's take. Note in the margin the definition of the word *thlípsis* we saw earlier in this lesson (translated "affliction" in 1 Thessalonians 3:3).

THLÍPSIS

To press together, compress, afflict ... to press as a person in a crowd; in the sense of to press together, compress ... figuratively, to oppress with evil, afflict, distress.

Complete this sentence from the definition of *thlípsis*: "Figuratively, to oppress w. evil, afflict, distress."

If we split hairs over the two terms—troubles and afflictions—I'd twice as quickly associate an affliction with a feeling of oppression. We may or may not sense the Enemy trying to take advantage of our troubles, but he rarely misses an opportunity to gnaw at the bones of our afflictions.

Read 1 Thessalonians 3:3 again. Paul says Timothy was sent so that they would not be "moved" by their afflictions. Process the definition of the Greek word *thlípsis* again, this time, in mental pictures as a visual learner would.

If you were watching the concept acted out by a group, what would be happening?

Mob the victim

The idea behind *thlípsis* is pressure pushing up against you so forcefully that you feel crushed. Mark 3:9 uses a form of the word in reference to Jesus.

What were the circumstances?

Jesus getting into the boat to escape the crowd.

Think about the last time something or someone pushed against you forcefully. Unless you had extremely firm footing, you were probably moved by it. That's precisely the point in 1 Thessalonians 3:3.

Consider this carefully: the one way we'd be less likely to move when something presses against us is if we knew it was coming. If you bumped me forcefully and I didn't see the bump coming, I'd stumble. I'd move. On the other hand, if you told me you were about to push me, I'd plant my feet solidly and bend my knees. I'd brace myself—unless you said it and I didn't really listen. Read this segment one more time:

> *[W]e sent Timothy, our brother and God's coworker in the gospel of Christ, to establish and exhort you in your faith, that no one be moved by these afflictions. For you yourselves know that we are destined for this. For when we were with you, we kept telling you beforehand that we were to suffer affliction, just as it has come to pass, and just as you know.*
>
> 1 THESSALONIANS 3:2-4, ESV

Did you catch it? "We kept telling you beforehand."

Jesus told us some things beforehand, but when they happen, we often act like we didn't really hear Him. For instance, He used the apostle Peter to say to us, "Dear friends, don't be surprised when the fiery ordeal comes among you to

"Dear friends, don't be surprised when the fiery ordeal comes."

test you as if something unusual were happening to you" (1 Pet. 4:12). But over and over again, we are surprised.

Today's lesson poses this question: what if we weren't surprised? What if we really did come to expect fiery ordeals, not as pessimists but as the prepared? What if we did come to expect that life was going to push us with pressure to compress us? What if we were ready in advance for things like peer pressure, cultural compression, and religious oppression? If we're not prepared, when they push, we are moved. But if we are prepared, we plant our feet, bend our knees, and hold tight with all our might.

What if we really did come to expect fiery ordeals, not as pessimists but as the prepared?

The beautiful part is that Scripture doesn't stop at telling us we'll have pressures and afflictions. It also tells us in advance that none of them will be wasted. They'll all work out for our good, and we are more than conquerors through Christ who loves us (Rom. 8:28,37). Without a shadow of a doubt, our perseverance will be rewarded (Heb. 10:35-36).

We've been told these things beforehand. What if we became proactive? Prepared? Immoveable? O God, that we would believe You and get prepared not only for pressures but for divine power.

Not far from our home in the country, a narrow path winds through the woods and opens up to a modest little creek. I've taken this trail no less than 150 times in the last 18 months and never once encountered another person. I often practice my memory work on my walks and, if I'm going to go to the trouble to recite the Scriptures, I'm usually going to throw a little passion and personality into it. This particular day, I went full-throttle into Psalm 25 at volume 10, complete with all manner of inflection and hand waving.

I made my usual turn at the creek just as I got to verse 16: "Turn to me and be gracious to me, for I am lonely and afflicted!" Right then I came face-to-face with a young couple fishing in the creek, so close that I nearly stepped on them.

Oh, for the vocabulary to freeze-frame their expressions in words for you. Picture something akin to terror.

That I wasn't lashed repeatedly with a worm-baited fishing pole is a wonder. There was no explaining to them that I was reciting Scripture. They appeared beyond verbal resuscitation. Furthermore, they obviously felt powerless to help me. What exactly do you do when someone is yelling, "I am lonely and afflicted!" The woman reached out and held her husband's arm, and he stuttered something unintelligible. And there I stood, looking like a cross between a tortured soul and a psychopath.

So I ran for it. What else could I do?

We may feel afflicted, but we need not feel lonely. We're all in this together. The persecutions are mounting, and the pressures are pounding, but thanks be to God, who gives us the victory through our Lord Jesus Christ!

"Therefore, my dear [sisters], be ... immovable" (1 Cor. 15:58). That's what.

Day Five

And Our Lord Jesus

FLASH-FORWARD: Now may our God and Father Himself, and our Lord Jesus, direct our way to you. ***1 Thessalonians 3:11***

Finally! You get to handwrite a portion we're actually studying today! Let's get straight to it.

Please read 1 Thessalonians 3:11-13 and copy it down on the appropriate page.

While you write verses 12 and 13, ask God to perform them in you. I'll do the same. Let's not just study the Scriptures. Let's practice actively receiving them.

Right before our very eyes, something huge has just taken place on the *sacra pagina*—a phenomenon that, to Paul, held significance without equal. We tumble past it because the terminology has been in place all our believing lives. For most of us, this kind of speech is all we've ever known as an approach to faith and Scripture. But it was not what these men had known.

In 1 Thessalonians 3:11, you are staring at "the earliest documented evidence of the profound change in prayer language that took place in Christianity as the early Christian community moved away from traditional Jewish prayers, where God alone was addressed or invoked, to the address and invocation of both God and Jesus Christ."[8]

- What profound change in prayer language is first introduced in 1 Thessalonians 3:11?

The prayer is directed at our God & Father + our Lord Jesus.

The year was A.D. 52 or close to it. The force of the words was titanic. The addition of the phrase was revolutionary, and to many disciples, the truth was wholly worth dying for. For the first time in writing, Jesus is seated right next to the Father, assigned with the "position and authority formerly held only by Yahweh."[9] To adequately wrap our minds around the all-glorious addition to the source of all blessing, let's grab hold of some Old Testament verses.

Write the two words "May God" in each of the blanks below. Underline the specific blessings spoken or sought in each one.

"May God give to you—from the dew of the sky and from the richness of the land—an abundance of grain and new wine" (Gen. 27:28).

"________ ________ Almighty bless you and make you fruitful and multiply you so that you become an assembly of peoples" (Gen. 28:3).

"________ ________ give you and your offspring the blessing of Abraham so that you may possess the land where you live as a foreigner, the land God gave to Abraham" (Gen. 28:4).

"________ ________ Almighty cause the man to be merciful to you" (Gen. 43:14).

"Then he said, '________ ________ be gracious to you, my son'" (Gen. 43:29).

"________ ________ be praised! He has not turned away my prayer or turned His faithful love from me" (Ps. 66:20).

"________ ________ be gracious to us and bless us; look on us with favor" (Ps. 67:1).

"God, You are awe-inspiring in Your sanctuaries. The God of Israel gives power and strength to His people. ________ ________ be praised" (Ps. 68:35)!

The LORD spoke to Moses: "Tell Aaron and his sons how you are to bless the Israelites. Say to them: 'May Yahweh bless you and protect you; may Yahweh make His face shine on you and be gracious to you; may Yahweh look with favor on you and give you peace.'"
NUMBERS 6:22-26

Inviting and invoking the blessing of God was the supreme grace and unmerited privilege of God's people. When they said it, they meant it. It was more than wishing someone well. Blessing had substance to it. Authority.

From the earliest flecks of formal worship, Yahweh commissioned His servants and priests to speak His blessings over the people. Although the practice pops up on the page numerous times in Genesis, Numbers 6:22-26 in the margin introduces it as a divine ordinance. Read the section carefully.

In Numbers 6:27, the very next verse, God describes what happens from His throne's perspective when the process takes place: "In this way they will pronounce My name over the Israelites, and I will bless them."

Draw an arrow from verse 27 above to the end of the Numbers 6 portion in the margin.

Picture the beauty of that. We cannot bear His name without His blessing or bear His blessing without His name. From a New Testament perspective, you might also think of the invocation of God's name through blessings as a means of asking for God's kingdom to come and His will to be done on earth as it is in heaven. In other words, may God do what only He can do. May God show what only He can show. May God give what only He can give. May God bless as only He can bless. May God empower with an energy He alone can possess. For hundreds of years that somersaulted into thousands, these same two words had been spoken: "May God."

Then one day there in the hustle and bustle of a pagan city named Corinth, the Holy Spirit fell on Paul, Silvanus, and Timothy to dip a quill in dark ink and write a letter to the nascent church in Thessalonica. Three chapters in, as we reckon chapters, the first of several invocations appears. Assuming Paul used an amanuensis, we don't have the privilege of knowing who took the actual dictation down on paper. Perhaps Peter's first epistle holds a clue since this man provided such a service for him.

Who is credited with the task in 1 Peter 5:12? Sylvanus.

○ What does the possibility that Paul may have dictated at least some of his letters through Silas/Silvanus contribute to your understanding of their relationship?

Trusted, intimate, respectful, mutual devotion to the gospel & care of the new churches.

We can be virtually certain that Paul dictated 1 and 2 Thessalonians since he refers to himself in the first person several times throughout these inspired documents. Imagine him coming to this portion of the letter and instead of saying "May God" as the Hebrews had always done, he said, "Now may our God and Father Himself, *and our Lord Jesus*, direct our way to you" (emphasis mine).

Maybe the concept was woven into his faith deeply enough that Paul spoke the phrase without special emphasis. On the other hand, perhaps he paused right there in the middle of that sentence and said all four words like a percussionist beating a base drum. The thrill of it may be lost on us, but I doubt it was lost on Paul. The paradigm shift was revolutionary.

Here's what strikes such wonder in my heart. Through all the time that the two words "may God" appeared on the Old Testament page and on the lips of the people, His Son was right there in front of Him in heaven. On the evening before His crucifixion, Jesus prayed, "Now, Father, glorify Me in Your presence with that glory I had with You before the world existed" (John 17:5). Throughout eternity, they'd been together sharing fellowship, oneness, and glory.

Don't you find it utterly amazing that God the Father had the patience to wait to reveal the very apple of His eye? His one and only Son? The Savior of the world? The Bright Morning Star? God can clearly keep a secret.

God the Father had the patience to wait.

With these thoughts stirred, read Ephesians 3:4-11. Give this section of Scripture a title of your own choosing.

God's plan for man

Write Ephesians 3:9 here please:

to bring to light for everyone what is the plan of the mystery hidden for ages in God who created all things

The ESV words verse 9 like this: "And to bring to light for everyone what is the plan of the mystery hidden for ages in God who created all things." Now read and compare Colossians 1:24-27.

What exactly was "the mystery hidden for ages and generations but now revealed to His saints"?

Christ, the Redeemer of all - Jews & Gentile.

All those years prior to the gospel revelation, God was keeping His Son hidden. He'd given glimpses, clues, and hints of Him through prophecies, theophanies, and foreshadowings. Then "when the fullness of time had come, God sent forth his Son, born of woman" (Gal. 4:4, ESV). Can you imagine the jubilant songs of the hosts of heaven when that baby was born? He'd been out of their sight for the first time since their creation and for nine laborious months. The Father alone could see Him inside Mary's womb. The further patience of God was demonstrated in His willingness to wait 30 solid years to baptize Jesus into His public ministry.

God watched the clock for the six longest hours in human history.

Then consider the patience of God to watch the clock for the six longest hours in human history while His Son bore a torturous cross. The seconds would have pounded by as loud as a hammer driving a nail. Perhaps nothing matches the patience of God, however, to wait one night, then two with Jesus hidden in the cleft of the rock and swaddled in burial cloths.

God's anxiousness to raise His Son from the dead may be most obvious in John 20:1—"On the first day of the week Mary Magdalene came to the tomb early, while it was still dark." The sun hadn't winked over the horizon when Mary Magdalene discovered the empty grave.

Perhaps even for God the Father, "Weeping may spend the night, but there is joy in the morning" (Ps. 30:5). A new day had come and it woke up early.

Please stay with our line of thought a moment longer and read John 20:26-28. How was Jesus proclaimed in verse 28?

My Lord & my God!

The written doctrines made their way to the page over a number of years, but the declaration of Christ's Lordship was immediate. Two decades later, Paul, Silvanus, and Timothy extended this blessed invocation to the church of the Thessalonians, and through them, to us: "Now may our God and Father Himself, and our Lord Jesus, direct our way to you."

Father and Son, side by side, name by beautiful name.

Every commentary I checked concurred that the use of the title "Lord" in the very next verse, 1 Thessalonians 3:12, is in reference to Jesus. "And may the Lord cause you to increase and overflow with love for one another and for everyone, just as we also do for you." Tuck that hope in your heart, because it will become important to us in our next session.

Until then, consider one final segment. It is taken from the very last book of the Bible.

> *Then the angel that I had seen standing on the sea and on the land raised his right hand to heaven. He swore an oath by the One who lives forever and ever, who created heaven and what is in it, the earth and what is in it, and the sea and what is in it: "There will no longer be an interval of time, but in the days of the sound of the seventh angel, when he will blow his trumpet, then God's hidden plan will be completed, as He announced to His servants the prophets."*
>
> REVELATION 10:5-7

For the sake of emphasis, what does the segment say about "God's hidden plan"?

will be completed.

I love the sound of that. Don't you? The mystery hidden for the ages will no longer be revealed only to His saints. He will be manifested for every eye to see. And the plan that has been underway since time began will be completed.

Patience, child of God! One day soon "there will no longer be an interval of time." Come, thou long expected Jesus.[10]

Group Session Four

REVIEW THE WEEK

Use these questions to guide your discussion of last week's homework.

● Principal Questions

DAY 1: Why did Satan hinder them from getting back to the Thessalonians? What do you think Satan was seeking to prevent by keeping them apart? (p. 65)

DAY 2: Exactly how did Paul go about proclaiming the kingdom of God and teaching the things concerning the Lord Jesus Christ? (p. 69)

DAY 3: What was Timothy sent to Thessalonica to do? (p. 72)

DAY 4: By what did Paul not want the Thessalonians to be moved? (p. 77)

DAY 5: What profound change in the language of prayer is first introduced in 1 Thessalonians 3:11? (p. 81)

○ Personal Discussion Questions

DAY 1: What examples illustrate the dangers of "legalism" and "license"? (p. 65)

DAY 2: Which of the equations on page 70–71 (including your own additions) speak to you most personally and specifically? (p. 71)

DAY 3: Do you ever feel like all the planning has flown the coop and you're just reacting? Describe a time you felt that way. (p. 76)

DAY 4: What maladies come to mind at the mention of the word "affliction"? (p. 77)

DAY 5: What does the possibility that Paul may have dictated some of his letters through Silas contribute to your understanding of their relationship? (p. 83)

VIEW THE VIDEO

Introduction

In today's session, we will return to the third chapter of 1 Thessalonians and consider the madness and the gladness of deep personal involvement.

Read 1 Thessalonians 3:1-5. Note the madness:

1. The ________________ to the ________________ (v. 1).

Check this definition: ________________: "from Latin *vulnerare* to ________________
(1) capable of being ________________ ________________
(2) open to ________________ or ________________."[1]

Capture Paul's frame of mind in 1 Corinthians 2:2-5 and 2 Corinthians 11:28.

2. The high-cost investment (v. 5). – labor in vain

3. The evaporating illusion of control (v. 5).

To be in control: a screaming testament to my distrust.

Madness.

Read 1 Thessalonians 3:6-8. Note the gladness:

1. The pure reciprocity (v. 6). – good news = gospel. James 4:5: long to see, yearning

2. The sheer relief (v. 7). John 14:2-3

3. The coloring of memory (v. 6).

4. The coming alive (v. 8).

Conclude with verse 12. From Chrysostom's Homilies on 1 Thessalonians 4.

"Do you see the unrestrainable madness of love that is shown by his words? Make you to increase and abound ..."[2]

1. *Merriam-Webster's Collegiate Dictionary,* 10th ed, s.v. "vulnerable."
2. Gene L. Green, *The Letters to the Thessalonians* (Grand Rapids, MI: Wm. B. Eerdmans Publishing Co., 2002), 177.

Week Four

Taught by God

Day One
Even More

FLASH-FORWARD: Finally then, brothers, we ask and encourage you in the Lord Jesus, that as you have received from us how you must walk and please God—as you are doing—do so even more. *1 Thessalonians 4:1*

One night my grandchildren—Jackson and Annabeth—and I stood side by side, staring into a bathroom sink full of water. I'd given them a couple of inexpensive surprises out of my toy stash and won copious kisses and hugs. Jackson's treat was a "magic towel" with a manly sports motif that was supposed to grow before our very eyes from a walnut-sized football. The football was meant to look like hard plastic so that the observer could be adequately awed when it began to split at the seams and emerge like a space alien from a small egg. The discerning eye, however, knows cellophane when it sees it, but wishes not to spoil the fun. The problem was the football refused to grow.

"Bibby, how long is this supposed to take?"

"It's going to happen any minute, Buddy," a claim to which Annabeth responded with an outbreak of applause, declaring, "I see it growing! I see! I see!"

Do you remember the play *Peter Pan*? In one part the villainous Captain Hook has poisoned Tinkerbell, and Peter says to the audience on the edge of their seats, "Do you believe in fairies? Don't let Tink die. Say that you believe! If you believe, clap your hands."[1] Remember all the blistering hand-clapping and earsplitting cries of "I believe! I believe!"? Let's just say the fairy would have survived with Annabeth that night but died a double death between Jackson and me. Even a football C-section with the scissors bore paltry results. Some things that were meant to increase flatly refuse to do so.

Today we're going to peel some of the cellophane off our souls.

Read 1 Thessalonians 4:1-10. Since the segment is longer than usual, handwrite only verses 1-5 in the back of your book. We'll write the remainder tomorrow.

We will save the most prominent subject in your 10-verse reading for our upcoming video session. Don't dread it, even if you feel like you've already blown it. We have some healthy discussion coming and some legitimate encouragement. If you know anything about my past, you know that I'm not about to throw a stone at you … but more on that in the next session. Today we are going to focus on a magnificent phrase found twice in the fourth chapter of 1 Thessalonians.

Carefully compare 1 Thessalonians 4:1 and 4:10. What phrase appears at the end of both verses?

to do so more & more

The HCSB words the phrase "even more"; the NASB, "excel still more." The NKJV, NIV, and ESV all translate the wording "more and more." In almost every translation, the wording at the end of verse 10 is consistent with the wording at the end of verse 1 because the Greek is nearly identical.

The phrasing illustrates the concept of abounding.

To my mind the phrasing illustrates the concept of abounding, like pulling the ends of a tape measure wider and wider. God has an affinity for lengthening cords and extending boundaries with a person willing to be stretched by Him. No matter who you are, where you've been, or what you've done, God has handpicked you to abound. The concept earns the right to be enormous to you, since Jesus explicitly stated that He came to this meager world to offer the very thing "abounding" embodies.

● What kind of life did Christ say He'd come to give in John 10:10?

I have come that they may have life, and have it to the full

If you know the verse by heart, don't let familiarity sift out the fresh wonder today. If you're like me, you can remember a verse long after you've forgotten to apply it. No matter how your version translates John 10:10, the Greek uses a form of the same word in 1 Thessalonians 4:1 and 4:10. We are each commissioned and empowered by the living Christ to "abound more and more."[2]

○ Before we go an inch further, how does the phrase "more and more" contradict the notion of a place of arrival in this earthly journey in which we simply maintain from there?

process of sanctification.

The propensity toward increase is found in all sorts of contexts in the Bible, both positive and negative. Many elements, situations, and characteristics by their very nature tend to increase or abound "more and more" unless something inhibits the process. Discover the broad radius for yourself so that you can draw your own conclusions.

Read the following verses and fill in the blanks with the two words "even more." Beside each verse, list the specific thing or exact condition that is described as growing "even more." I'll supply the first one so you get the idea.

GENESIS 37:5—"Then Joseph had a dream. When he told it to his brothers, they hated him even more. ➜ Hatred can grow even more.

JUDGES 2:19—"[T]he Israelites would act even more corruptly than their fathers." ➜ going after other gods, serving them, bowing down to them

1 SAMUEL 18:29—"[A]nd [Saul] became even more afraid of David. As a result, Saul was David's enemy from then on."
→ Knew that the Lord was w. David & that Michal loved him.

2 SAMUEL 6:22—"[A]nd I will humble myself even more."
→ David turned away from Michal & she died childless.

EZEKIEL 8:15—"And He said to me, 'Do you see this, son of man? You will see even more detestable things than these.'"
→ v18. God will act in wrath

LUKE 5:15—"But the news about [Jesus] spread even more, and large crowds would come together to hear Him and to be healed of their sicknesses." → More people become aware of the miracles done by Jesus.

LUKE 11:28—"[Jesus] said, 'even more, those who hear the word of God and keep it are blessed!'" →

LUKE 12:48—"Much will be required of everyone who has been given much. And even more will be expected of the one who has been entrusted with more." → faithful & wise manager.

ROMANS 5:20—"But where sin multiplied, grace multiplied even more" → the law increased the trespass, but grace abounded all the more.

2 CORINTHIANS 3:9—"For if the ministry of condemnation had glory, the ministry of righteousness overflows with even more glory." → law – ministry of death, ministry of righteousness from the H.S.

2 CORINTHIANS 7:13—"For this reason we have been comforted. In addition to our comfort, we rejoiced even more over the joy Titus had, because his spirit was refreshed by all of you."
→

2 CORINTHIANS 8:22—"We have also sent with them our brother. We have often tested him in many circumstances and found him to be diligent—and now even more diligent because of his great confidence in you." → Titus & ?

PHILIPPIANS 1:14—"Most of the brothers in the Lord have gained confidence from my imprisonment and dare even more to speak the message fearlessly."
→

HEBREWS 2:1—"We must, therefore, pay ________________ attention to what we have heard, so that we will not drift away."

These final two verses convey the same meaning but use the terminology "more and more." Please fill in the following blanks with "more and more."

EPHESIANS 4:19—"They became callous and gave themselves over to promiscuity for the practice of every kind of impurity with a desire for ________________." ➔

PHILIPPIANS 1:9 (ESV) —"And it is my prayer that your love may abound ________________, with knowledge and all discernment." ➔

I hope this Scripture-spanning theology of abounding was thought-provoking for you as it was for me.

Based on the Scriptures you've just read and the kinds of elements or conditions that can abound, how would you summarize your findings?

Which abounding element or condition spoke most loudly to you, and why?

I was struck by how few human conditions are genuinely static. In so many ways, we are in constant flux. For instance, compare the first verse in the above list (Gen. 37:5) and the last verse (Phil. 1:9).

What conclusion could you draw from these two verses?

Human emotions have an inherent propensity to grow. We can hate more and more or we can love more and more. Organic beings that we are, we have trouble maintaining one steady condition over the long haul.

Were you as disturbed as I was over the innate propensity of sin and corruption to increase? We can both thank God that "where sin multiplied, grace multiplied even more" (Rom. 5:20). Perhaps you also compared 1 Samuel 18:29 and Philippians 1:14 and noted that fear has an overwhelming tendency to increase even more but, praise God, so has courage. Darkness is intensifying across this globe, but look at what God's Word says about glory: "We all, who with unveiled faces contemplate the Lord's glory, are being transformed into his image with ever-increasing glory, which comes from the LORD" (2 Cor. 3:18, NIV).

In these days of burgeoning hatred, violence, madness, and terror, we are a people called to more and more love and more and more diligence while reflecting more and more of God's glory.

"Where sin multiplied, grace multiplied even more."

Something is going to grow. Something will get "more" of us. Will it be hatred? Coldness? Addiction? Sensuality? Perversion? Devotion? Affection? Belief? Blessing? Ask yourself this question as I do the same: knowing the propensity of things to grow, which way do I want to go? "More and more" one direction will force its antithesis into "less and less." We get to decide which we want to feed and which we want to starve.

We can give up trying to control our whole worlds, but many things in our lives are well within our charge. In many respects, we get to decide which parts of our lives we will release to abound. Jesus already made it possible for us. We don't have to beg Him for abundant life. He sanctioned it by His expressed will, declaring it as the gift of His coming. We simply open up our lives to Him day after day and receive the Holy Spirit without limit (John 3:34). Abundant life is our re-birthright, unmerited and unrestrained.

Let's give our closing attentions to a remarkable exception. The God who beckons you to love more and more cannot love you more. No matter how you grow in diligence and obedience, you cannot increase His affection for you. No matter how faithful you become, you won't get a boost in your lovability. At your darkest moment, you were loved to the fullest measure; the same is true at your lightest moment.

You and I have no power to affect divine love. It is perfect. All we are left to do is ask to know it more and more. And right there in the increase, a miracle of decrease is forced into play: as we are more and more aware of His love, we fear less and less.

For "perfect love drives out fear" (1 John 4:18).

Day Two

Inside Out

FLASH-FORWARD: About brotherly love: You don't need me to write you because you yourselves are taught by God to love one another. ***1 Thessalonians 4:9***

If you were part of our opening video session, do you remember wrapping up with a Greek compound word we asked God to apply to our whole nine-week experience? You'd find that mouthful at the end of your listening guide. The word is *theodidaktoi* (pronounced they-ah-DEE-dak-toy). Is it ringing a bell? If your last three weeks held all the tranquility of an ant bed, don't stress. The term jumps back where it belongs in its original context in today's segment.

Please write 1 Thessalonians 4:6-10 in the back of your book.

- Exactly why did the Thessalonians have no need for anyone to write to them about brotherly love? (See verse 9.)

For you yourselves have been taught by God to love one another

There you have the meaning of the Greek compound word. *Theodidaktoi*: "taught by God." In the first four letters, you see *theo*, which translates into "God," just as in the more familiar word "theology"—the study of God.

We touched on this fascinating piece of information in our opening session, but this time let's really grab hold of it: this mention is the only occurrence of the word *theodidaktoi* in the New Testament and the earliest known occurrence in any body of Greek literature. Paul may well have coined the word himself.[3] Aren't you a little intrigued that the Holy Spirit dropped a brand-new word right into the brain of the apostle Paul?

Paul was a man of the Scriptures and, this early in the New Testament era, the only completed canon he could have held in his hands was the Old Testament. The New Testament was under construction by the Holy Spirit at the very moment the ink was landing on the page of the letter we're studying. God used His hand like a broom, sweeping the words of Isaiah 54:13 from the back of the apostle's mind to the front at this moment of inspiration, adding a nuance the Old Testament prophets couldn't have fathomed.

Write Isaiah 54:13 in this space:

All your sons will be taught by the Lord, and great will be your children's peace.

Isn't it beautiful? If you're in a parental role, even spiritually speaking, don't you wish you could write it like a claim on the foreheads of your children? If you check the context in Isaiah 54, much of what God promised Israel in that portion is yet to come. However, the verse already encircles us because Jesus Himself threw it like a hoop around everyone who comes to Him.

Please read John 6:41-48. What is the context of Jesus' application of the phrase "taught by God"?

I was one of those kids in class who constantly stuck her hand up to ask questions, so I continually imagine what questions might come from your side of the page. Right now, somebody is throwing her hand in the air, asking how Paul could have coined the word *theodidaktoi* when Jesus already clearly used the phrase "taught by God" in John 6:45.

Here's the resolution. The usage in the Gospel of John is two separate words: *didaktoi theou.* After the birth of the church, however, the Holy Spirit (of Jesus Himself, Rom. 8:9) rolled a one-word version of the term right off of the tongue of the apostle Paul: *theodidaktoi.* In fact, if you really want to get technical about the arrangement of the words, *theodidaktoi* would literally read "God-taught" rather than "taught by God."

Here's the fabulous part: something of paramount significance happened between Christ speaking the words recorded in John 6:45 and the penning of 1 Thessalonians 4:9. God sent the Holy Spirit on the day of Pentecost to dwell within the temples—the very bodies—of all who received Jesus Christ as Savior (1 Cor. 6:19).

God sent the Holy Spirit on the day of Pentecost to dwell within temples.

So when we use the terminology of "I received Jesus as my personal Savior," we describe reality. We are not just using a figure of speech or a metaphor or a way to say we embraced a certain belief system. Whether or not we sensed a shred of divine activity at the time, when we received Jesus as our Savior, we literally received His Spirit into our beings. Sometimes I can go about my day as though that whole idea is an ordinary part of Christian living. On other days, like today, the wonder of it almost splinters my skull.

The Gospel of John records Christ's promise of the indwelling Spirit to His followers (John 14:17) and, in the same chapter and context, His description of a pertinent work "the Helper" (John 14:26, ESV) would accomplish.

No matter which formal translation of John 14:26-27 you consult, you can fill in the following blank:

"But the Counselor, the Holy Spirit—the Father will send Him in My name—will ______________________________ and remind you of everything I have told you. Peace I leave with you. My peace I give to you."

The apostle Paul would have been well within Christ's own gospel bounds to see the activity of the indwelling Spirit as at least a partial fulfillment of Isaiah 54:13. Take a look at it in the ESV: "All your children shall be taught by the LORD, and great shall be the peace of your children."

Here in 1 Thessalonians 4:9, the concept of God-taught is particularly captivating. Look at Paul's context and lean into his tone. He viewed the new Thessalonian believers' love as something so uniquely Christ-tattling, that he didn't tie it to a page, presentation, or the parroting of any godly person. All three of those are valid avenues the Holy Spirit uses to instruct His children, but something different seemed to happen with those nascent believers. They learned to love from the inside-out. And that they learned it straight from God is remarkably clear.

And He personally gave some to be apostles, some prophets, some evangelists, some pastors and teachers, for the training of the saints in the work of ministry, to build up the body of Christ, until we all reach unity in the faith and in the knowledge of God's Son, growing into a mature man with a stature measured by Christ's fullness.
EPHESIANS 4:11-13

To make sure we appreciate the slice of uniqueness, read Ephesians 4:11-13 in the margin for the sake of a gentle contrast. What setup did God ordain for the primary equipping of His people?

apostles, prophets, evangelists, pastors & teachers,

That we received the instruction through a secondary source does not make it a second-class lesson. God set pastors, speakers, evangelists, and teachers in place for exactly that purpose, and His Spirit unquestionably remains the impetus. A divine work is still required for the process to take, just as Paul described in 1 Corinthians 2:13—"We also speak these things, not in words taught by human wisdom, but in those taught by the Spirit, explaining spiritual things to spiritual people."

The Thessalonians, however, learned to love one another in a little different way. That's the point of our fascination today.

Thank God, not everything has to be learned the hard way. On blissful occasions, we don't even have to learn the long way. I was about 40 years old before those refreshing possibilities ever really occurred to me. Please don't wait that long. Sometimes something even more extraordinary takes place. We develop a know-how only God could teach us and yet the process isn't latched to the usual methods. God's Spirit bypasses all the formal routes of the learning curve and the lesson comes straight from Him.

We read whispers of a similar phenomenon from parts of the world where Christianity is forbidden by law, where training is virtually nonexistent, and where most believers are first-generation. One solitary Bible may be smuggled into an area where believers receive single pages of Scripture, handling them like hidden treasures, folding and unfolding them until they crack at the seams.

These believers may know little more than how to be saved, yet the fruit of the Spirit sprouts and they love and worship and pray and fellowship in ways most of us learn in formal discipleship. It's a mercy from God. Extraordinarily *theodidaktoi.*

A young woman I love grew up in an agnostic home with no exposure whatsoever to Jesus. She came to know Him in early adolescence through a novel that wasn't even overtly Christian. Right there in her small bedroom speckled with stuffed animals, God Himself taught her to pray and stirred up a genuine love in her heart for Him.

My friend pours out her lifeblood today to disciple people in Christ, but she never forgets how He pursued her for that sacred length of time apart from more common means.

I'm getting tears in my eyes just thinking about it. Could God be any better? Any more merciful? Would He stop at nothing to get to us?

○ Do you have a similar example from someone you know or have read about (or perhaps seen in the mirror this morning) who seemed to have learned some biblical truth straight from God without textbook, training, or human teacher? If so, share the story here.

Some people believe that to truly come away with a viable understanding of the Bible requires a grasp of original languages and that the New Testament is properly studied only in Greek. I am profusely thankful for scholars who have gone to the arduous task of learning and poring over the original languages. Rarely does a workday pass that I don't benefit from their labors, through commentaries and dictionaries. They are appointed by God for profound contributions to equip His church. But, Sister, God can also reveal Himself to the simpleminded, to the partially educated, to the uneducated, and, oddly, even the missionally unreached.

God can also reveal Himself to the simpleminded.

Jesus commissioned His followers to go into the entire world and make disciples, and we are without excuse to disobey. But sometimes when we get there, we might come to the startling discovery that those very people have been taught something by God that we still struggle to learn.

It may be contentment. It may be unselfishness. It may be compassion.

Or, like the Thessalonians, it may just be love.

Day Three

Stop in the Name of Love

FLASH-FORWARD: Seek to lead a quiet life, to mind your own business, and to work with your own hands, as we commanded you. ***1 Thessalonians 4:11***

Prior to his death, one of my uncles spent several years in a storage unit stacked to the ceiling with canned goods and lined with plastic jugs of water. Adjacent to his cot stood a large freezer wrapped in a heavy rusted chain joined by a padlock the size of a man's palm. My uncle did not pay taxes and had not for many years, a choice that forced him to live off the grid of formal employment and in a bafflingly unnecessary state of poverty and filth. He was a perfectly capable, able-bodied man and a source of untold anxiety to an older brother who often bailed him out financially. "I'm terrified that he's going to die in that storage unit," the big brother once told me. Tragically, he did.

Please read 1 Thessalonians 4:9-12 and add verses 11 and 12 to your handwritten portion.

In addition to loving one another more and more (v. 10), what three directives did the apostle Paul give in verse 11?

1. lead a quiet life
2. mind your own business
3. work w. your hands.

What two reasons did Paul give in verse 12 for the directives he issued in verse 11?

1. win the respect of outsiders
2. not be dependent on anybody

The two reasons you listed above were almost certainly intended to point toward two distinct groups of people: (1) unbelievers in the larger community (called "outsiders" in the text) and (2) fellow believers in the smaller Christian community (whom we'll call "insiders"). The latter is less obvious, but implied in Paul's insistence that the Thessalonians "not be dependent on anyone."

The unbelieving community and civil government couldn't have been depended on to support the Thessalonian believers, particularly for what the officials considered seditious beliefs. The issues on the table in this Scripture segment revolve around responsible love and the responsible reputation of Christ's people. Simply put, how the Thessalonians lived their believing lives bore ramifications that involved both outsiders and insiders. Two thousand years later, the same is true for us. In this respect, "I don't care what anybody thinks about me or how this looks" is an irresponsible Christian ethic.

My uncle lived in such bizarre conditions because of his rabid obsession with end-time events. Day and night he listened to radio broadcasts, read materials, and watched television programs centered on Bible prophecies about the end of the world. He left streams of voice mails warning his family members, friends, and fellow church members about emerging fulfillments of various Bible predictions. Sadly, few people returned his phone calls.

The irony is that several of us shared his strong belief in the Bible and his conviction that we were part of an era of prophetic fulfillment. We had different philosophies, however, about what to do with the time we had left.

He had lost his perspective.

Some might reason he'd lost his mind, but those of us who knew my uncle knew that he was very capable of taking care of himself. What he had lost was his perspective. He measured devotion to God on the scale of fanaticism.

In days 4 and 5 of this week, we'll transition into the subject of end-time events. We'll see the connection between Paul's directives in today's segment and an appropriate expectancy of Christ's return. Before we chalk up all such fanatical end-time living to what is at least an admirable single-mindedness toward Scripture, let's consider how quitting work in the name of advanced eschatology could be particularly convenient if we're lazy.

Lately I've been facing a little unsound thinking of my own, which also ties into today's lesson. Does anyone besides me ever keep saying yes to people because you assume that yes is the loving answer even when your insides are screaming no? I get wound up in a knot of neurotic processing right there. I catch myself with the attitude that *whatever I want to do the least is probably what God wants me to do the most.* I start assuming that the harder thing is always the godlier thing.

When I'm in this line of thinking, I imagine forgiveness always demands reconciliation and occasions never arise to cut myself off from someone who keeps squeezing me dry. Automatic assumptions like these grow from such a fundamental self-distrust that, if I'm in a neurotic mind-set, it rarely occurs to me that my preference in the situation could possibly reflect God's.

Can you relate to these lines of reasoning? If so, explain in the margin.

In numerous letters, Paul called believers to take care of one another, to bear one another's burdens and to, in effect, be their brother's keeper. In 1 Thessalonians 4:9-12, he summoned followers of Christ to love one another more and more but, in the very same context of community, he warned them not to take advantage of love by being inappropriately dependent on other believers. Dr. C. A. Wanamaker puts it this way:

> Thus, while on the one hand Paul sought to encourage familial love and responsibility among his converts, on the other he did not wish to allow his instructions regarding familial love to be exploited by anyone. [4]

Because God calls us to love lavishly and share generously, we who want desperately to please God can be at considerable risk of exploitation. Paul placed the burden of responsible community in this matter right where it should be: squarely on the shoulders of those who would otherwise be overly dependent. The problem is, sometimes unnecessarily dependent people remain unnecessarily dependent. Dependency keeps working so they don't have to.

Dependency keeps working so they don't have to.

Over-dependency isn't limited to finances. It can be seen in emotional, physical, psychological, and spiritual arenas, but it always comes down to the same thing: one person ends up doing the other person's work.

When we find ourselves in a dependency situation, the following question might be beneficial: *Is saying no and drawing a line coming from selfishness or good sense?* If it's a blend of the two, the motive is suspect and needs to be carefully sorted out with God in prayer. But if selfishness is genuinely not in play and your good sense is saying no, think twice before you override that logic.

The Holy Spirit lives in us if we belong to Christ. That "good sense" may at times be our human nature's rationale, but it could also be the urging of the Holy Spirit Himself. Yes, we are called to live sacrificially and told by Christ that "if anyone takes away your coat, don't hold back your shirt either" (Luke 6:29), but let's listen for an inner alarm to go off if we're about to sacrifice biblical wisdom in an attempt to act biblically.

James 1:5 is the only perfect solution. What does it say?

If any of you lacks wisdom, he should ask God who generously gives to all without finding fault

How much we want to say no is an unreliable indicator of how much Jesus wants us to say yes. If we've hit a nerve today, you and I could talk for hours, but our Scripture segment beckons us to turn our thoughts to walking "properly in the presence of outsiders" (1 Thess. 4:12). The NIV rendering is particularly powerful: "so that your daily life may win the respect of outsiders."

To keep this discussion from remaining theoretical, write in the margin the first names of unbelievers who have peered closely into your life—whether at work, in family gatherings, in your neighborhood, or in social settings.

With them in mind, consider each of the directives in 1 Thessalonians 4:11.

1. **"SEEK TO LEAD A QUIET LIFE."** The NIV translates the original language this way: "Make it your ambition to lead a quiet life." Dr. Leon Morris calls the wording "a striking paradox," explaining that "Paul's remark would be something like 'be ambitious to be unambitious'" or possibly even "seek strenuously to be still."[5] The bottom line is to avoid drawing unnecessary and unhelpful attention. For the Thessalonians, it could have been a matter of life and death or easily a matter of home and prison.

Michael W. Holmes notes a similarity for some today:

> In some countries today Christianity is, like the church in Thessalonica, a persecuted minority movement. Public attention to one member of the group can and often does result in a spotlight being cast on others as well. The wrong kind of public activity on the part of one believer can have devastating consequences for the entire congregation ... In many countries and regions, however, Christians form a substantial part of cultural majorities. In these circumstances the consequences of public involvement are substantially different, and it may be that engagement with rather than withdrawal from the public arena is called for.[6]

Most of us taking this journey are not in threatening circumstances. Our greater temptation is to remain quiet when we should speak up. However, we do still encounter environments or situations when the Holy Spirit fills us with the conviction to choose quiet over loud.

Share a personal example in the margin if you have one.

2. "MIND YOUR OWN BUSINESS." There we have it in black and white. I'm a curious people-person by nature, but I'm learning that some things we simply do not want to know. Some things we cannot handle knowing and still love like we are called to love. Only Jesus can maintain an unwavering, healthy affection while knowing all things, reading all hearts, and seeing behind all doors.

Sometimes we insist on knowing something that we then cannot get past. I'm not advocating denial and certainly not supporting deception; I'm talking about details that we can't erase from the marker board of our minds—details that exceed our coping abilities and disintegrate our commitment to love.

○ What is the most prominent lesson you've had to learn about minding your own business? Respond in the margin.

We need to do our jobs.

3. "WORK WITH YOUR OWN HANDS." We need to do our jobs. If we stay busy with edifying activities, we have less time to get wrapped up in things that impede the spread of the gospel, undermine community, and inhibit brotherly love. Be a giver, not a taker. Add, don't subtract. The admonition is for those who are dependent by convenience and refuse to take appropriate responsibility for themselves. People who have to be dependent are not the ones on the hot seat in today's lesson or anywhere else in Scripture. Why all these directives? "So that your daily life may win the respect of outsiders" (NIV).

Let it never be said of us that people disrespected Christianity because they disrespected us. Let's carry the reputation of Christ well.

Day Four

Since We Believe

FLASH-FORWARD: We do not want you to be uninformed, brothers, concerning those who are asleep, so that you will not grieve like the rest, who have no hope. ***1 Thessalonians 4:13***

Keith and I are newcomers to the country woods where we live. A year passed before some of our neighbors acknowledged our presence as we drove up and down the dirt road loosely connecting our houses. They would have rightly considered us "city folks," but we have worked hard to prove ourselves over the last two years. Around here, being neighborly has nothing to do with waving at one another. It is about doing. If a tree falls in someone's yard, you help clean it up. You repair a hole in the road, put a rabid varmint out of its misery, and buy your fresh vegetables out of a woman's backyard—all this with a cell phone in your Wranglers in case you need to text or check your email.

A couple of years may seem like ample time for acceptance until you start counting the decades our neighbors have on us. The family at the top of the road was planted on that very acreage in the mid-1800s. They were German immigrants who built and sold wagon wheels and caskets.

Let your mind turn on those two products for a moment. You might say those carpenters specialized in coming and going. In whatever direction you were headed, they could help take you there. Today we begin breaking in to the best-known portion of the letters to the Thessalonians. Notice that I didn't call it the best understood. We'll reap vastly more from 1 Thessalonians 4:13-18 if we continually observe Paul's original intention in the short, potent discourse: it's about coming and going. Wagon wheels and caskets. See for yourself. Read 1 Thessalonians 4:13-18 but handwrite only verses 13-15.

How could you use verse 13 to build an argument against the colloquialism "ignorance is bliss"? Respond in the margin.

Knowledge is power.

How would you define grief (skip the dictionary)? In your explanation, point out how you'd distinguish grief from sadness.

Extended, painful, overpowering, despair

"Fallen asleep" in verse 14 was a way of describing believers who had died. Compare 1 Corinthians 15:17-18. What if Christ were not raised from the dead?

your faith is futile, you are still in your sins

Write 1 Corinthians 15:20 in the margin.

Now read 1 Corinthians 15:3-8 and sharpen your basic math skills. How many people saw the resurrected Lord Jesus? "Cephas" is another name for "Peter," so subtract one from the Twelve and subtract another for the absence of Judas Iscariot. Use the margin for your equations. Then put the total here: ________

Good job, Sister. Those early followers who died gruesome deaths for the sake of gospel did not follow through because they *thought* He'd been raised from the dead. They *knew* He had. Once you believe to your bones that Jesus died and rose again, you know with everything in you that nothing is too difficult for God. That's Paul's point in 1 Thessalonians 4:14.

● Reread 1 Thessalonians 4:15-16. What group of people has the first access at the coming of the Lord?

They expected Christ's coming at any time—just as we can.

Christ's return was proclaimed to those early believers with such authority and unshakable confidence that they expected it at any time—just as we can. "For this we declare to you by a word from the Lord" (v. 15, ESV). This was no rumor. No fool's hope. No claim of men. Christ's second advent is as certain as His first. Both were on schedule before the voice of God pitched the planets into orbit.

The Thessalonians obviously feared that those who'd believed in Christ yet died before His appearing had fallen into an unfortunate vacuum of time and would forfeit all participation. Paul's assurance was they'd not only be there for the big event; they'd get there first.

Tomorrow's lesson will focus the lens on the promised coming of the Lord Jesus Christ as expressed in these passages. Today we center on the motivation prompting this part of the letter: the bewilderment of death. Notice a striking difference in terminology used for Jesus and His followers in reference to the end of their mortal lives in verse 14.

Most formal translations use the same two words for the following blanks, so fill them in to draw the contrast: "Since we believe that Jesus ________ and rose again, in the same way God will bring with Him those who have fallen ________ through Jesus."

Meditate on this powerful commentary excerpt:

> Paul speaks of Christ not as sleeping, but as dying. In the New Testament there are two distinct strands of teaching about death. On the one hand it is the most natural of all things and is an inevitable part of the conditions of our earthly existence. On the other hand it is completely unnatural, a horror, the result of sin. Christ in his

> death bore the wages of sin. He endured the worst that death can possibly be. Thereby he transformed the whole position of those who are in him. It is because there was no mitigation of the horror of death for him that there is no horror in death for his people. For them it is but sleep."[7]

○ What might be gained through thinking of death in terms of sleep?

So if death is "but sleep," should we not mourn? Fix your gaze on 4:13 and do not let it go until this lesson draws to a close. Through His servant Paul, God subtly extends two hands of solace. In one hand He gives us permission to grieve, a gift of inestimable value to our human souls.

As much as we may despise and dread the need to grieve, imagine being disallowed to grieve, too dead inside to grieve, condemned or ridiculed because you grieved. Consider the gift of tears cradled in the palm of that hand of solace. Tears take us somewhere words cannot. Tears are liquid language set to the tune of the Holy Spirit's groanings (Rom. 8:26). Grief is the sacred love seat where we fellowship acutely in the sufferings of Christ. We are not glad to be drawn to that seat, but there we find Him if we're willing. Oddly, we also find a faith beyond what we thought we'd lost. There He seems to say, "Put your finger here, and see my hands; and put out your hand, and place it in my side" (John 20:27, ESV). The wounds of Christ are never more sacred to us than when we feel the stab of this fallen world's blade and hasten to Him.

I don't mean to romanticize grief. But the way God fashioned us with capacity to feel, to muse, to experience and respond to life, grief denied would be a terror to the soul. We would be image bearers reduced to animal instinct. To the degree we have loved, we often mourn; but we can be whole again piece by piece if we accept what 1 Thessalonians 4:13 holds in its other hand.

For a child of God, hopelessness is the most unnecessary condition.

If one hand of solace holds permission to grieve, the other hand contains insistence of hope. A hand empty of hope can cast us headlong into the only place blacker than grief. Nothing is like hopelessness. No physical pain is like it, though it can lead to it. No fear is like it, though it can feed it. No feeling of loss, as terrible as it may be, can compete with it. You feel dead while wide awake. You bide your time while something buries you a teaspoon at a time.

Hopelessness is accepting that you are doomed and, as the condition advances, it is not only you—the whole world is doomed. News can only be bad. Fights can only be lost. Things can only get worse. With its chin embedded in its chest, hopelessness mutters robotically "It's too late" and "It's no use."

For a child of God, hopelessness is the most unnecessary condition in the entire bag of mind tricks, but even the most righteous can crater to it. See if the following words from Job 6 call out any response from you.

Circle each word or phrase that you think contributes to hopelessness.

What strength do I have that I should continue to hope? What is my future, that I should be patient? Is my strength that of stone, or my flesh made of bronze? Since I cannot help myself, the hope for success has been banished from me.
JOB 6:11-13

Job's words are especially insightful because they whisper the secret root of human hopelessness: *I have no strength. I cannot help myself. Therefore, all hope of success has been banished from me.*

As spiritual people, we tend to tie our hopelessness to our belief that God has somehow let us down or refused to come through. Job's raw confession conveys that he felt hopeless because he could not help himself. Let this one go deep, Sister: God is your help. He is your strength. This whole thing is not dependent on you. In Him is your future and it is bright with His countenance.

"Be strong and courageous, all you who put your hope in the LORD" (Ps. 31:24).

"I will praise You forever for what You have done. In the presence of Your faithful people, I will put my hope in Your name, for it is good" (Ps. 52:9).

"(Insert your name)____________, *put your hope in the LORD. For there is faithful love with the LORD, and with Him is redemption in abundance." (Ps. 130:7)*

"Rejoice in hope; be patient in affliction; be persistent in prayer" (Rom. 12:12).

"I pray that the perception of your mind may be enlightened so you may know what is the hope of His calling" (Eph. 1:18a).

"Let us hold on to the confession of our hope without wavering, for HE WHO PROMISED IS FAITHFUL" (Heb. 10:23, emphasis mine).

Life can be painful here. Loss is inevitable. So let us grieve when we must, but God forbid that we grieve as the hopeless do. In His hands, we find solace. In His heart, we find rest. In His time, we find meaning. In His eyes, we are blessed. In His strength, we're made mighty. In His light, morning breaks. In His Word, He has promised. In His coming, sleepers wake.

Day Five

All Caught Up

FLASH-FORWARD: Then we who are still alive will be caught up together with them in the clouds to meet the Lord in the air and so we will always be with the Lord. *1 Thessalonians 4:17*

All of us, regardless of our Christian traditions, creeds, or systematic theologies, stand to be slack-jawed by the way God ultimately fulfills end-time prophecies. We sometimes confuse His unwavering loyalty to His Word with His limitation to His Word. Wait one second before you light a match to me. Without question, God will do exactly what He said and His Word will be unequivocally upheld and every prophecy fulfilled. But He has all the room in the universe to perform His Word in ways not yet disclosed to us and that exceed the finite constructs of human language.

To us, to be "caught up ... in the clouds" means that we'll be suspended midair with our feet dangling and our shoes dropping like hailstones. To us, the resurrection of the dead seems less complicated if you're not cremated, as if we could somehow make it harder on God. To us, our bodies cannot "fall asleep" while our souls remain wide-eyed and awake. To us, souls can only be comprised of intangible substance, ghostlike and ethereal.

How do you explain a rocket ship to a caveman? Or a satellite to a shepherd? Or the color orange to a blind man? Or a sonic boom to someone who has never heard a pin drop? If we insist on end-time events making perfect sense to us in advance and maintaining a precise order of detailed service that we can wrap our minds around, we will weaken the wonder right out of the pursuit and perhaps come no closer to the truth. We are called to study Scripture. The moment we think we've mastered it, we've manipulated it.

"The Bible was not written to gratify our curiosity."

Leon Morris said it so well, "There are many things that we would like to know, but the Bible was not written to gratify our curiosity."[8] Curiosity is good, but let's not confuse divine revelation with God owing us an explanation.

○ What are you most curious about concerning end-time events?

Questions like these are advantageous. They drive us to study. Let's just stay open to the fact that the reward of our pursuit may not be our sought-out answer. Our reward may be the inestimable gift of answerless awe.

Though clearly God has method, methodology is not the point of most end-time discourses in Scripture, including Christ's masterpiece in Matthew 24. We're invited to marvel and exhorted to prepare and, as we do, we can bank on this: God will do everything He says He will. Numbers 23:19 says, "God is not a man who lies, or a son of man who changes His mind. Does He speak and not act, or promise and not fulfill?"

How God meticulously fulfills His Word, however, is a matter of His creative perfection and infinite wisdom. God did not spend the total of His imagination on Christ's first advent. The prospect of a measureless sky rolling back like a scroll ought to be enough to silence the volume of mortal hubris (Rev. 6:14).

When God's kingdom comes and His will is done on earth as in heaven, a whole new reality will break in before our eyes. When He who is enthroned in the heavens returns to claim the earth, we will see and experience things we've never had the capacity to imagine. It will be a new era of Let There Be Light.

Now let's read 1 Thessalonians 4:13-18. Handwrite verses 16-18 on the appropriate page.

Write the first four words of verse 16 from any formal Bible translation in all capital letters in the margin. FOR THE LORD HIMSELF

This won't be the mighty angel Gabriel coming through the skies in swift flight like he rushed to Daniel in Babylon (Dan. 9:21). "For the Lord Himself will descend from heaven" (1 Thess. 4:16). Exodus 19 (below) is the first context in which the NIV translates the phrase "the LORD descended."

- Just for joy's sake, as you read Exodus 19:16-20 below, jot any resemblance to 1 Thessalonians 4:16-18 on the right and the major differences on the left.

DIFFERENCES	RESEMBLANCES
Specific time	Loud trumpet
Thunder lightning	Clouds
Trembled - people	Meet God
Moses led	Lord descended
Smoke fire	went up.
Mountain trembled	

On the morning of the third day there was thunder and lightning, with a thick cloud over the mountain, and a very loud trumpet blast. Everyone in the camp trembled. Then Moses led the people out of the camp to meet with God, and they stood at the foot of the mountain. Mount Sinai was covered with smoke, because the LORD descended on it in fire. The smoke billowed up from it like smoke from a furnace, and the whole mountain trembled violently. As the sound of the trumpet grew louder and louder, Moses spoke and the voice of God answered him. The LORD descended to the top of Mount Sinai and called Moses to the top of the mountain. So Moses went up.

EXODUS 19:16-20, NIV

1. YOU NO DOUBT RECORDED THE TRUMPET AS A RESEMBLANCE. Trumpet sounds have a longstanding history in the Scriptures. They were used to summon an ingathering, to signal an oncoming proclamation or presentation, and to herald official festivities. Most intriguing of all, trumpet sounds in the Bible do not always come from trumpets.

> Glance at Revelation 1:10, and then at Revelation 4:1. What were the sources of those sounds?

Voice

2. YOU PROBABLY ALSO LISTED CLOUDS AS A COMMON DENOMINATOR. The Scripture often depicts the glory of God with a cloak of clouds. Clouds both bear a visible witness to His presence and simultaneously spare the witnesses from suffering death by glory.

- Matthew 17:5 records God's voice emanating from a cloud on the mount where Christ was transfigured.
- Acts 1:9 records Jesus, before the eyes of His disciples, ascending from the Mount of Olives, wrapped in a cloud, and taken "out of their sight."
- Revelation 1:7 (ESV) says of Christ's return, "Behold, he is coming with the clouds, and every eye will see him, even those who pierced him, and all tribes of the earth will wail on account of him."

Consider the Old Testament account of the Lord's descent in Exodus 19:20. I see something gloriously powerful about the Lord having to go south to reach the tip-top of an earthly mountain. At man's highest heights, God's lofty presence still has to stoop to touch our ground.

Note a point of vast contrast between the Lord's descent to meet His people in 1 Thessalonians 4:16 and His descent to meet with Moses in Exodus 19. Moses had to climb the mountain. We will be swept up into thin air. Ain't no mountain high enough. Leon Morris notes, "The verb Paul uses for 'caught up' is one that means 'to seize, carry off by force.' There is often the notion of a sudden swoop, and usually that of a force that cannot be resisted."[9] That means we're all going to meet Christ in the air when He says so, no matter how we expected the event to take place.

"Caught up" is a translation of the lexical Greek *harpazō*. The Latin equivalent of the Greek is the word *raptus*, from which comes our most common English term for the occurrence, the rapture.[10]

Another amazing difference between the scene in Exodus 19:16-20 and the one in 1 Thessalonians 4:16-18 involves the participants. While the camp stood at the foot of the mountain and Moses alone ascended to the meeting place with God, quite a crowd will gather in the air with Jesus. Several Greek words are used in reference to the appearance or coming of Christ (and we will set those terms side by side in week 7). The one translated "coming" in the phrase "the coming of the Lord" in 1 Thessalonians 4:15 (ESV) is the beautiful word *parousia* (pah-roo-SEE-ah). Of it, Leon Morris says:

> One more point remains to be determined in this verse, and that is the meaning of "bring with Jesus." Some understand it to signify that Jesus will take these people with him into glory, but this does not seem to be justified. Paul is talking about the Parousia. It is their share in the events of that great day that is in view. It is best to understand the words to mean that Jesus will bring the faithful departed with him when he comes back. Their death does not mean that they will miss their share in the Parousia.[11]

So will Christ bring the resurrected with Him to get believers who are alive at the time, and then take them all back in brand-new bodies to heaven for an interval? Or will both groups meet the triumphant, returning King as ancient celebrants would do—but this time in the air—and then escort Him on to earth for every eye to see? The question represents a great big capital Y in the road of end-time enthusiasts: is the event in 1 Thessalonians 4:17 secret and separate from the coming of Christ when all will see Him?

Many of those who view the rapture as a distinct event from the globally visible return of Christ believe that the occasions are separated by seven years of tribulation. Some believe the seven years are literal, while others consider the years symbolic. God-seeking, Jesus-loving, Scripture-believing people can be found all over the spectrum in their stands on this aspect of eschatology. In the end, proving right in our ordering of events will not matter an iota. If our thorough understanding was either necessary to us or pleasurable to Him, God could have dictated His plan line by line in pristinely paralleled texts. He didn't. God obviously chose to leave this subject cloudy on purpose.

God obviously chose to leave this subject cloudy on purpose.

All that will matter at the end of the Day is that we will forever be with the Lord. The justified will finally live by sight. We will know every line in His gorgeous face. We will know the pitch of His voice and the iris of His eyes. And we will know once and for all why angels splendorous and awesome in their own right endlessly declare, "Worthy is He!" Jesus is the Dayspring (Luke 1:78, KJV) who will end all nightfall. One shout from His mouth and the dead shall be raised.

Therefore, encourage one another with these words.

Maranatha.

Group Session Five

REVIEW THE WEEK

Use these questions to guide your discussion of last week's homework.

● Principal Questions

DAY 1: What kind of life did Christ say He'd come to give in John 10:10? (p. 90)

DAY 2: Exactly why did the Thessalonians have no need for anyone to write to them about brotherly love? (p. 94)

DAY 3: What two reasons did Paul give for the directives he issued in verse 11? (p. 98)

DAY 4: What group of people has the first access at the coming of the Lord? (p. 103)

DAY 5: What similarities and differences did you note between Exodus 19:16-20 and 1 Thessalonians 4:16-18? (p. 107)

○ Personal Discussion Questions

DAY 1: How does the phrase "more and more" contradict the notion of a place of arrival in this earthly journey in which we simply maintain from there? (p. 90)

DAY 2: Do you have an example of someone who seemed to have learned biblical truth straight from God without textbook, training, or a human teacher? (p. 97)

DAY 3: What is the most prominent lesson you've had to learn about minding your own business? (p. 101)

DAY 4: What might be gained through thinking of death in terms of sleep? (p. 104)

DAY 5: What are you most curious about concerning end-time events? (p. 106)

VIEW THE VIDEO

Introduction

This week in our homework, we purposely dodged portions of 1 Thessalonians 4:3-8 so we could save them for today's session. This countercultural segment of Scripture centers on ______ ______.

Keep the following continuum in view as we move through our discussion:

There are ______ ⟷ There are ______ ______

regarding ______ ______ regarding ______ ______

1. What God dictates here is ____________ ____________ and it was pertinent ____________ (v. 3). The Greek word for sexual immorality is ____________.[1]

2. What God dictates here is ____________. See v. 1: "just as ____________ are ____________"

3. What God dictates here is ____________. See v. 4: "that ____________ of you ____________"[2]

4. What God dictates here is ____________. See v. 4. God does not ____________ of us what cannot ultimately ____________ us.

1. S. Zodhiates, *The Complete Word Study Dictionary: New Testament*, s.v. "porneía."
2. F. F. Bruce, *1 and 2 Thessalonians*, Word Biblical Commentary, vol. 45 (Dallas: Nelson Reference and Electronic, 1982), 83.

CHILDREN OF THE DAY

The 28-Day Challenge

In the session five video I introduced the 28-day challenge. If the Holy Spirit has convicted you that you are to any degree trapped in a sexual stronghold, this could be part of your path to freedom. On page 225 you will see Scripture prayers that make up the 28-day challenge. The prayers are the words of Scripture, personalized into prayers you may return to Christ. I encourage you to begin using them each day as the basis for your conversations with Him about freedom from this stronghold. And keep your chin up! You are deeply loved and highly esteemed by Christ.

Do not allow Satan to discourage you. You can do this. Begin the next 28 days with a Scripture prayer. Through the day, talk with the Father about His truth in the Scripture and seek to follow Him in sexual purity. If you struggle or fall, He will not abandon you. Continue the journey. If He leads you to repeat the challenge, please do so.

At *www.lifeway.com/28daychallenge* you will find a video message and email address especially for you from me. The email address is just for the challenge. Send me a note so we at Living Proof Ministries can be praying for you.

Satan has done a masterful job of shaming those of us who have been caught in sexual strongholds into a continuous cycle of defeat. He seduces, and then he shames, keeping his eye steadfastly on the goal of scandal. Satan cannot take our salvation from us, so he does everything he can to steal, kill, and destroy our character, testimony, and effectiveness. Defeated Christians work far more effectively in Satan's scheme to undermine the church than successful non-Christians ever will!

None of us will question that Satan is having a field day in our present generation in the area of sexual strongholds. His attacks on healthy sexuality have become so outright and blatant that we're becoming frighteningly desensitized and are unknowingly readjusting the plumb line to a state of relativity. Instead of measuring our lives against the goal of Christlikeness, we measure ourselves against the world's depravity. We can point to the trash heaps around us and say, "I'll never be as bad as that." A Christian teenager might reason, "At least I sleep only with my boyfriend. Anyway, we're going to get married one day." A Christian spouse might justify his or her lusts with words like, "I may not get to order the dish, but there's no harm in checking out the menu."

The virus of relativity is especially contagious in the media industry. We're tempted to choose one compromising movie over another because it's not nearly as bad as the other. We are wise to become very alert to the venomous snakebite of relativism. Satan is increasing the dosage of sexually immoral provocation with such consistency that we don't realize how much poison we're swallowing.

We must begin with the basic truth that sexual intimacy is an absolute gift of God given to a husband and wife for their mutual joy and satisfaction. Most of us realize that sex itself is not the problem. It's what we're doing with it beyond its stated purpose that becomes the problem. Incalculable numbers of believers suffer from sexual strongholds. Even believers who really want to live victoriously often find themselves caught in a cycle of sin. Many who fall into sexual sin are extremely remorseful about their actions and suffer terrible guilt, but they can't seem to avoid falling back into the trap.

Satan traps his pawns in secret shame. Please read this carefully: we are being sexually assaulted by the Devil. The church must keep mentioning the unmentionable and biblically address issues that are attacking our generation. God's Word applies to the strongholds of promiscuity, perversity, and pornography just as it does to any other. God is not shocked. He has the remedy. He is awaiting our humble, earnest cry for help.

No matter what kind of sexual stronghold you seek to overcome, God's remedy is His truth. As you pray and claim these Scriptures through prayer throughout the next 28 days, choose to believe God's truth even when you still feel the lie. Even state out loud when possible, "God, I know what Your Word says is true even though I still have feelings to the contrary. Your Word will remain the same, but my feelings will change. Help me to know that the first step is to believe with my mind and soon my heart will change too."

You can do it, believer, because God will do it through you if you'll let Him. Give Him time and truth and there's nothing He can't do. Reject Satan's lies that you can never be free. Don't you see? He is afraid of you! He is afraid of what you'll become and the power of your testimony if God sets you free. Go to whatever lengths God takes you. He's already provided the blood. Now you be willing to provide the sweat and tears.

I promise you based on the authority of the Word of God that your liberation will be worth it. I love you and am praying for you!

Week Five

Children of Light

Day One

Like a Thief in the Night

FLASH-FORWARD: For you yourselves know very well that the Day of the Lord will come just like a thief in the night. *1 Thessalonians 5:2*

My funny, quirky mom died 15 years ago today, all five of her children by her side. We watched a homicidal cancer kill her a day at a time for several years until she was swept home in the strong arms of Jesus. We siblings love each other tremendously, but we've struggled somewhat to roll to a center. Mom was the axle spinning our relational wheel, and we've done a good bit of swerving in her absence. When the officer directing the family traffic is gone, collisions occur. Thankfully, many of us know from personal experience what God can do with wrecks.

My mom was a churchgoing, Bible-carrying believer who developed her systematic theology primarily from her life perceptions. She believed God oversaw global events, but that the suffering and madness in the world were proof He remained at arm's length. And she saw His arms as apishly long.

Many people had let my mom down. Colossal disappointment and disenchantment tinted her perception of God. She didn't think God was unkind but, until the last year of her life, she tended to find Him a tad aloof.

My mom was not alone in the way she formed her theology. We're all prone to develop perception-driven beliefs. What we see, hear, and experience can be so glaringly persuasive that we end up scribbling invisible addendums and corrections all over Scripture. Like the half-man/half-goat in Greek mythology, our theology ends up in the shape of a mythical half-us/half-God. We create our own blend based on the parts of Scripture that match our perceptions. Fusion becomes the answer to our confusion.

○ Does this resonate with you? If so, what part of your personal experience fights hardest to distort your biblical beliefs?

We can be a bundle of philosophical contradictions, can't we? Life is too hard to be approached with a wispy-thin confidence in the character of God. In a world that has lost its way, we must have the fidelity of His heart, the rightness of His judgments, the certainty of His love, and the inseparability of His presence as our north, south, east, and west. When life sends us headlong into a cartwheel, if we'll stretch our hands out in each direction, He will land us back on our feet.

If we allow the world to set our standard, we'll rewrite a theology in which humanity is the victim of a god's jealous love. Such a god becomes more terrifying than hell and more dangerous than evil. We may as well be cockroaches running under a couch, our only hope being to get swept up in that god's dustpan with our legs barely kicking when he cleans up this mess. Imagine this basic equation for a systematic theology:

god = insatiable appetite for acclaim + blood thirst for vengeance

In that case, salvation is just a lesser evil than destruction, and heaven is only better because it beats hell. A perception-driven, Bible-snipping systematic theology is demoralizing, but that's not the only risk it runs. We can keep our heads buried in Scripture and believe everything we read, but if we study only God's acts and not His character, our sum-total god still won't be the God of the Bible. A lesser god is not our God.

A lesser god is not our God.

With this dust intentionally kicked up, read 1 Thessalonians 5:1-3 and handwrite the verses in the back of the book. How do we know that the topic was not a new one for the Thessalonians?

- Exactly what will come "like a thief in the night"?

In John 6:39, the same time is called "the last day." In 1 Corinthians 1:8, "the day of our Lord Jesus Christ." In Philippians 1:6, "the day of Christ Jesus." In 2 Peter 3:12, "the day of God." In Jude 6, "the great day." In 2 Thessalonians 1:10, succinctly put: "that day."

What one word do you see as the common denominator in every reference to it? ________

Don't miss the paradox. This is a "day" that will come like a thief in the "night." This Day will eclipse every other day in history and make the noonday sun seem as dark as midnight. The white-hot brilliance of the Holy One will rip through the skies like lightning slicing black construction paper. His brightness will expose evil and incinerate adversaries. It will also heal the land, purify the dross, and gleam with hallowed love on the rescued and redeemed. The Day of the Lord will be the ultimate reenactment of Exodus 6:6 (ESV), "I am the LORD, and I will bring you out ... and I will deliver you ... and I will redeem you with an outstretched arm and with great acts of judgment."

The righteous Judge and the redeeming Deliverer are one and the same. As our heels drag over the threshold of the second half of our study, let's not rip out the carpet between the fourth and fifth chapters of 1 Thessalonians. The "Day of the Lord" belongs to the same One who will "descend from heaven with a shout, with the archangel's voice, and with the trumpet of God" (4:16) to resurrect the dead and meet believers in the air. He is the same Lord who dispatches hope in our darkest grief and the same Lord who sent His Son into our ruptured world to save our fallen lives. "For God did not send His Son into the world that He might condemn the world, but that the world might be saved through Him" (John 3:17).

That is why we need our Bibles wide open today. Beware of taking a single page of Scripture and trying to fold God tightly up in it so you can make Him more definable. He is irreducible and uncompressible. "The unfolding of [His] words gives light" (Ps. 119:130, ESV). The Bible is meant to fold Him out, not fold Him up.

The Bible is meant to fold God out, not fold Him up.

Remember how we started our journey together in Acts 17 with Paul's visit to Thessalonica? We're not informed in that early narrative exactly what doctrines he taught besides the death and resurrection of Jesus. We can conclude, however, that he talked about Christ's return, because he clearly referred in his letter to certain facts the Thessalonians knew "very well" (1 Thess. 5:2). Only a short time later Paul preached the following message in Athens, suggesting the kinds of teachings that were stirring in his soul:

> *Therefore, having overlooked the times of ignorance, God now commands all people everywhere to repent, because He has set a day when He is going to judge the world in righteousness by the Man He has appointed. He has provided proof of this to everyone by raising Him from the dead.*
>
> ACTS 17:30-31

The "day" He has set is the "Day of the Lord." Prophets foretold the event centuries before a young virgin nestled the infant Son of God against her neck and sang Him the songs of Zion.

Go back to 1 Thessalonians 5:1-3. What will people be saying when sudden destruction comes upon them?

According to Dr. Gary S. Shogren, "It seems more than coincidence that Paul echoes a well-known slogan of the Roman Empire, *Pax et securitas* ('Peace and Security'), which comes from living under the *Pax romana* [meaning Peace of Rome] ... Not even the Roman Empire, with its Caesar who proclaimed himself the divine savior, would protect them from God's judgment."[1]

At this point in documented history, surely we know that any peace brought about by human government has all the permanence of a handshake between two enemies posing for a photo. The following Scripture segments are stunningly telling. The contexts concern the divine judgment God warned He would bring through the Babylonians. His people did not listen or repent and, true to His Word, He brought it.

Read each portion and record their basic message:

Jeremiah 6:13-14 "peace, peace" is a false message—greed, false deals

Ezekiel 13:10-16 misleading by proclaiming peace

Saying "Peace and security" when there is no peace is not only unhelpful; it is woefully harmful. Imagine the level of betrayal in having a matter with eternal consequences misrepresented to you.

In 1 Thessalonians 5:3, Paul likens the sudden destruction of the Day of the Lord to ___labor___ pains coming upon a ___pregnant___ woman.

The analogy did not originate with Paul. Christ's disciples well remembered going to Him privately on the Mount of Olives and walking through the door of the dialogue in Matthew 24:3-8 (see in the margin).

"Tell us, when will these things happen? And what is the sign of Your coming and of the end of the age?" Then Jesus replied to them: "Watch out that no one deceives you. For many will come in My name, saying, 'I am the Messiah,' and they will deceive many. You are going to hear of wars and rumors of wars. See that you are not alarmed, because these things must take place, but the end is not yet. For nation will rise up against nation, and kingdom against kingdom. There will be famines and earthquakes in various places. All these events are the beginning of birth pains.
MATTHEW 24:3-8

Once her pregnancy is confirmed, typically the first question out of a mom's mouth is "When's the baby due?" Christ explicitly told His disciples that no one knows the day or hour, "neither the angels in heaven, nor the Son—except the Father only" (Matt. 24:36).

So what were the disciples' instructions? The same as ours: "be ready, because the Son of Man is coming at an hour you do not expect" (Matt. 24:44).

Christ offered a powerful meter to gauge the general timing: "As the days of Noah were, so the coming of the Son of Man will be" (Matt. 24:37). Rewinding to Genesis 6:11-12, we'd find record of an earth seeded with corruption, watered by violence, and harvesting every evil. "God saw how corrupt the earth was" (Gen. 6:12). Note the verb "saw." We suppose, but God actually sees.

That God waits to bring judgment while His piercing eyes penetrate a world off its axis with depravity and injustice is the greater wonder. The time has not yet come for one glorious reason: The Lord is patient, "not wanting any to perish but all to come to repentance" (2 Pet. 3:9).

We will not "think lightly of the riches of His kindness and tolerance and patience ... knowing that the kindness of God leads [people] to repentance" (Rom. 2:4, NASB).

Day Two
Wide Awake

FLASH-FORWARD: For you are all children of light, children of the day. We are not of the night or of the darkness. ***1 Thessalonians 5:5, ESV***

My friend Sue, her husband, and young boys were each tucked under their warm covers, sound asleep in their rooms, when the sound of crashing glass popped their eyes wide open. It was 3:00 in the morning.

A few days earlier, their pastor and fellow neighbor had mentioned that several break-ins had occurred recently in their neighborhood. So, one night, Sue and her husband, Jim, threw around a few "what ifs" and talked through a dry run. The actuality proved messier than the plan, but they were on their feet in full activation within seconds. Jim flew down the hall and jerked both boys out of bed, stuck them in a closet, and stood guard. Sue dialed 911 then, to the sound of burglars tearing through the front room like wild carnivores, she dropped to her knees in the den and yelled repeatedly, "I plead the blood of Jesus!" That part wasn't planned. It erupted like a volcano from the liquid fire of her faith.

I sat across from Sue in a café, listening to her story with my jaw hanging and tears welling. My kids were the same age and we'd recently been in their cozy home. "Thank God you guys weren't hurt."

We pitch our tents on the soil of a dark, scary world.

We'd give anything if every attack resulted in minimal harm. We pitch our tents of brick on the tremulous soil of a dark, scary world. The peculiarity of their nick-of-time warning and courageous run-through caused their story to spin back through my mind recently. I picture myself at that age, piling my whole family into one bed, shoving the dresser in front of the door, and kicking anyone under the covers who started nodding off. In the words of my beloved mother, "somebody give me a nerve pill."

Please read 1 Thessalonians 5:4-8 and handwrite the verses in the back of the book.

Fill in the next four words according to the translation in today's "Flash-Forward": "For you are all children of light, children of the day."

We finally step both feet into the wet cement of our study title. When it dries, I pray that our prints leave a lasting impression.

What a lovely and poetic identity. The beams of the sun have broken through the darkness of an icy atmosphere, found our faces, and lifted our chins to see the countenance of Christ. Our identity is not only breathtaking in the imagery of light; to be reminded that we are children—abiding, laboring, and resting in that light—is oxygen to our heaving lungs.

Sometimes being a grownup is wearying. All the bill paying, problem solving, and reality facing can be exhausting even though they're necessary. Coddling folks who should've long-since grown up is taxing too.

What is the most wearying part about being a grown-up right now? If you're under 20, what's the hardest part of leaving childhood behind?

The title *Children of the Day* sings a melody with two simple lyrics:

We are not in charge, but our Father is.

We are not in darkness, but our world is.

The former stands guard over our security; the latter stands guard against our complacency.

Read this carefully: If you are in Christ, you are not of the darkness. If you are camped somewhere in the dark (I've been there too) and feeling pegged to that ground, Jesus is calling you out of the rift into the broad rays of day. "He has rescued us from the domain of darkness" (Col. 1:13).

That means if you have trusted Christ as Savior, darkness cannot force you to stay. It can only harass you into believing that you belong there.

You don't.

Since God fashioned our bodies to function with adequate sleep, 1 Thessalonians 5:6 can't mean that we never shut our bloodshot eyes. What do you think it means?

Be prepared, wary, focused

Eugene Peterson's translation pastes these words in this portion of Paul's letter:

> *But friends, you're not in the dark, so how could you be taken off guard by any of this? You're sons of Light, daughters of Day. We live under wide open skies and know where we stand. So let's not sleepwalk through life like those others. Let's keep our eyes open and be smart. People sleep at night and get drunk at night. But not us! Since we're creatures of Day, let's act like it. Walk out into the daylight sober, dressed up in faith, love, and the hope of salvation.*
>
> 1 THESSALONIANS 5:4-8, THE MESSAGE

Life on this whirling top can be like bellying up to a bar lined with shot glasses. We set out to feel something good and end up feeling nothing at all.

We have so much stimulation that we're going numb. We stumble into the fog, letting go of the rope of real relationships as we unravel thread by thread. Our detachment renames itself rejection, and so we do what rejected people do best: we further detach and throw back the next shot.

We sleepwalk to a place where nightmares replace dreams. There we collapse in the dark, passing out under the smothering blanket of a two-sided lie: the world gives and God takes.

The two-sided lie: the world gives and God takes.

Then, blessed be the Name of the Lord, something wakes us up. Maybe we'll never be thankful for what shook us out of our slumber, but we can be thankful at least to feel wide-awake.

Awake to the activity of God around us.

Awake to His Word on the surface of that page.

Awake to the lightning before we hear the thunder.

Awake to our present season. Awake to our people. Awake even to our pain lest it end up meaning nothing. Awake to the clock ticking, conscious of the critical hour in which the soles of our shoes are glued to this globe. Awake and aware of what is to come, both the beautiful and the frightful.

To be awake is to still have questions and not just tidy summations. Our Creator knows that, once we figure anything out entirely, we sigh so deeply that our lungs fill with water and we sink to the bottom with boredom.

To be awake is to still grapple with mystery. How else could we appreciate certainty? This is the paradox of the crucified life: to lose ourselves in Christ is to find our very lives.

○ What one event in your life shook you to your most awakened state?

You'd think those kinds of things would keep us alert for the rest of our lives but, if you're like me, you can still get drowsy. We can get lulled back to sleep by routine and dulled by endless comforts. But our faithful God won't leave in endless hibernation those of us who still show a pulse for Him. He seeks to break into our awareness and restore our vision. God can use a fresh dream to wake us up.

A steady diet of behavior modification makes up one part of our religious lives that is prone to make us sleepy. When behaving ourselves becomes the only point of our Christianity, no wonder we turn to the world to wake us up.

If you were part of our most recent session, you'll recall that we talked about keeping the call to morality in our biblical theology. You'll find no contradiction here. Morality is a priority, but as the outward beam of the brilliant theme of light in the darkness. It's not just discipline; it's dignity. And it's not just chastity; it's charity.

- Give 1 Thessalonians 5:8 (ESV) another look. What two pieces of attire do children of the day "put on"?

Those are not the kinds of things you wear strolling down the beach in your swimsuit. You wear a breastplate and a helmet where danger lurks. We wear love and faith to guard us from being gutted by coldness and unbelief.

We clamp down our racing minds with the helmet of salvation because this world is spinning toward a harrowing end, and, in the black of night, we need to know we're not going with it.

We are not called to be sober for sobriety's sake. We're called to be sober because a drunk soldier on a dark battlefield could get himself slaughtered.

Bits of dialogue from J. R. R. Tolkien's *The Hobbit* are flying around in my head like pages in front of an open window.

Gandalf the wizard says to the hobbit Bilbo Baggins: "I am looking for someone to share in an adventure that I am arranging, and it's very difficult to find anyone."

Bilbo Baggins replies: "I should think so—in these parts! We are plain quiet folk and have no use for adventures. Nasty disturbing uncomfortable things! Make you late for dinner!"[2]

In the movie *The Hobbit,* a disgruntled Gandalf speaks: "You've been sitting quietly for far too long. Tell me; when did doilies and your mother's dishes become so important to you? I remember a young hobbit who always was running off in search of elves and the woods, who would stay out late, and come home after dark, trailing mud and twigs and fireflies. A young hobbit who would have liked nothing better than to find out what was beyond the borders of the Shire. The world is not in your books and maps; it's out there."[3]

Adventure awaits us, and Jesus is looking for people to share in it.

We don't have to snore to sleepwalk. All we have to do is get distracted by doilies and dishes. There are droves of lost people beyond the borders of our Shires who need reaching. Adventure awaits us out there, and Jesus is looking the whole world over for people to share in it. If you're game, grab your armor on the way out the door. In the words of J. R. R. Tolkien, "It does not do to leave a live dragon out of your calculations, if you live near him."[4]

And grab an apple. You may be late for dinner.

Day Three

Wrestling with Wrath

FLASH-FORWARD: For God did not appoint us to wrath, but to obtain salvation through our Lord Jesus Christ. *1 Thessalonians 5:9*

A couple of days ago I received a vicious note from a professing believer who told me publicly and colorfully to shut my mouth and repent of my heresies. Normally I'd find that kind of assault from a fellow Christian fairly wounding, but on this rare occasion, I did something I hope God found refreshing. I rolled my eyes and trashed it. I got up the nerve to dismiss the whole paragraph because of the last sentence: "God hates you."

Christianity 101: "For God so loved the world" (John 3:16, ESV). According to Romans 5:8, God didn't even hate us in our unredeemed condition: "But God proves His own love for us in that while we were still sinners, Christ died for us!" At times He disapproves, disciplines, and redirects us ... but hates us? No, not on His Son's life. In the folds and shadows of our misshapen hearts, however, most of us have entertained that bleak prospect.

Take your pen and write these words in the margin: "God does NOT hate me. He loves me."

In the words of the apostle John, let's "know and rely on the love God has for us" (1 John 4:16, NIV).

Read 1 Thessalonians 5:9-11 and handwrite the verses in the back of the book.

The news this segment nails to the page is magnificent for those of us in Christ, but the word "wrath" may be so disturbing that we can hardly get past it.

- What are a few words or concepts that pop into your mind when you think of "wrath."

revenge, intolerance, hate

The Greek term translated "wrath" in 1 Thessalonians 5:9 and in Colossians 3:6 where it is qualified as the "God's wrath" is *orgé* (pronounced or-GAY). Read the definition carefully: "anger as a state of mind. Contrast *thumós,* [meaning] 'indignation, wrath as the outburst of a vengeful mind.' Aristotle says that *orgé* anger is desire with grief (see also Mark 3:5; Rom. 12:19; Eph. 4:31; Col. 3:8)."[5]

How could contrasting *orgé* and *thumós* be especially important in an accurate understanding of God's wrath?

anger vs. hate

Another definition of the Greek term exhibits a similar concept. "The word 'wrath' (*orgé*) means anger, but it is not the outburst of anger that quickly blazes up, not the anger that arises solely from emotion. Rather, it is a decisive and a deliberate anger."[6]

I don't know if these definitions taste differently in your mouth from our English connotations of "wrath," but they carry a distinct flavor in mine. I think of "wrath" as the explosive unleashing of a fury so feverish that it cannot help exceeding its target. You too, perchance? If so, no wonder we can hardly fathom God in this context. Though the wrath of God is described at times as a fury, He is not like man. God never whirls out of control. His wrath is tempered by the steadfastness and blamelessness of His character.

God never whirls out of control.

Glance back at the first definition in today's lesson and fill in the following blank accordingly:

Aristotle says that *orgé* anger is desire with grief.

Mark 3:1-5 sets a perfect stage for a dramatic interpretation of Aristotle's explanation. Read the segment please.

Now He entered the synagogue again, and a man was there who had a paralyzed hand. In order to accuse Him, they were watching Him closely to see whether He would heal him on the Sabbath. He told the man with the paralyzed hand, "Stand before us." Then He said to them, "Is it lawful on the Sabbath to do what is good or to do what is evil, to save life or to kill?" But they were silent. After looking around at them with anger and sorrow at the hardness of their hearts, He told the man, "Stretch out your hand." So he stretched it out, and his hand was restored.

MARK 3:1-5

The Greek word *orgé* is translated "anger" in verse 5 in virtually all formal translations and is used, as you can see, in reference to Christ.

What additional word is used in Mark 3:5 to describe Christ's emotions in the context?

sorrow

The coupling of words in both the Greek and the English wrestles the concept of divine wrath into something a human can more capably grasp. God cannot set aside His love to render His wrath. In anthropomorphic terms, He cannot detach the arteries in His outstretched arms from the chambers of His heart. God is holistic in His holiness. Unlike ours, His soundness of mind cannot be trampled by a stampede of emotions.

If we're willing to do a little extra reading today, we could dramatically tighten our understanding of the biblical concept of "wrath."

Read each portion and record any information you feel is pertinent to a proper understanding of God's wrath.

Revelation 6:9-11

Revelation 6:12-17

Revelation 16:5-7

Romans 1:18; 2:5

Romans 5:6-10

In Scriptures like Romans 12:19-21, we clearly see that God's wrath is altogether different from ours.

> *Friends, do not avenge yourselves; instead, leave room for His wrath. For it is written: Vengeance belongs to Me; I will repay, says the Lord. But [i]f your enemy is hungry, feed him. If he is thirsty, give him something to drink. For in so doing you will be heaping fiery coals on his head. Do not be conquered by evil, but conquer evil with good."*
>
> ROMANS 12:19-21

Would God expect us to exceed Him in mercy? Would He apply the scriptural maxim "mercy triumphs over judgment" (Jas. 2:13) to us while judgment triumphs over mercy to Him? He would not.

Would God expect us to exceed Him in mercy?

Just in case we're tempted to picture God seated on His throne, licking His chops in wrath, these verses jump off the page in the Book of Ezekiel: "'Do I take any pleasure in the death of the wicked?' This is the declaration of the Lord GOD. 'Instead, don't I take pleasure when he turns from his ways and lives?'" (Ezek. 18:23). "Tell them: 'As I live'—the declaration of the Lord GOD—'I take no pleasure in the death of the wicked, but rather that the wicked person should turn from his way and live'" (Ezek. 33:11).

If we have placed our faith in Jesus, we are not destined for wrath.

If we have placed our faith in Jesus Christ as our Savior, we are not destined for wrath. Based on many of the verses we've seen today, our relief could be palpable. Hebrews 2:3, however, keeps interrupting my lesson like a persistent student, waving her hand wildly with a question: "how will we escape if we neglect such a great salvation?"

Let's take two crucial actions with the remainder of the lesson to halt that waving hand. First, let's confirm that we are each in Christ. Do you know to your core that your salvation has been secured through the acceptance of Christ as your Savior? As faithful as our parents may have been, we cannot be born from our mother's womb into Christianity. Christ teaches that we must be reborn into eternal life with Him. This rebirth happens when we repent of our sins, confess with our mouths that "Jesus is Lord," and believe in our hearts "that God raised Him from the dead" (Rom. 10:9-13; see 2 Tim. 2:19).

We cannot earn it. Our good works cannot attract it.

These brush strokes from the apostle Paul are to the New Testament what the central frame of Michelangelo's masterpiece is to the Sistine Chapel. This is the portrait of salvation as clearly as we can see it painted:

> *We too all previously lived among them in our fleshly desires, carrying out the inclinations of our flesh and thoughts, and we were by nature children under wrath as the others were also. But God, who is rich in mercy, because of His great love that He had for us, made us alive with the Messiah even though we were dead in trespasses ... For you are saved by grace through faith, and this is not from yourselves; it is God's gift—not from works, so that no one can boast.*
>
> EPHESIANS 2:3-5,8-9

Did you notice the mention of "wrath"? What did it say?

we were by nature children under wrath

○ How does God's wrath differ from ours?

it is anger w. love & mercy.

How does it change how you feel about Him?

Praise & thank him.

How does that change how you feel about yourself?

To God I'm precious.

The entire trajectory of our lives changes the moment we receive this gift of God's grace. If you do not know for certain that you are in Christ, would you accept this glorious salvation by faith and confess Jesus as Lord and Savior today?

Once we make this deliberate decision, we don't ever need to doubt it again. All the angst of uncertainty can vanish because nothing can snatch us out of God's hand (John 10:28). Even when we think we've let go of Him, His grip holds us fast. Settle the matter this very moment, and then walk forward with Jesus in full assurance, come what may, until you see His face. Hear Christ's straightforward approach in John 20:27 to stop doubting and believe.

Then He said to Thomas, "Put your finger here and observe My hands. Reach out your hand and put it into My side. Don't be an unbeliever, but a believer."
JOHN 20:27

Absorb Paul's words in our current text to "put on a helmet of the hope of salvation. For God did not appoint us to wrath, but to obtain salvation through our Lord Jesus Christ, who died for us, so that whether we are awake or asleep, we will live together with Him" (1 Thess. 5:8-10).

The second crucial action is to earnestly pray together for many more to miss the wrath to come. I'm not talking about exercising our faith toward hundreds or even thousands. I am asking you to partner with me in prayer for the power of the gospel to explode all over this globe in our generation, so that millions of people will experience salvation. I'm about to get on my knees right here at my desk, and I wonder if you'd consider bowing right where you are. Intercede spontaneously as the Holy Spirit leads you. In the margin, record several specific parts of your prayer along with today's date.

Partner with me in prayer for the power of the gospel to explode all over this globe.

At the end of today's lesson you will also find a prayer for awakening and revival that God placed on my heart several months ago along with an explanation of my own repentance. I do not want to put any words in your mouth but, if the prayer resonates with you, would you consider also praying it with me? You may not have time to do it now, but perhaps you could turn to it soon, and we could come together in agreement for God to do whatever it takes to crack open the heavens with a downpour of His Spirit.

I respect you so much. Thank you for the privilege to seek Christ with you.

Intercessory Prayer for Awakening

Several months ago, I was overcome in a way I've rarely experienced with a burden for people who do not know Christ. I confessed my longing for fresh awakening to God and grappled in prayer, wondering why it tarries in many parts of the world. He has already told us in Scripture that His desire is for none to perish and for all to have eternal life through faith in Christ yet many lost people die daily. What on earth is the hold up?

My heart began to burn with a sense that part of this ceiling over our heads is our demand for God to bring awakening and revival within our means, keep our rules, and respect our boundaries. If Christ is to do what He longs to do, it's time to relinquish our expectations and formulas for revival. Passages like Matthew 13:58 and Mark 6:5-6 make troublingly clear that we can put a leash on a work that God would otherwise be willing to perform.

Perhaps one reason awakening waits is that we are afraid for God to do whatever it would take. We fear the uncertainty of revival. We don't trust God with the work of His own Spirit. What if He embarrasses us? Or makes us change our minds? God won't work contrary to His Word but, if you're like me, your greater worry may be that He could work contrary to your tastes. We are worried that He will not use our methods. Perhaps many reasons cause a fresh awakening to wait. We could write more articles and list possible hindrances. We might deliberate over them and debate them. But we would only exert more and more energy while we have less and less time.

Or maybe we could say today, Lord, if Your time is now—and it's the only time countless millions have—remove the obstacles, whatever they are. Shove them out of the way and COME, Lord Jesus, with a torrential downpour of Your Holy Spirit.

I'm looking for anyone willing to echo a prayer something like this. I bring it to you in humility, in lack, and in want. I do not wish to put words on a tongue detached from a heart. Vocabulary is meaningless without volition. If this is not you and if these sins are not yours and these aches find no place in your soul, please don't own them. If, on the other hand, these words could flow from your own pen, pray them with me. For where two or three are gathered in His name, crying out for a cracked-open heaven, that ceiling over our heads could shatter to our feet.

Most glorious all-powerful, merciful God,

Your Son died for more than these. We thank You for what You've already done, but we beg You to do infinitely more. Look upon this ailing planet, pulsing with the hopeless, the helpless, the hiding, and the dying. You have willed that people would not die in their sins but be saved and redeemed through Your Son, Jesus Christ. You promised that the cross was big enough for us all, with everlasting arms reaching to the ends of the earth. We know what Your Word says You can do, and we confess to You that many of us have not yet seen it with our eyes, but we feel it stirring in our souls. Hosanna, Lord! Save now!

We willingly confess to You our sinful arrogance. We have prescribed to You by what means You, the solitary Healer, should heal souls. You have refused to sign Your name to our prescriptions. We ask You this day to write Your Name across our sky and bring revival! Save by whatever means brings You glory. Bring it any way You like, but bring it, Lord. We free You from using our methods. We free You from using our denominational names. We free You from using our buildings, though we welcome You to them. We free You even from using us, though we cast ourselves before You at Your complete disposal and beg that You would. Use none of us. Use all of us. Use whatever people and whatever means honor You most, but do it, Lord. Please do it!

We confess to You our appalling narcissism in asking You to mirror us. We confess to You our oversophistication and snobbery. We confess to You that we are terrified of Your Holy Spirit. We confess our pathetic arrogance for having forbidden signs and wonders when there could be no greater sign and wonder than a tidal wave of salvation rolling on our dry banks. Oh, Jesus, that we would not leave You to marvel that You could do so few miracles among us because of our unbelief.

We repent this day for not trusting You with what revival should look like. We repent this day from prioritizing our dignity over Your downpour. We confess to You that we have torn pages from our Bibles and handed them back to You and demanded that You work through what was left. We confess to You this day that the tent pegs of Scripture are vastly wider than our imaginations and our expectations.

Lord, if souls are saved by the thousands of thousands and millions of millions, we pledge to You this day that we will not, in our sectarianism, pick apart the process and reason how it was not legitimate. We are ready even if it's messy. Even if, atop the beautiful feet carrying the good news are bruised and broken bodies of willing evangelists.

Open heaven. Rain down, Holy Spirit. We repent for having asked You to respect our boundaries. We bow now to Your boundless Spirit and make room over our lowered heads for You to fall upon us with power and might and a firestorm of Your great affection. You have loved us so. You have loved us well. Scar our hearts with Your cross and love through us, Lord. Oh, Holy Spirit of the Living Christ, come without limit. We have known You were able but begged You to be willing. All the while, we have been disabled because we have been unwilling.

To what conceivable degree we could have held them in our hands, we turn the reins of revival back over to the Rider who is Faithful and True, and we plead that You would not let them rest on the neck of that great horse but that You'd bid him run.

Do what You want, but we plead for You to do it now. Do it here. Make Your name glorious. Save now.

In the holy name of Christ our King, amen.

Day Four

An Open Connection

FLASH-FORWARD: And we exhort you, brothers: warn those who are irresponsible, comfort the discouraged, help the weak, be patient with everyone. ***1 Thessalonians 5:14***

Today, boys and girls (minus the boys), we're going to play Connect the Dots. Imagine bold, black dots that seem almost randomly scattered on a page of unbleached newsprint. Each black freckle has a number next to it. As you draw the lines from dot 1 to 2 to 3, you have no idea what shape you're drafting, but as you zigzag across the page, a form emerges. By the last dot, the frame of a church pops up from the page. A steeple didn't give it away. The numbers did, as each reconfigured into a name.

> *Church wasn't about attending. It was about attaching.*

The early New Testament believers didn't think of church as somewhere they went; they saw it as something they were. Church wasn't about attending. It was about attaching. Engaging. Without connecting the dots, each Christian is like a square-inch island scattered haphazardly over an ocean of humanity. Linked, we're transformed into a tightly woven net to which fingers can cling, and in which lives are not lost at sea.

Write 1 Thessalonians 5:12-15 in the back of the book, and then we'll get our game off the ground.

First connect the dots of community believers to their lead-laborers as Paul does in verse 12. These leaders are identified in three ways in verse 12. They are those who labor among you
and are over you in the Lord
and admonish you.

Paul summons the community to respond to their leaders in two ways—one in verse 12 and the other in verse 13. What are they?

V12: respect those
V13: esteem them very highly in love

In a social-media world where servants can turn into celebrities, the idea of giving further recognition to Christian leaders could be a bit repelling. We shouldn't have much trouble, however, respecting and, in love, esteeming the kind of leaders our text describes.

Let's take the segment apart briefly using the HCSB. "Now we ask you, brothers [and sisters], to give recognition ..."

"TO THOSE WHO LABOR": Note that Paul does not say to give recognition "to those who crave it" or "to those who get all the attention while the others do all the work." That's a relief, isn't it? According to verse 13, the catalyst for recognizing and esteeming leaders is their work, not their title.

I can testify that nothing will heighten your esteem for the labor-intensive side of church leadership like a new senior pastor in the family. And don't even get me started on the responsibilities of a pastor's wife. I have a whole new appreciation these days. We will never waste ink, time, or energy on a note of encouragement written to a hard-working leader. God times those notes perfectly, having them delivered when a weary laborer is right about to give up.

"AMONG YOU": The leaders who engender the most affection are invariably the ones who serve among us and not so far above us that we have to squint at the sun to see them. Having no boundaries or safeguards over time and family is slow suicide to effective, enduring leadership. No one can be at a congregations' constant beck and call. Still, our most beloved leaders are often those we see as fellow sojourners just steps ahead, hacking through the thorny brush for our easier passage. I so hope you have someone in your congregation who fits that picture.

Who would that be for you and why?

"AND LEAD YOU IN THE LORD": Not "in the flesh" or "in the competition." Individuals who lead us "in the Lord" practice authority as those under authority.

"AND ADMONISH YOU": The Greek term translated "admonish" in verse 12 is the compound word *noutheteó. Noús* means "mind" and the remainder of the word *(títhēmi)* means "to place." *Noutheléō* means "to warn, admonish, exhort."[7]

This aspect of leadership can be a balancing act on a very thin tightrope. Those who are most trustworthy with admonitions tend to be the ones who are neither too anxious to give them nor too afraid. Over time I've come to believe that a warning can be one of the most loving gifts of grace we could ever receive from a good leader. It can turn the steering wheel away from a fast-approaching freight train.

Reflecting on some of the most foolish decisions of my believing life, I'm haunted by warnings that, had I heeded them, would have diverted me from indescribable heartache.

○ Share an admonition you accepted and a reason why you're so thankful you did.

Draw doubly thick lines to connect the dots between lead-laborers and the members of the believing community, because they are drawn twice, once from each direction. The picture we're drawing is about to get far more interesting, however. In the next portion of Connect the Dots, the lines we'd expect to be slanted vertically are surprisingly horizontal. Read 5:14-15 again.

- To whom are the responsibilities listed in 1 Thessalonians 5:14-15 assigned? brothers

Note with great care that these responsibilities are not assigned to leadership. These lines are drawn straight across, from community member to community member. I love the HCSB translation on this portion: "And we exhort you, brothers: warn those who are irresponsible, comfort the discouraged, help the weak, be patient with everyone. See to it that no one repays evil for evil to anyone, but always pursue what is good for one another and for all."

Fellow believers share in the tasks of warning the irresponsible, comforting the discouraged, helping the weak, and showing patience to all. Seeing to it that no one repays evil for evil is not just the job of the leadership; it's a community affair. On a shore of Scripture still wet with the words "mind your own business" (1 Thess. 4:11), Paul calls us to a notable measure of meddling. The primary difference is this: 1 Thessalonians 4:11-12 puts binoculars in the hands of outsiders looking in. Our present text sets glasses on the noses of insiders looking side to side. What Paul's letter to the Thessalonians would label "interaction," we are apt to call "interference."

What Paul would label "interaction," we may call "interference."

The social ethics of our culture have turned the way we communicate inside out. We feel free to ask astonishingly personal questions to complete strangers, yet we've grown increasingly timid face to face. And by "we," I do mean me. Just recently, I fretted about a good friend who seems to have something on her heart that's heavier than her circumstances suggest. I was reluctant to ask her a straight question, stricken by the irony that, had we been more superficial, I might have been less hesitant.

What implications do you see from getting into the habit of drawing fewer boundaries with the wider social arena and airtight boundaries with your closest companions? Think about it and offer your thoughts.

lack of support
estrangement.
lack of true loving care

I did end up asking my friend a straight question, by the way, and while I was at it, I told her how much I love her. She didn't divulge anything more (maybe she was afraid I'd use it as an illustration!), but she at least knows that I care.

The easiest explanation for our increasing hesitancy toward those closest to us is that we don't want to pry, yet we often feel free to pry into the lives of virtual strangers. You'd be slack-jawed to know the kinds of questions I'm asked by people I've never met, sometimes from the next stall in the public restroom.

I'm not convinced our emotional distance from those who are physically close has much to do with minding our manners. I think we feel so overwhelmed with our own problems that we are afraid to open ourselves up to those we'll continue to see. After all, to care is to bear, and we feel buried already. That seems like fair-enough reasoning until we take stock of the skewed lines on our relational map. We're connecting dots with people who may as well live on Pluto, while trying to avoid the ones planted right next to us.

I like tidy lessons. I don't mind stirring things up if I know how it's going to smooth out by the end. For the life of me, I can't see how to tidy this lesson up with black-and-white answers. In all this line-drawing we're doing today, where is the line between caring and prying? At what point do we shift from a tending body to a busybody? When does godly patience with someone downshift into the gear of poor judgment? And how on earth do we warn someone who is irresponsible without the person feeling judged?

Closeness carries risk.

As much as we want to insulate ourselves, closeness carries risk. The lines aren't always straight or perfectly clear. After all, Christ entrusted these charges to frail flesh and blood, but we do have His Spirit. We can ask to be crucified to our selfishness and filled by the Holy Spirit in our interactions. We can even tell the person how nervous we are and how much we care. With the same courage it takes to ask someone how she's really doing, we can look her in the eyes and say, "I just love you so much. Please tell me how I can help."

I keep thinking about the way one commentary translates the Greek into English in 1 Thessalonians 5:15, "See that no one renders meanness for meanness, but always keep pursuing the thing that is good in regard to one another and in regard to all."[8]

A year ago, someone with whom I'd been very close left me a series of vicious voice mails. By the tenth one, I felt mauled by a bear. I told a dear friend what had happened and she listened compassionately and shared my offense. She gave me about a month, then she thoughtfully posed this question: "Beth, do you still have those voice mails saved on your phone?"

"Yes."

"You know it's time to erase them now, don't you, Sister?"

"Yes."

I erased them. And I started getting over it and moving on. All because a good friend had the courage to meddle.

There comes a time.

Day Five

He Will Surely Do It

FLASH-FORWARD: He who calls you is faithful, who also will do it.
1 Thessalonians 5:24

I'm already a smidge on the defensive because I'm about to annoy you, and natural-born people-pleasers dearly hate to annoy. I'd butter you up first, but we don't have the space for all that extra fat, so I'll just blurt it out:

> You need to handwrite 13 verses in the back of your book today.
> That's right: 1 Thessalonians 5:16-28.

Does it help that six verses in the segment each contain five words or fewer? How about the satisfaction of knowing that, as of today, you've handwritten an entire book of the Bible? May that be sweet consolation for your trouble. Please finish before I tap my fingers to nubs.

We'll study verses 19-22 in our next video session, so we can excuse them from our present discussions. The remaining verses are still too many to cover, so we will hit and miss in such a way to taste the tenor of this letter's closing.

Just before saying good-bye to my daughters in their college dorm rooms for the first time, I spat out exhortations in choppy sentences like a person hyperventilating.

"Call me every day."

"Don't oversleep."

"Don't be messier than your roommate."

"Make your bed."

"Study hard."

"Don't skip class."

"Don't walk on campus alone at night."

"Don't trust weird people." (Of course, that one carried a certain irony.)

"I love you."

"I'm so proud of you."

"God will be with you." (And then I cried.)

Often when we're wrapping up something of significance—be it a letter, message, or meeting—we feel the urgency to say as much as we can in as little time as possible. The difference is that the breathy good-byes of Paul, Silvanus, and Timothy were ventilated by the Spirit and permanently etched ever-warm onto the window of Scripture.

Those good-byes are meant to change the way we see our worlds.

○ Which of the exhortations in 1 Thessalonians 5:16-22 do you think you need most to apply in your present circumstances? Explain why.

Now may the God of peace sanctify you completely.

Something happened one weekend that I can't get off my mind. We were serving in Tulsa, Oklahoma, at a Living Proof Live event. As we wrapped up our final hour, God led me to call for intercession over two specific age groups.

First I asked those who were 20 years and younger to stand and, if they felt comfortable doing so, for others nearby to lay hands on them (see Acts 6:6) as we prayed. We asked God to grant them supernatural love for Jesus and for His Word. And we requested that He set them apart, protect them, and raise them to be mighty in Christ.

As they were seated, I asked women 65 years and older to stand. I'd anticipated this moment since God placed it on my heart. I thought how often those in that age bracket feel overlooked, irrelevant, or undervalued in the work of the gospel. I hoped we could pray some fresh zeal over those discouraged by a church culture that appears as youth-obsessed as the world surrounding it. Whatever my preconceived notions were about that age group in Tulsa, I could hardly have been more mistaken.

Human vocabulary insufficiently describes something sensed in the Spirit more than seen with the eyes, but go with me this far: Almost before I got the age group for the second intercession out of my mouth, the women 65 years and above jumped to their feet. The room literally roared with the sound of them leaving their seats.

Contrary to my expectation, the women who stood before us were not beaten down by a youth-obsessed culture nor were they gearing down for spiritual retirement. Their heads were raised high, their necks unbowed and stately. They weren't proud but, make no mistake, they were confident. These women had managed homes, raised families, fostered children, taught classes, fed masses, run businesses, volunteered services, served pastors, fought injustice, nursed the sick, buried loved ones, lost breasts, endured radiation, hauled grandchildren, sacrificed the unimaginable, and endured enough hormonal ups and downs to qualify for a medal of honor.

They smiled ear to ear, the lines on their faces drawing rays around their eyes like a child's illustration of the sun, causing them to gleam. Their expressions were almost mischievous—like they were in on a secret the rest of us could only imagine.

When those women stood to their feet, power surged in that room. Not the power of flesh and blood. It was as if the Holy Spirit shot up from the ground in a geyser ceiling-high. The hair stood straight up on my arms and the room broke into cheers and applause. Before us all stood a force to be reckoned with.

What made these women of such a challenged demographic defy the odds? They'd suffered too much and lived too long to pretend to the rest of us that life turns out like a Disney movie. Even with optimum health, aging well is a battle never won by cowards. As I'm just a few steps behind them, I've tasted and seen. If you pinned me down and gave me three seconds to offer you an explanation, I'd give you 11 words that could have flown like a banner over that group of women in Tulsa, Oklahoma: "He who calls you is faithful; he will surely do it" (1 Thess. 5:24, ESV).

"He who calls you is faithful."

If we, in the words of Hebrews 10:23, "hold on to the confession of our hope without wavering," filled to the brim with the conviction that He who promised is faithful, we become free to let God do His job. Ours is to choose joy—with the maturity of an adult who claims her birthright combined with the determination of a 2-year-old grabbing a toy and yelling, "Mine!"

No season or suffering can prohibit the kind of joy Paul talks about because it is not of this world. This joy is of the Holy Spirit and, like a tear on the floor of heaven, it spills something utterly divine into the air of earth. This joy is the fragrant "oil of gladness instead of mourning" (Isa. 61:3, ESV) and the midnight song in its very midst (Acts 16:25). It represents the bold declaration nailed to the door of despair that reads, "Nobody's home."

To crippling circumstances demanding the right to rule, this joy is the banging of the gavel: "Motion denied." Joy is the gravity-defying grace to know that what we see is not all there is, and doom is not our destiny. Unceasing rejoicing is a song on constant replay that sings, "I know my God will be faithful. I know He will turn this out well. I know what my God has promised. I know that He cannot fail." Joy throws the heavy cloak of hopelessness on the floor and pulls the "splendid clothes" (Isa. 61:3) from the closet. It says that what we bear need not be what we wear.

Knowing that God is doing His job, ours is also to "pray without ceasing" (1 Thess. 5:17, NASB). The exhortation in 1 Thessalonians 5:17 cannot mean that we never sleep a wink, shut our mouths, quiet our minds, concentrate on our families, recreate, or do our jobs.

● How should a believer pray? What might "pray constantly" mean?

I'd love so much to hear your thoughts in response to that question. I'll add a few of my own to yours.

- Unceasing prayer is consciously leaving open the door that adjoins God's throne room and our personal lives.
- It is a day lived in a long run-on sentence that's built a line and a phrase at a time.

- It is hearing God speak through His Word and responding right back in conversational symbiosis.

Prayer is our open expressway with God, even when our words are uninvolved (Rom. 8:26-27).

In 1 Thessalonians 5:18, we're not told to give thanks *for* every circumstance. We're told to give thanks *in* every circumstance. How would you describe the world of difference between the two?

Giving thanks in every circumstance sends us on the hunt for God's goodness right there in life's difficulty. It shifts our gaze and strengthens the gait of our walk. We, not God, are the beneficiaries of thankful lives. He remains the benefactor. We're not commanded to feed His ego. In the beautiful words of Psalm 37:3, we "feed on His faithfulness" (NKJV).

All of this sounds fabulous in the pep rally, but it's harder on the field in a pileup, isn't it? In the midst of writing this lesson, I went in for my annual mammogram, full of faith for another "see you next year!" like I'd had in the last three. My mom died of breast cancer, so I never have the luxury of being pressed between those two pieces of plastic nonchalantly.

Instead of being happily sent on my way, I was called in from the waiting area for a second set of pictures and told to sit tight in my hospital gown. Then I was called in for an ultrasound and told again to wait.

I had a second ultrasound, followed by a personal visit from the radiologist. Within three hours, I was on the table, under the surgical light for a biopsy on a mass in the left breast.

Don't try telling me the timing is coincidental as I conclude this lesson during the 72-hour wait for test results. Whatever they are, they do not smudge or budge the ink on the sacred page.

The directive remains fixed: "Rejoice always! Pray constantly. Give thanks in everything, for this is God's will for you in Christ Jesus." Meanwhile ...

Now may the God of peace Himself sanctify you completely. And may your spirit, soul, and body be kept sound and blameless for the coming of our Lord Jesus Christ. He who calls you is faithful, who also will do it.

1 THESSALONIANS 5:23-24

Group Session Six

REVIEW THE WEEK

Use these questions to guide your discussion of last week's homework.

● Principal Questions

DAY 1: Exactly what will come "like a thief in the night"? (p. 116)
DAY 2: What two pieces of attire do children of the day "put on" (1 Thess. 5:8)? (p. 122)
DAY 3: What words or concepts pop into your mind when you hear "wrath"? (p. 123)
DAY 4: To whom are the responsibilities listed in 1 Thess. 5:14-15 assigned? (p. 132)
DAY 5: How should we pray? What do you think "pray constantly" means? (p. 136)

○ Personal Discussion Questions

DAY 1: What part of your experience fights to distort your biblical beliefs? (p. 115)
DAY 2: What one event in your life shook you to your most awakened state? (p. 121)
DAY 3: How does God's wrath differ from ours? (p. 126)
DAY 4: What is an admonition you accepted and a reason you're glad you did? (p. 131)
DAY 5: Which of the exhortations in 5:16-22 do you think you need most to apply in your present circumstances? Why? (p. 135)

VIEW THE VIDEO

Introduction

Today we are going to narrow the lens on four rapid-fire verses toward the conclusion of the First Letter to the Thessalonians. First Thessalonians 5:19-21 encapsulates a segment sparse on words and immense in implication and application.

1 Thessalonians 5:19 (ESV)—Do not ____________ the ____________.

1 Thessalonians 5:20 (ESV)—Do not ____________ ____________.

Let's throw some questions out on the table:

What are prophecies, how do they rank, and what is their purpose?

What are they? Consider these two definitions:

- **Prophecy:** "Reception and declaration of a ____________ from the ____________ through a ____________ ____________ of the Holy Spirit and the human instrument thereof."[1]

- ***Prophēteúō:*** "To prophesy ... To foretell things to come ... to declare truths through the inspiration of God's Holy Spirit whether by prediction or otherwise ... To tell forth God's message, hence the noun *prophḗtēs*, prophet, is the proclaimer, one who speaks out the counsel of God with the ____________, ____________, and ____________ which spring from the consciousness of ____________ in ____________ ____________ and having received a direct message from Him to deliver. Thus one may prophesy without being a prophet in the strict sense of the word. A *prophḗtēs*, both in the Old Testament and New Testament, is not primarily one who foretells things to come, but who (having been taught of God) speaks out His will (Deut. 18:18; Isa. 1; Jer. 1; Ezek. 2; 1 Cor. 14:3)."[2]

How do they rank? We can set no ____________ ____________ on the same standard with ____________.

What is their purpose? 1 Corinthians 14:3 (NIV)—"But everyone who prophesies speaks to men for their ____________, ____________ and ____________."

Must knows:

- Prophecies can be quite ____________. They are by their ____________ nature ____________ (1 Cor. 13:9).

- Prophecies ____________ be ____________. Keep in mind how much easier it is to ____________ than to ____________ (Acts 17:11; Matt. 7:15).

Dr. Gordon Fee: "Despite the fact that the ministries of the Spirit can be ____________ in the Christian community, Paul's own deep appreciation for the central role of the Spirit in individual and corporate life will not allow for ____________ ____________ by ____________ ____________. Rather, the antidote for ____________ is proper ____________."[3]

Concluding bottom line

Believers in Christ cannot be both ____________ and ____________.

1. *Holman Illustrated Bible Dictionary,* edited by Chad Brand, Charles Draper, Archie England (Nashville, TN: Holman Bible Publishers, 2003), s.v. "prophecy."
2. S. Zodhiates, *The Complete Word Study Dictionary: New Testament,* s.v. "prophēteúō."
3. Gordon D. Fee, *God's Empowering Presence* (Peabody, MA: Hendrickson Publishers, Inc., 1994), 59.

Week Six

Mobilized Ministry

Day One

You Have One

FLASH-FORWARD: **And in view of this, we always pray for you that our God will consider you worthy of His calling, and will, by His power, fulfill every desire for goodness and the work of faith.** *2 Thessalonians 1:11*

Today we slide the letter opener under the seal of the second letter of Paul, Silvanus, and Timothy to the church of the Thessalonians. I'm anxious to walk with you through this week of study and filled with faith that God will cause it to bear fruit.

The first chapter of 2 Thessalonians is only 12 verses long, so please read all of it for context, then write verses 1-4 on the appropriate page.

Our next two video sessions center on end-time events in 2 Thessalonians. Saving the most climactic portion of chapter 1 for week 7 means that we get to narrow the focus all week to portions that stir up fresh resolve for our God-ordained ministries. Over the months of memorizing the letters, I've found 2 Thessalonians 1:11-12 fascinating and motivating each time I've come to it. We'll take the week to explore why.

For now, what did Paul, Silvanus, and Timothy pray for God to fulfill in the lives of recipients in 2 Thessalonians 1:11?

every resolve for good & every work of faith by his power.

What is the exact purpose for this divine fulfillment (v. 12)?

so that the name of our Lord Jesus Christ may be glorified in you, and you in him.

Over the last several years, God has fanned an insatiable flame in me to keep growing and developing as a servant of Christ and to see others mobilized in their callings and propelled forward in their effectiveness. Some of you are already actively and effectively fulfilling your life's work and, for you, parts of this week may not be new. Please press on with us for two reasons:

1. For a fresh reminder that your life has great significance and perfect timing
2. For encouragement to train and mobilize others with your own adaptations of similar concepts

If you are effectively serving, then you are called to help others do likewise. We'll start with the basics and transition throughout our week of study into more complex concepts. First, we can't move forward into a fresh equipping and increased anointing for what we've been called to do until we're convinced that we have a ministry.

Read 1 Corinthians 12:4-7. What is the main idea of the portion?

What exhortation is recorded in Colossians 4:17?

Have you placed your faith in Jesus Christ as your personal Savior?

Your ministry is the collection of your life works for the glory of God.

If your answer is yes then, child of God, you have a ministry. We will use the word "ministry" this week as the overarching title for the way we've each been called to serve Christ. Your ministry is the ever-accruing collection of your life works for the glory of God. It's not about where you receive a paycheck; it's the means by which you live out your divine purpose. It can take place in secular or sacred environments. In fact, God fulfilling in you what you were born to do can render a secular environment beautifully sacred.

Please fill in the following blank with your whole name.

I, ______________________________, have a God-ordained ministry.

You do indeed—it is the reason God left you on this planet after you received Christ and became a citizen of heaven. You won't be satisfied until you are living it out because God wired you with a compulsion to do it. Speaking to Paul, Jesus referenced this inner compulsion with a figure of speech He used when He converted the former persecutor. Jesus said, "'It is hard for you to kick against the goads'" (Acts 26:14).

> In the many instances where the proverb occurs in Greek literature, it always has the meaning of resisting one's destiny or fighting the will of the gods. That meaning fit Paul's situation. In persecuting Christ, Paul was fighting the will of the One who had set him apart from birth (Gal. 1:15). Like a beast of burden kicking against his master's goads, he would only find the blows more severe with each successive kick. He was fighting the will of God (Acts 5:39). It was a futile, senseless task.[1]

We kick against the goads too when we resist our God-ordained destinies. The more we ignore His will for our works, the more discontented and out of sorts we'll be. Sometimes we can misread our squirming as discontent with our human relationships. If you're married and dissatisfied, don't leave your husband. Embrace your calling.

Read the following verses and write a corresponding statement of fact in the first person (use "I" and "my") about your God-ordained works.

Ephesians 2:10 For I am his workmanship, created in Christ Jesus for good works, which God prepared beforehand, that I should walk in them.

1 Peter 4:10
As I have received a gift, use it to serve another, as good stewards of God's grace.

1 Peter 4:11
I speak, as one who speaks oracles of God, I serve, as one who serves by the strength that God supplies - in order that in everything God may be glorified through Jesus Christ.

Your spiritual gifts are means by which you have been distinctively and divinely equipped to manifest God's presence and power. No one else can fulfill your calling. Other people can do what you've been called to do but, child of God, they cannot be you doing it. That's what makes your footprint here unique.

No one else can fulfill your calling.

What you have been called by God to do is beyond your natural abilities, skills, or talents. God will use those as well as you yield them to Him, but unbelievers also possess those qualities. They are premiums that accompany being created in God's image. Only believers in Christ have spiritual gifts, however. Your divine calling cannot be fulfilled without their activation.

As you read Romans 12:4-8, highlight the gifts Paul mentions.

Now as we have many parts in one body, and all the parts do not have the same function, in the same way we who are many are one body in Christ and individually members of one another. According to the grace given to us, we have different gifts: If prophecy, use it according to the standard of one's faith; if service, in service; if teaching, in teaching; if exhorting, in exhortation; giving, with generosity; leading, with diligence; showing mercy, with cheerfulness.

ROMANS 12:4-8

What gifts has God given you? How can you use them to serve others?

Fill in the following blank with your whole name:
I, Martha ________________________, am immensely gifted by God. My ministry is something I cannot fulfill on my own. In the words of 2 Corinthians 3:8, it is a "ministry of the Spirit." Only the Spirit of Christ activated and energized in me can perform my God-ordained life works. I cannot serve Jesus without Jesus.

Our sixth week of study is about letting Scripture say to us what Paul said to Archippus in Colossians 4:17, "'Pay attention to the ministry you have received in the Lord, so that you can accomplish it.'" Whether you are brand new to this concept or you've served Christ actively for decades, all authentic, effective ministry begins and persists the same way.

Memorize these eight words: "Pursue love and earnestly desire the spiritual gifts" (1 Cor. 14:1, ESV).

Circle those first two words.

By all means, we are to "pursue love" for people. That's the entire point of 1 Corinthians 13, but let's back up one more step to what Christ termed the single most important commandment in the entire canon. "Love the Lord your God with all your heart, with all your soul, with all your mind, and with all your strength" (Mark 12:30).

Go ahead. Tell me about it now. What does loving God with all your heart look like for you? If you aren't certain, write what you imagine it would look like.

Social networking has allowed us a bird's-eye view—however distorted it may be—into all sorts of servants' lives and, more to the point, into all sorts of ministries. If you want to be motivated to serve, just get out there on the web and see how Christians are serving. Or if you want to feel lame and ineffectual and boring, do the exact same thing. Depending upon our frame of mind in our web search, other lives and ministries can look so adventurous that our contributions seem pathetic.

○ Have you found other people's contributions encouraging or discouraging lately? Explain why.

Recently my mind traveled to hosts of people I admire who are serving the kingdom. I thought of Bible professors who spend all of their work lives training up students in the Scriptures and then get to see them take their places and serve. That's huge. I thought of dear friends who courageously fight the atrocities of human trafficking. That's enormous. Then I thought of people who've adopted numerous orphans and others who put their hearts at risk over and over as loving foster parents. What could be more Christlike than that? My mind then jumped oceans and eyed missionary friends who have left every worldly comfort for the sake of Christ, sometimes at the daily risk of their lives. What could be more honorable than that?

But which cause do we take up?

Which ministry do we build?

Where do we begin?

Which one is God's favorite?

The works of God taking place out there are astounding, but they can leave us bewildered as we try to figure out where we fit in. We can decide we don't fit at all and quit trying. Here's the key that unlocks the call: what do you look like when you love the Lord your God with all your heart, soul, mind, and strength? That's who He's looking for in you.

What are you bursting to do when your heart is flooded with divine affection?

When you are teeming with love for the Lord your God, who are you right then? What is your passion? What are you bursting to do when your heart is flooded with divine affection? That's very likely the stream of your calling. Take a step and get your feet wet.

You following Christ will not look exactly like someone else following Christ. Why on earth would He bother to form you in your mother's womb with your own DNA and life experience ahead just to copy what someone else is doing? You're supposed to look like the version of you that loves Jesus with every particle. That's the real you.

You don't have to figure out what to surrender to. Just surrender every ounce of your heart to Jesus. Ask Him to give you a supernatural love for Him that surpasses anything in your human experience.

If you're a writer, your exploding love for Him will bring it out. If you're a liberator, you will not be able to resist fighting for the oppressed. If you're a teacher, you won't stop studying except to share what you've learned. If you're a counselor, you'll find yourself counseling before you even know what to call it. If you're an administrator, your love for Him will lead you to lead.

Whatever area of service you are called to fulfill, if it is fueled by fiery love for Jesus Christ, you'll be effervescent in the Spirit and effective. If you love Him with your whole heart and that heart bursts to sell everything and move to China, Girl, get your passport!

Who would you be if you loved Jesus with your whole heart, soul, mind, and strength? That's what you're meant to look like.

Let that person follow Him, and He will make you a fisher of men.

Day Two

You Can't Do It Alone

FLASH-FORWARD: We must always thank God for you, brothers. This is right, since your faith is flourishing and the love each one of you has for one another is increasing. ***2 Thessalonians 1:3***

We are devoting this entire week of study to seeking a fresh equipping and increased anointing in the ministries God has assigned to each of us. Are you in?

Bring your faith to our lessons this week. Never confuse unbelief with humility. In John 15:8 Jesus said, "My Father is glorified by this: that you produce much fruit and prove to be My disciples." He inspired the apostle Paul to write this: "For God has not given us a spirit of timidity, but of power and love and discipline" (2 Tim. 1:7, NASB). Likewise, He gave the apostle John this: "The anointing you received from Him remains in you" (1 John 2:27).

So let's get to some obedience to see that anointing and gifting stirred up and fanned into a flame through the power of Jesus. Don't make me sit here and have revival all by myself.

Paul, Silvanus, and Timothy: To the church of the Thessalonians in God the Father and the Lord Jesus Christ. Grace to you and peace.
1 THESSALONIANS 1:1

Please handwrite 2 Thessalonians 1:5-8 in the back of your workbook.

You read all of 2 Thessalonians 1 yesterday, but please review verses 1-4 and 11-12. Now compare the greeting of each book (in the margin). Document every difference between the two greetings.

Paul, Silvanus, and Timothy: To the church of the Thessalonians in God our Father and the Lord Jesus Christ. Grace to you and peace from God our Father and the Lord Jesus Christ.
2 THESSALONIANS 1:1-2

A key fact we've learned is how early in the New Testament formulation of the church the letters were written. You can see the bonds growing in the second letter as Paul refers to God the Father as "God our Father." The family blood is thickening and its temperature rising.

- Compare 1 Thessalonians 3:12 to 2 Thessalonians 1:3. What answered prayer do you see reflected?

sanctification growing.

What is a Bible-sanctioned form of boasting according to 2 Thessalonians 1:4?

among believers to build them up.

In today's lesson, we'll see how important we are to one another in fulfilling our callings. We are going to discover that, whatever we've been called to do, we cannot do it by ourselves. Other people are strategic to our development.

One reason God designed us to need each other was to force the issue of unity. Yesterday we put first things first: all obedience and giftedness of calling is initiated by divine love. "We love Him because He first loved us" (1 John 4:19, NKJV). In loving Him with our whole heart, soul, mind, and strength (Mark 12:30), all else will fall into place piece by piece, "grace after grace" (John 1:16), and "from faith to faith" (Rom. 1:17).

We don't need to look like any other human on this earth. Jesus rejoices in the version of us that loves Him with everything in us.

Jesus rejoices in the version of us that loves Him.

While we don't need to look like other people in the fulfillment of our callings, our premise today is that we do indeed need other people to fulfill our callings. Let's research several ways.

First read Ephesians 4:11-16. Then write verses 11-12 in this space:

And he gave the apostles, the prophets, the evangelists, the shepherds, and teachers to equip the saints for ministry, for building up the body of Christ.

God ordained that a sizable measure of our equipping (ESV) or "training" (HCSB) come no other way than through the Spirit-gifted, actively functioning leadership of the church. Christ designed this to take place in a local body of believers comprised both of mature Christians fully functioning in their spiritual gifts and young converts being raised up under their leadership to serve.

A few days ago a dear brother in Christ told me he'd become really close to a group of strong believers active in various ministries. He wondered if I found anything objectionable about the fact that none of them attend a church.

"Should I be flagging in any way?" he asked.

The city has a population of around two million and is home to many Bible-believing churches. God, help me not lapse into legalism but, as I live and breathe, I cannot fathom how it can be healthy for believers to be detached from any local church for years on end in an area where many exist.

We sidestep a vital part of our equipping when we scoot out from under the shepherding and teaching designed by God. I'm going to just go ahead and put myself out there and say that, from what I've observed, people who can never find a body of believers where they can both give and receive measures of gifting are often those who resist authority. The resulting dysfunction often does not surface right away but, sooner or later, soundness, effectiveness, and credibility almost invariably wane. No church is perfect, but biblical leadership and active discipleship do exist in numerous local bodies. Jesus taught us the best way to put leadership to the test.

How can we determine quality according to Matthew 7:15-20?

You will recognize them by their fruits

The equipping described in Ephesians 4:11-12 is God-designed, and we will lack crucial training and preparation in our ministries if we sidestep it. But Scripture also intimates several other gorgeous ways we can be vital to one another in the fulfillment of our callings.

A Jew named Apollos, a native Alexandrian, an eloquent man who was powerful in the use of the Scriptures, arrived in Ephesus. This man had been instructed in the way of the Lord; and being fervent in spirit, he spoke and taught the things about Jesus accurately, although he knew only John's baptism. He began to speak boldly in the synagogue. After Priscilla and Aquila heard him, they took him home and explained the way of God to him more accurately. When he wanted to cross over to Achaia, the brothers wrote to the disciples urging them to welcome him. After he arrived, he greatly helped those who had believed through grace. For he vigorously refuted the Jews in public, demonstrating through the Scriptures that Jesus is the Messiah.
ACTS 18:24-28

Look up each of the following and record the impact:

Hebrews 10:24-25 not neglecting to meet together

2 Timothy 1:5-6 faith of T. from grandmother & mother.

Acts 13:2-3 blessing of the gathering of believers.

Read Acts 18:24-28 in the margin. What mutual impact do you see depicted in the passage?

Priscilla & Aquila instructed Apollos
Apollos helped believers in Achaia.

It's thrilling, don't you think? God is so pro-community and pro-family that He designed us to be trained by others in our works, encouraged by others in our works, sent forth by others in our works, blessed by others in our works, and taught the way of God more accurately by others in our works. We cannot operate in the same anointing autonomously.

As an insecure young woman in my late twenties, I had Bible study teachers who encouraged something in me I could never have stirred up in myself. At every strategic point in my ministry life, God has brought someone along to say, "Have you ever thought God might be calling you to ____________________?"

If I sought Him and did not sense His nod, I usually shrugged the suggestion off. But over and over again, He used the body of Christ to affirm any shred of gifting in me, sharpening and stewarding it more effectively. Despite my innumerable weaknesses and self-doubts, I studied hard under several teachers, took notes on my pastor's sermons, and watched how each of my leaders served.

I could cry reflecting on the patience of my early Bible classes and how much room they gave me to make mistakes. When I taught something inaccurately, I was rerouted without feeling shamed. Mind you, I didn't say without being embarrassed. I remember a woman staying after class once and correcting my grammar. It worked. Thirty years later and counting, I'm batting a thousand on the use of that one word. If we won't let a little embarrassment kill us, it just might equip us. We don't have to fall dead just because we turned red.

Throughout the years I've also received (and sometimes earned) volumes of criticism and you may too, but we have to get back up, dust ourselves off, and go on with God. I often tell myself, *You can't quit now. You're almost Home!* We all are. Our time lines are an inch long against the backdrop of eternity. We can do this thing for the five minutes we're here.

The titanic impact of others on my calling is ongoing. Two years ago I saw such great courage and anointing on a woman in Christ that I pleaded with Him to do that great work in me too, if it would bring Him glory. I'm a work in progress with a long way to go, but as a result of that journaled prayer and the appetite for Christ that sister stirred up in my bones, my courage has increased exponentially. Her example threw me right into a fresh awakening.

We can do this thing for the five minutes we're here.

○ OK! It's your turn! Testify in this space to ways God has used others to encourage, train, or direct you in your works or your calling. Get specific, using names and describing means. Be ready to share what you've written with your small group.

Praise God for the paths He's braided. Without them, imagine the impact of cultural narcissism invading the body of Christ. What if each servant of God were just out for herself? What if she were too territorial and insecure to encourage and train others? Or just too self-consumed?

What if everybody were to get their shepherding and ministry training on line and local functioning bodies of believers became obsolete? What if the young didn't respect the old? What if the old didn't train up the young? The rippling ramifications would drown our witness.

A body torn apart hemorrhages to death. Every tear in our fabric offers our anointing a route to bleed out.

Day Three

Eat This Book

FLASH-FORWARD: He said to me: "Son of man, eat what you find here. Eat this scroll, then go and speak to the house of Israel." So I opened my mouth, and He fed me the scroll. "Son of man," He said to me, "eat and fill your stomach with this scroll I am giving you." So I ate it, and it was as sweet as honey in my mouth. Then He said to me: "Son of man, go to the house of Israel and speak My words to them. *Ezekiel 3:1-4*

This week of our journey is about getting mobilized with a fresh awareness and an increased anointing in the ministries God has assigned to us. Let's keep up with our handwritten portions as we go.

Please write 2 Thessalonians 1:9-10 in the back of your workbook, putting us exactly where we need to be on day 4.

Take a moment now to bask in today's "Flash-Forward." Don't you love it?

- What did God tell the prophet Ezekiel to do before he spoke to the house of Israel?

Eat this scroll

At the risk of redundancy, what did Ezekiel do?

He ate it

How did Ezekiel describe it?

as sweet as honey.

Let's emphasize that order again. God told Ezekiel to "eat this scroll," then "go and speak to the house of Israel."

Circle the word "then" in the last sentence and in the "Flash-Forward."

God etched the message He entrusted to Ezekiel on a scroll, and the prophet would not be prepared to fulfill that measure of his calling until he'd consumed it. God gave similar instructions to the apostle John in Revelation 10:8-11. We're meant to picture the servants of God in both visions putting the scrolls in their mouths, then chewing and swallowing them.

Often in Scripture, particularly in the Psalms, "eating" the Word of God is metaphorical for finding it so delectable and satisfying in your reading or hearing, that it is "sweeter than honey, which comes from the honeycomb" (Ps. 19:10).

The Message translates the wording in Ezekiel 3:1-2 in a way easily relatable to us: "Eat this book." Gorgeous, isn't it? I'd love those three words engraved in gold on the front of my Bible. Second Timothy 3:16-17 doesn't use the same dining metaphor, but it suggests a very similar order in the ongoing fulfillments of our divine assignments.

Read 2 Timothy 3:16-17 and write verse 17 in the margin.

Receive some well-earned affirmation, my friend. You are obviously studying Scripture or you wouldn't be six weeks' deep into a Bible course. Still, we'd leave a gaping hole in our discussions about ministry mobilization, increased anointing, and fruitfulness if we did not give primacy to a hungry relationship with God, fed by His Word.

Obviously, "eat this book" does not mean that we need to start at Genesis and read all the way through Revelation before we go out and minister to people. However, the passages in 2 Timothy 3 do tell us that we can't be thoroughly equipped for every good work without ongoing exposure to Scripture.

We can't be thoroughly equipped without ongoing exposure to Scripture.

Whether this is your 1st in-depth Bible study journey or your 25th, this is a perfect context in which to stir up appreciation for the privilege of opening a Bible. "All Scripture is breathed out by God." That's the way the ESV words it. It doesn't say it *was* breathed out. It says it *is* breathed out. Every time we open the Bible, it breaks forth with fresh breath of the Spirit. If God is going to exhale, Sister, we want to inhale.

For discussion's sake, in what language is your copy of the Bible?

The language of your Bible has a rich story—one you'll want to know. Do some research and discover it. If yours is English, I hope to whet your appetite here. Let's sit up straight, shake off every shred of casualness and smug entitlement, and pitch ourselves into the following scene.

It's Friday, October 6, 1536. A crowd is forming around a barricaded circle.

> Inside the circle, two beams were set up in the shape of a cross, which would project from the ground to a man's height. At the top of this structure were iron chains. Brushwood, straw, and logs were packed tightly around the upright beam in a kind of hut. The prisoner was brought in and given a last chance to recant. His feet were then bound to the stake. Gunpowder was added to the brush for the quick burn.[2]

The prisoner was William Tyndale. In early August of the same year, he'd been ceremonially and publicly stripped of his priesthood before a gathering of bishops and condemned to die.[3]

> He was made to kneel. His hands were then scraped with a knife or a piece of glass—anywhere he would have been anointed with oil at his ordination. The office was withdrawn from him, the anointing removed ... He then stood before the bishops and the crowd below as a layman, and suffered a final curse. "We commit your soul to the devil."[4]

Tyndale translated the Scriptures at great loss and constant risk.

In the eyes of many, Tyndale had committed the most heinous of crimes. He'd dared to translate the Scriptures into English. And he'd done so at great loss and constant risk. Proficient in multiple languages, including Hebrew and Greek, he labored tirelessly, moved constantly, and evaded authorities until, finally, the New Testament was birthed in 1526 with the distinct cries of an English infant.

Picture a man with rounded shoulders, poring over a Greek New Testament by the light of a lamp, taking his quill, dipping it in the dark ink, and first writing these familiar long-loved words:

"No room for them in the inn."

"Give us this day our daily bread."

"For thine is the kingdom and the power and the glory forever."

"Blessed are the poor in spirit."

"Take, eat, this is My body."

"Let this cup pass from Me."

Discipline alone lacks the heat to keep a long, arduous work aflame amid the ruination of reputation and the loss of home, country, and companionship. Love drives such a man. God drives such a man. Tyndale penned these words to his accusers: "Christ is the cause why I love thee, why I am ready to do the uttermost of my power for thee, and why I pray for thee. And as long as the cause abideth, so long lasteth the effect; even as it is always day so long as the sun shineth."[5]

If those words paint the self-portrait of William Tyndale, then these by author David Teems, paint the portrait of his works:

> Even his Englishing of the Scripture has something to tell us. To William Tyndale, the Word of God is a living thing. It has both warmth and intellect. It has discretion, generosity, subtlety, movement, authority. It has a heart and a pulse. It keeps a beat and has a musical voice that allows it to sing. It enchants and it soothes. It argues and it forgives. It defends and it reasons. It intoxicates and it restores. It weeps and it exults. It thunders but never roars. It calls but never begs. And it always loves. Indeed, for Tyndale, love is the code that unlocks and empowers the Scripture. His inquiry into Scripture is always relational, never analytic.[6]

Pick two of the following questions to answer in light of the excerpt:

Which verse has "sung" to you recently and why?

Which verse have you found most soothing recently and why?

Which verse has reverberated with profound authority to you recently?

On that sixth day of October in 1536, the accused heretic was brought forth in the public square to fulfill the last requirements of his sentencing. Before the kindling at his feet was lit, the rope around his neck was tightened until all breath was blocked from his lungs. The mouth of the Englishman was silenced. His accusers exhaled with relief that he would speak no more.

But God used his vocal cords again this very day to wrap divine breath in the crisp linen of language you and I could understand. This is what we hold to our breast and consider dearer than our daily bread. As months turn into years, some of its pages are stained with our tears, its corners curled up with our turning. Even the question marks we've scribbled in its margins evidence enough intelligible understanding to boldly enter a dialogue with the Divine.

In closing today, picture yourself in this scenario: A friend or acquaintance is baffled by your love for the Bible and became a bit incredulous in a recent conversation. She asked you what you loved so much about it, but you were too caught off guard to respond thoughtfully. You sit down now to write her a letter. You don't have time for a lengthy diatribe or a quick course on Bible apologetics. You know you can't force her to understand. You simply want to convey in a paragraph what Scripture has meant to you personally.

○ Compose your letter here and consider sharing it with your small group.

Day Four

A Fresh Resolve

FLASH-FORWARD: "To this end we always pray for you, that our God may make you worthy of his calling and may fulfill every resolve for good and every work of faith by his power." *2 Thessalonians 1:11, ESV*

Our previous lesson drew an arrow straight to the Word as the source of and equipment for "every good work" (2 Tim. 3:17). Sometimes the connection between God's Word and our work is beautifully blatant. For instance, the Book of Proverbs speaks plainly and boldly about work ethics as well as caring for the poor. If you're looking for a mandate to rise up on behalf of the oppressed, Isaiah 58 speaks unflinchingly, specifically, and gorgeously. You don't have to meditate long on how a number of Scriptures apply to your pursuit of God's will in your assigned calling.

The connection of a correction can also be easy to spot. If we come to the portion of 1 Peter 5:5 that says "clothe yourselves with humility toward one another" and the Holy Spirit convicts us about a present work, we don't need to be sages to conclude that pride is in the equation. Left in place, pride will block the grace utterly necessary to accomplish the work.

Let's take Galatians 3:3 (NIV) as another example. What if you or I came upon this verse in the midst of a long-term work and looked up from the page with the clear sense that God was talking to us? "After beginning by means of the Spirit, are you now trying to finish by means of the flesh?"

How could the verse prove enormously vital to our equipping?

Having begun by the Spirit, are you now being perfected by the flesh?

If opposition is rising against you in a work God called you to accomplish, what equipping could 1 Corinthians 16:9 offer you?

a wide door for effective work has opened to me, & there are many adversaries.

Scripture is effectively at work even when a verse does not tie directly to our task.

Often the connection between God's Word and a specific good work is less obvious, but here's the wonder of it: Scripture is effectively at work even when a verse does not tie directly to our task. In 1 Thessalonians Paul spoke brilliantly of its effectiveness.

Fill in the remainder of 1 Thessalonians 2:13 (NIV, though you should be able to complete it based on any Bible translation):

"And we also thank God continually because, when you received the word of God, which you heard from us, you accepted it not as a human word, but as it actually is, the word of God, which is at work in you believers."

Scripture is at work in our works even when it doesn't speak a specific word toward our tasks. That means that my morning reading could be the genealogy of Matthew 1, but I can still get up from my kitchen table better equipped as a ministry employer because the Word possesses inherent strength and shapes character. An open Bible also awakens our ears (Isa. 50:4).

○ OK, let's get specific. In what present or impending task could you use some equipping from the Scriptures? Respond in the margin.

This portion of Psalm 119 in Eugene Peterson's translation is itching for a place in today's lesson. Read it aloud, if possible, and make your own personal prayer out of it.

> *Let my cry come right into your presence, God; provide me with the insight that comes only from your Word. Give my request your personal attention, rescue me on the terms of your promise. Let praise cascade off my lips; after all, you've taught me the truth about life! And let your promises ring from my tongue; every order you've given is right. Put your hand out and steady me since I've chosen to live by your counsel. I'm homesick, God, for your salvation; I love it when you show yourself! Invigorate my soul so I can praise you well, use your decrees to put iron in my soul. And should I wander off like a lost sheep—seek me! I'll recognize the sound of your voice.*
>
> PSALM 119:169-176, THE MESSAGE

Fellow student, God's decrees are putting iron in our souls even when we still lack specific direction in our task. Try to resist forcing Scripture to fit or reading your situation into every verse, sermon, or devotional. An egocentric approach to Scripture—eyeing it chiefly with ourselves in mind—will throw us off course and dramatically increase our tendency to misapply it.

God's decrees put iron in our souls even when we lack specific direction in our task.

If we'll ask God to fill us with the Holy Spirit as we read and study, He will alert us when He's speaking to our situation through a precept that doesn't blatantly fit. Our inner man will bear witness with His Spirit.

Reading in panic mode can also throw off a sound application of Scripture. It's my least effective frame of mind for receiving direction and equipping from the Bible. That's when I'm most apt to use the day's Scripture reading like a crystal ball. By all means, when we're panicked, let's cry out to God and ask for help and tell Him how desperate we are to hear from Him. But hacking through the Scriptures with a mental machete is hazardous.

When we are in panic we end up blaming God for misdirection when we wrap the wrong word around our steering wheel. Times of fright or distress present us an opportunity to get on our faces before God and request a trade-in for trust mode. Don't try to make Him speak. *Let Him speak.* He wants to, and He will when the time is right. We don't need to put words in God's mouth. Whatever the task at hand, it will not come down to achieving; it will come down to receiving.

These two words can be deep breath to an asthmatic soul: "calm down" (Isa. 7:4). Go for a walk and reflect on God's goodness and faithfulness. Praise Him and profess confidence in His commitment to equip you for every good work. Quiet yourself in Him for a while. Sometimes we'll find that we're trying too hard. Often the equipping will follow the calming because God honors a posture of trust.

But what if I blow it? What if I fail? What if I miss the calling?

I've waited all week for us to get to those questions. Now we're finally ready to throw our arms around 2 Thessalonians 1:11-12 and hold the verses tight.

Handwrite verse 11 in the back of your workbook. Save verse 12 for day 5. Then glance back at today's "Flash-Forward" where you'll find 2 Thessalonians 1:11 (ESV). Fill in the following blanks accordingly:

"To this end we always pray for you, that our God may make you worthy of his calling and may fulfill ______________ ______________ and ______________ ______________ by his power."

We'll unpack the second phrase tomorrow. For the rest of our time today, let's bask in the first: "every resolve for good." Forget setting out to do something great. That goal entangles our egos every time. Instead, let's resolve to do some *good* in Jesus' name. If our good turns out great, then give glory to God. It was all about Him anyway. If we feel like it failed to achieve the fruit we hoped for (I've been there many times), did we do anyone any good?

To find your niche, go meet some needs.

To find your niche, go meet some needs. There's no end to them. Students need tutors. Shut-ins need visitors. Sick people need someone to pick up their medicine. Demoralized people need someone to listen. Pastors need encouragement before they pass out or pass on. Small group Bible studies need places to meet. Ministries need volunteers. Church nurseries are desperate for workers. Kids' ministers are clamoring for servants who can keep commitments. Hungry people need food collectors. People who live out on the streets need shelter and, if they're too trapped in addiction to desire it, they could use a blanket when it's cold. So many young women need mothering. Elderly women need to matter. And everybody needs spiritual mentors. Don't worry about doing something great. Resolve to do some good.

As you willingly and humbly serve in ways that do some good, eventually you're going to start noticing that certain works seem to energize you more than they exhaust you. Always take notice of those occurrences, because you're probably stumbling onto your spiritual gifts and heading toward your foreordained path. When the Holy Spirit's anointing is on us for a work, we're using His energy and not just our own.

- How did Paul describe this symbiosis in Colossians 1:29?

As you can see, Christ's energy working powerfully within us doesn't mean we'll never struggle. After all, we live on a planet where struggling is standard. But we'll often feel emotionally and spiritually satisfied after a work handpicked and infused by the Holy Spirit.

If you're on the right track for your spiritual gifting, you'll start getting snippets of feedback that affirm your contribution. God will use people to tell you that what you're doing helps. And give it time! I still have plenty of growing to do as a Bible teacher, but my first year was a train wreck. I'd made a 12-month commitment to teach, intending to get to the end of it and run for my life. Just as I approached the final few Sundays, God began to enlighten my heart with His Word and use a handful of women to affirm the track I was on.

God will even use a disastrous attempt at serving as part of our equipping. Nothing will be wasted. Realizing where God *hasn't* sent us is strategic to figuring out where He *has.*

Never underestimate the power of ruling out. That's qualified equipping. Did we learn anything from it? Were we humbled by it? Were we led elsewhere by it? Every yes implies an equipping.

God looks past our scorecard to our sincere resolve to do some good in His great name. Stay after it, Sister. Stay willing, flexible, and teachable, and God will not let you miss what He put you on this planet to accomplish. If you're on the wrong road, He'll take you to the right place. He will raise you up out of a rubble of confusion, so that you're trained and equipped for works that work.

Because we know that this extraordinary day is just ahead, we pray for you all the time—pray that our God will make you fit for what he's called you to be, pray that he'll fill your good ideas and acts of faith with his own energy so that it all amounts to something. If your life honors the name of Jesus, he will honor you. Grace is behind and through all of this, our God giving himself freely, the Master, Jesus Christ, giving himself freely.

2 THESSALONIANS 1:11-12, THE MESSAGE

Day Five

Every Work of Faith

FLASH-FORWARD: "[S]o that the name of our Lord Jesus will be glorified by you, and you by Him, according to the grace of our God and the Lord Jesus Christ." *2 Thessalonians 1:12*

Today we'll wrap up a week of study dedicated entirely to fulfilled ministries teeming with fresh anointing and effectiveness for one splendorous purpose.

Please handwrite 2 Thessalonians 1:12 on the appropriate page, recording that purpose boldly.

Before we add the last few brush strokes to the canvas of the ministry portrait we're painting, let's go back and see the landscape we have so far.

Flip through the pages of days 1–4 and jot down one thing from each day that you believe God wanted to say to you personally:

Day 1: God has called me to glorify him.

Day 2: I am part of the body of Christ.

Day 3: Bible study equips me for God's service.

Day 4: Do something good.

20 Now may the God of
peace, who brought up
from the dead our Lord
Jesus—the great Shepherd
of the sheep—with the
blood of the everlasting
covenant, 21 equip you
with all that is good to
do His will, working in us
what is pleasing in His
sight, through Jesus Christ.
Glory belongs to Him
forever and ever. Amen.
HEBREWS 13:20-21

The benediction to the Book of Hebrews is not only an appropriate blessing for the end of our emphasis, it also cradles an embraceable treasure.

Please read Hebrews 13:20-21 in the margin. What does the blessing involve? Equip w. all that is good.

● Who is in charge of providing what we need to do God's will through our works?

The God of peace

That's a relief, isn't it? Our responsibility is to stay willing, keep doing some good, and not quench the Spirit with so much worldliness that we wouldn't know divine direction if God spelled it on a banner and flew it over our heads.

Most formal translations use a word we've repeated often this week. It is the first word in verse 21. Please circle it.

The Greek word translated "equip" is defined as follows:

> *[K]atartízō*, from *katá*, "with," and *artízō* "to adjust, fit, finish" ... The fundamental meaning is to put a thing in its appropriate condition, to establish, set up, equip, arrange, prepare, mend ... To refit, repair, mend that which is broken such as the nets (Matt. 4:21; Mark 1:19). Metaphorically, of a person in error, to restore, set right (Gal. 6:1). By implication and in the proper force of *katá*, meaning to make a perfect fit, suitable, such as one should be, deficient in no part. Of persons (Luke 6:40; 1 Cor. 1:10; 2 Cor. 13:11; Heb. 13:21; 1 Pet. 5:10); of things, e.g., to fill out, supply (1 Thess. 3:10).[7]

Circle the parts of the definition that stand out to you the most.

○ The grace-glaring dimension of the term is that God's equipping can take the form of *preparing* or *repairing*. From your experience, how are the two distinct?

Even the mending is part of the sending.

When our assignments here on earth are complete and we see Jesus face to face, our works will have been a blend of the gloriously proactive and gracefully reactive. The God who calls us knows the end from the beginning and sees our entire life story as an open pop-up book before page 1 is turned. That means even the mending is part of the sending.

If your past is like mine, think of all we've done to blow it—all the harm we've brought on ourselves through foolish decisions, all the derailments, and all the times He's had to put us together again. Maybe, like me, you've felt shamed by the long list of repairs you've required, and your prayer life often amounts to one long apology. Maybe you feel like God prepared something for you and placed it in your hands, then you dropped it. The spilling doesn't have to end your story. God can do something far more personal than repair your calling. He can repair you. God mends our pasts to tend to our futures.

Every time we've been broken and then allowed God to repair us, that mending becomes part of our equipping. All the pain we've endured. All the abuse and misuse. Every betrayal. Every wound. Where God mends, He equips. We embrace a hurting woman with far greater empathy because we've been one. We're equipped to minister to her precisely because God has sewn up our similar wounds.

Do you see it? If we still have life and breath, God can repurpose every shred of havoc the Devil wreaks.

If you think, *I wish I could believe that*, then take heart.

Near the midpoint of day 4, you filled in two blanks for 2 Thessalonians 1:11 (ESV). The first one was "every resolve for good." What was the second one? Every work of faith.

Just as we walk by faith, we work by faith. Even when we don't see the connection between where we've been and where we're going, God is at work. He knows how a hurt will equip us. He knows how a doubt will end up building our faith. He knows who we need to be to do what He's called us to do. We can't always tell if what we're doing is working, but we can rest assured God is doing His job with our resolve for good. In John 5:17, Christ said, "My Father is still working, and I am working also." He hasn't quit on you.

God hasn't quit on you.

I remember a season when I couldn't sense the presence of God in the works I believed He'd called me to do. I became heartsick, scrambling for answers and searching for the place I'd veered from the path. In my morning reading one day, God led me to these unexpected words in Haggai 2:5 and bound them around my heart like a bandage: "My Spirit remains in your midst. Fear not" (ESV). I wept with relief and, though it was still a while before I could discern His activity, I hung on tight to those words and worked by faith. Matthew 28:20 is the matching promise in the New Testament: "And remember, I am with you always." Let both verses breathe fresh life over you.

Every task Christ puts on our docket requires a measure of faith, because "without faith it is impossible to please God" (Heb. 11:6). If, as we've seen in Hebrews 13:21, He is constantly "working in us what is pleasing in His sight" and we cannot please Him without faith, then our progressive works will entail our progressive faith.

If you've known Jesus long, you've probably seen a work materialize that required tremendous faith. Once faith becomes sight and serving fits a formula, go fetch your swimsuit because, as sure as God is working in you what is pleasing to Him, He'll call you back out of that predictable boat and offer you a fresh walk on wind-tossed waters. That's His way. Nothing on earth puts us in a serving rut like replacing faith with a formula does.

Substantial equipping still awaits us over our final two weeks, but today we wrap up our single-minded focus on mobilized ministry. In doing so, I'd like to take you to some wording that leapt off the page at me while reading a familiar story in Luke's Gospel in less familiar terminology. Read Luke 13:10-17 below.

As He was teaching in one of the synagogues on the Sabbath, a woman was there who had been disabled by a spirit for over 18 years. She was bent over and could not straighten up at all. When Jesus saw her, He called out to her, "Woman, you are free of your disability." Then He laid His hands on her, and instantly she was restored and began to glorify God. But the leader of the synagogue, indignant because Jesus had healed on the Sabbath, responded by telling the crowd, "There are six days when work should be done;

> *therefore come on those days and be healed and not on the Sabbath day." But the Lord answered him and said, "Hypocrites! Doesn't each one of you untie his ox or donkey from the feeding trough on the Sabbath and lead it to water? Satan has bound this woman, a daughter of Abraham, for 18 years—shouldn't she be untied from this bondage on the Sabbath day?" When He had said these things, all His adversaries were humiliated, but the whole crowd was rejoicing over all the glorious things He was doing.*
>
> LUKE 13:10-17

Because this week's subject matter was spinning in my mind, I thought of disabilities that cripple our capacity to do the "good works, which God prepared ahead of time so that we should walk in them" (Eph. 2:10). I thought of all the ways the Enemy tries to thwart our effectiveness and kill our fruitfulness because he does not want our Father in heaven to be glorified (John 15:8).

The woman in the account probably wasn't demon possessed or Christ would have cast the demon out of her. Instead, "He laid His hands on her." She'd been so oppressed and bound by Satan that she could not straighten herself up. I know the feeling. I haven't experienced her physical malady, but I have most certainly battled the kind of oppression that gnarls a person's backbone until she can't stand up straight.

Maybe our theme has been frustrating this week because you're willing to work but can't find a place you fit. You can't seem to find your niche and you feel bereft of a single spiritual gift. Or maybe you were certain you had what it took and surrendered publicly to your calling, but nothing ever materialized. Either way, I'm praying with all my heart for a change on your horizon.

You are powerfully gifted by God. He prepared in advance for your contribution to this world. He is willing to use every repair, so that you'll be prepared. If Christ is your Savior and yet your works seem anemic and ineffective, you do not have an *inability;* you have a *disability.* In spiritual terms, inability comes from being unable; disability comes from being disabled.

Describe the difference between inability and disability.

inability: impossible to do.
disability: a barrier prevents from doing.

If the enemy is standing in between you and your fruitfulness, Daughter of Abraham (Gal. 3:29), it's time for him to move. I'm going to get down on my knees right here at my desk and pray for you. Get down on yours too. Cry out with everything in you for Jesus to free you of any disability oppressing or suppressing your calling. Ask Him to untie you from your bondage. Then, Sister, get up, go out there, and work by faith.

Group Session Seven

REVIEW THE WEEK

Use these questions to guide your discussion of last week's homework.

● Principal Questions

DAY 1: What exhortation is recorded in Colossians 4:17? (p. 142)

DAY 2: Compare 1 Thessalonians 3:12 to 2 Thessalonians 1:3. What answered prayer do you see reflected? (p. 146)

DAY 3: What did God tell the prophet Ezekiel to do before he spoke to Israel? (p. 150)

DAY 4: How did Paul describe the symbiosis in Colossians 1:29? (p. 157)

DAY 5: Who is in charge of providing what we need to do God's will? (p. 158)

○ Personal Discussion Questions

DAY 1: Have you found other people's contributions encouraging or discouraging lately? Explain. (p. 144)

DAY 2: How has God used others to encourage, train, or direct you? (p. 149)

DAY 3: Would you like to share your letter with your small group? (p. 153)

DAY 4: In what task could you use some equipping from the Scriptures? (p. 155)

DAY 5: From your experience, how are *preparing* and *repairing* distinct? (p. 159)

VIEW THE VIDEO

Introduction

In our homework this week, we began to unravel the sacred parchment of the Second Letter to the Thessalonians. Six words from the center of chapter 1 will preoccupy us today: When the ______________ ______________ is ______________.

The lexical Greek word is *apokálupsis*: "______________, uncovering, ______________, disclosure. One of three words referring to the Second Coming of Christ (1 Cor. 1:7; 2 Thess. 1:7; 1 Pet. 1:7,13). The other two words are *epipháneia*, appearing (1 Tim. 6:14), and *parousía*, coming, presence (2 Thess. 2:1). *Apokálupsis*, a ______________ and more comprehensive word, includes not merely the thing shown and seen but the ______________, the unveiling of the same. The *epipháneiai*, appearances, are contained in the *apokálupsis*, revelation, being separate points or moments therein. Christ's first coming was an *epipháneia* (2 Tim. 1:10); the second, an *apokálupsis*, will be far more ______________."[1]

We'll invite the apostle Peter to come alongside Paul through his own inspired letter and help us broaden our grasp of those six words. Savor the NET Bible translation of 1 Peter 1:1-2:

> From Peter, an apostle of Jesus Christ, to those ____________ ____________ ____________ (in Pontus, Galatia, Cappadocia, the province of Asia, and Bithynia) who are chosen according to the foreknowledge of God the Father by being set apart by the Spirit for obedience and for sprinkling with Jesus Christ's blood. May grace and peace be yours in full measure!

Now read 1 Peter 1:3-9. Note three distinct time periods:

1. ____________

2. A ____ ____________ ____________

3. When Jesus is ____________

According to 2 Thessalonians 1:6-10, when the Lord Jesus is ____________ ...

- ____________ will ____________ to the "____________."
- "Relief" in the Greek is ____________. Find the term also in 2 Corinthians 2:12-13 and 2 Corinthians 7:5-7. Reflect on this relief in view of Matthew 24:21-22.
- ____________ ____________ will be assigned.
- ____________ will occur (v. 10).
- He will be ____________ in His ____________ (v. 10; Rom. 8:18-19).

1. S. Zodhiates, *The Complete Word Study Dictionary: New Testament,* s.v. "apokálupsis."

Week Seven

To Love the Truth

Day One

Let No One Deceive You

FLASH-FORWARD: Don't let anyone deceive you in any way. ***2 Thessalonians 2:3***

Our homework this week sits encased between two video sessions spotlighting the astounding arrival of our Lord Jesus Christ. To say that the winds pick up slightly on the end-time landscape in 2 Thessalonians is like calling a hurricane a breeze.

Please read 2 Thessalonians 2:1-3 and handwrite this segment in the back.

With verse 1 in mind, peruse the First Letter to the Thessalonians. Where in the letter did Paul describe our being gathered together with Jesus?

1 Thess 4:16-18.

His Second Letter slips into an envelope also addressing the future. F. F. Bruce translates the Greek in the first half of verse 2 like this: "We beg you not to be quickly shaken out of your wits or disturbed."[1] I can get shaken out of my wits with shocking swiftness at times. You too? Just when we feel completely focused and sound of mind, a situation can drop a grenade that sends all our certainties flying like shrapnel. Paul's exhortation to his spiritual son in 2 Timothy 4:5 is sublime in its brevity: "But you, keep your head in all situations" (NIV).

Maybe that's somebody's word today. Everybody around you may lose complete control, but you keep your head. Imagine how often those five words would apply in a dialogue with God:

Lord, I have no idea what's going on here.
But you, keep your head.
Lord, what they're doing is not right!
But you, keep your head.
Lord, it looks like he's getting away with this!
But you, keep your head.
Lord, I've worked too hard for this to happen now.
But you, keep your head.

Where are you most at risk of losing control right now? Write the statement here as if you are bringing it straight to God.

But you, keep your head.

That's what I need to hear today. Maybe you do too.

● Now, what three sources of potential alarm did Paul list in 2:2?

1. a spirit
2. a spoken word
3. a false letter.

The inclusion of the word "spirit" in the list of three is fascinating, isn't it? F. F. Bruce explains that it could convey either of two things: "a prophetic utterance made in the power of the Spirit of God or of another spirit." Bruce goes on to say, "The prophecy might be a false prophecy or it might be a genuine prophecy misunderstood ... Prophecy was encouraged in the Thessalonian church (1 Thess 5:19,20) and no doubt things to come figured largely in such prophecy ... But discrimination was necessary (1 Thess. 5:21,22) and nowhere more so than with prophecies relating to future events."[2]

At first I assumed the spirit in this context could only be demonic. The reminder that the Holy Spirit can speak something that we falsely apply may be even more relevant to us than a warning about evil spirits. A prophetic word can be right, yet we can wrongly interpret it. Something from the Spirit of God can be errantly understood by the mind of man. This brings us to our key concept for today's lesson. From verse 3: "Don't let anyone deceive you in any way."

Know and love the truth.

The singular guard against deception is truth. This week, one overriding message is meant to bounce loudly from the walls of our study halls: know and love the truth. We are blessed to have limitless opportunities to study under many pastors and teachers but, if we do not go diligently to the Scriptures for ourselves, the question is not whether we'll be deceived, but how often.

One subject ranks above all others in the Bible (including end-time events). We absolutely must know who Jesus really is.

If it's been a while, I suggest you set aside a six-month period to read all the way from Matthew 1 through Revelation 22. When you get to the final word of the New Testament, the Savior quoted and depicted in those pages is the real Jesus. He alone is "the way, the truth, and the life" (John 14:6). He's the one sitting at the right hand of God, interceding for us. He's the one in whose omnipotent name we pray. He's the one who can do the impossible. The New Testament's Jesus is our Jesus. What He did, our Jesus can do, because they are one and the same.

Glance at Matthew 16:15 and record Christ's question to His disciples.

But who do you say that I am?

The query resounds to every generation: "But you, who do you say that I am?" Does our Jesus have the same authority? The same ability? The same affinity for lost and broken people? The same aversion to religious pride?

Staying under good teaching and preaching is vital, but we can't let others spoon-feed us Jesus. Let's keep turning our faces back to the sacred pages.

Second Thessalonians 2:3 places the burden of lie-proofing ourselves on us. "Let no one deceive you in any way" (ESV). Let's broaden the topic from being deceived in our doctrine to being deceived in any way. No exhortation in the entire letter is more relevant to our current era. That, Sister in Christ, is a verse begging to be memorized.

Take a moment to read 2 Timothy 3:1,12-13. What does verse 13 say regarding imposters?

Flip through your mental Rolodex and think of all the opportunities our society offers to imposters. List as many as possible.

Social media is rife with misrepresentation. But we're talking about something more slack-jawing than spinning our personas to look more interesting or impressive than we are. Exaggeration is a form of deception that elbows its place among acts of wrongdoing. For the next few moments, however, let's talk about lies that are contrived virtually *ex nihilo*.

We have imposters out there who are making up identities, accounts, and memoirs out of thin air. Some of them scam for the money, but many of them do it for the sheer satisfaction of drawing attention. We have mourned the deaths of infants and young children who never existed. We have pleaded passionately with God to heal people of diseases that we later learned were pretended. You can smell some hoaxes from the start. They're predictable long before they're provable. Others hoaxes are elaborate and well executed by minds so brilliant they should be studied by science.

With our magnetic draw toward drama, you can imagine how many imposters I've encountered in 30 years of women's ministry. The recent ones could have earned Academy Awards. One young woman came all the way to our Bible study in Houston, faking stage IV cancer so she could entrap my involvement. She shaved her head and apparently carved scars in her own body to present herself convincingly. She claimed to be a patient at MD Anderson, the world-renown cancer center in Houston, a sleek part of her story that earned some credibility because we have frequent visitors to Bible study who are in town for treatment. In a large sanctuary with several thousand women present, she made sure she knelt at the altar for prayer right in front of me, so I wouldn't miss her. She was the living embodiment of a pretty little liar.

We might reason that the young do foolish things for attention, but some people never grow out of it. Make no mistake: old liars can give the young liars a run for their money. A woman much older than I came into my life several years ago claiming to be a Jewish holocaust survivor. She said she had been saved in one of my Bible studies in Colorado. She had duped her entire small group with her false identity and moved in with one of the families. Most impressively, she partnered with a historian to write a book on her heroic story, which also included competing in the Olympics as a teenager.

Here comes the complication: I suspected both of them early on. I let the woman's book influence me because I assumed facts had been verified. Still, I couldn't shake the feeling that she was lying. Even when we went to a great deal of trouble to participate in her baptism, my insides were doing somersaults. In the same way, I felt something was off with the young cancer pretender from the first time I knelt beside her to pray.

Why didn't I do anything? I had no proof. In both cases they'd covered their bases beautifully, and I've lived long enough to know that my heart can deceive me. I also had moments with them both when I wanted to believe them and love them. *I've seen Jesus do dramatic things, so why not these?* I asked myself.

If I were going to err, it seemed better to fall on the side of acceptance and compassion until any proof surfaced. That may sound like a spiritual answer, but it also was defective. Second Thessalonians 2:3 says, "Don't let anyone deceive you in any way." For the life of me, I do not know what the perfect answer would have been.

"Don't let anyone deceive you in any way."

What answer do you think would have been best?

○ Now it's your turn. Have you ever been duped by someone who proved to be an imposter? If so, without using any names or identifiable details, describe the situation.

The human need to be significant and noticeable is insatiable. Social networking has exponentially increased our connections to people—that's one of the things we love about it—but it simultaneously offers multiple stages for performing actors.

The human need to be significant is insatiable.

The compulsion to be compelling in our culture is overwhelming and almost irresistible. It invites the inner charlatan in all of us to come out and play. Our exposure to more people will always invite our exposure to more imposters. Scripture promises us that in the last times, "evil people and impostors will become worse, deceiving and being deceived" (2 Tim. 3:13).

Let's zealously ask God to grant us spiritual discernment and protection from both deception and cynicism. Above all, let's ask Him to make us true—to slay the charlatan in us and to convict us to the core when we lead people to believe lies about ourselves. If we don't get our inherent need to be significant met by Jesus, we will shape a deceptive persona from the malleable clay of our vain imaginations.

Jesus provides everything we need spiritually and psychologically to be whole people who know our value. The answer is to become who we really are in Him. Only in Christ can the extraordinary woman He foresaw in each of us emerge from her hiding.

I know, dear God, that you care nothing for the surface—you want us, *our true selves—and so I have given from the heart, honestly and happily.*
1 CHRONICLES 29:17, THE MESSAGE

Day Two

The Man of Lawlessness

FLASH-FORWARD: For that day will not come unless the apostasy comes first and the man of lawlessness is revealed, the son of destruction. *2 Thessalonians 2:3*

In 1983, Christian psychiatrist M. Scott Peck did something gutsy. He went on record to say that some individuals are not just troubled; they are evil. What may not be news to us was a highly provocative stand in Peck's field. He stated his claim in a day when evil had, in his own words, "been generally thus far off-limits to psychiatric investigation." In his soul-prying *People of the Lie*, Peck talks about revulsion as a healthy reaction in an encounter with an evil person.[3]

Keep in mind that, while all evil should be revolting, not all revulsion is caused by evil. Michael Jackson, for example, apparently found aging to be revolting, yet aging fails to qualify as evil, despite its challenges. Peck clarifies the relationship between evil and revulsion:

> Revulsion is a powerful emotion that causes us to immediately want to avoid, to escape, the revolting presence. And that is exactly the most appropriate thing for a healthy person to do under ordinary circumstances when confronted with an evil presence: to get away from it. Evil is revolting because it is dangerous. It will contaminate or otherwise destroy a person who remains too long in its presence. Unless you know very well what you are doing, the best thing you can do when faced with evil is to run the other way. The revulsion ... is an instinctive or, if you will, God-given and saving early-warning radar system.[4]

Fill in the remainder of this sentence clipped from Peck's excerpt: "Evil is revolting because it is dangerous. ______________."

That may sound obvious, but it's a profound bottom line. When was the last time you felt the compulsion to run the other way?

Many of us believe Scripture teaches that a man who is the embodiment of evil will rise on the blood-red horizon of end-time events. He will assume such a seat of global authority that many will run themselves to death in their attempt to run away. This personification of evil will wrap the claws of Satan in the skin of man, and most of the escapees will become martyrs. In this harrowing counterfeit of the divine incarnation, the son of destruction will emerge chock-full of satanic power—supernaturally endowed to perform false signs and wonders.

Please read 2 Thessalonians 2:1-7 and handwrite verses 4-7.

- According to the passage, what specific events occur before the Day of the Lord?

Let's take them in order. First, "that day will not come until the rebellion occurs" (v. 3, NIV). When we hear a reference to the Depression, we picture the era from 1929 through the early years of World War II. The rebellion—with emphasis on the definite article—is the name given to the era of open opposition to God that will precede the return of Christ.

The original word translated "rebellion" is *apostasia,* and you can see its similarity to our English word "apostasy." In both languages the word denotes a revolt that could be either political or religious but with a dimension that lends it distinctive flavor: "*Apostasia* indicates an act of abandoning or moving away from a position formerly held."[5]

This element of apostasy is key to understanding the rebellion, because it flags more than your run-of-the-mill opposition. It conveys brash abandonment of former values.

By no means am I down on our country, but those of us who call it home don't need much imagination to picture institutions, platforms, and people of position publicly distancing themselves from God. We're already witnessing departures that would have been unthinkable to the average U.S. citizen a century ago. A postcard of our present spiritual landscape wouldn't have even looked like America to most of them. The difference between now and the time to come is that worldwide departures from Christianity won't just occur during the rebellion; they will blatantly characterize it.

The apex of this era of apostasy will be the rising of the "man of lawlessness" who will lead and feed the viral rebellion against God. That's second on the list of prerequisites. All we have to do to start rolling our thoughts along the track of lawlessness is to scratch the Ten Commandments off society's tablets.

The apex of this era of apostasy will be the rising of the "man of lawlessness."

Christ said that "[a]ll the Law and the Prophets depend on these two commands" (Matt. 22:40): "Love the Lord your God with all your heart ... love your neighbor as yourself" (Matt. 22:37,39). If the entire law of God hinged on love, swing your head the opposite direction and picture the exact reverse. In the light of that darkness, you'll begin to formulate the basic structure of lawlessness. Feel the temperature of warm hearts plummet to frozen tundra. Picture a world where people couldn't care less about their neighbor. Picture cold, calculated madness fleshed out and fed by a megalomaniac the likes of which this world has yet to meet.

Hebrews 10:1 tells us that "the law has but a shadow of the good things to come" (ESV). The law poured concrete into God's mold for human relationships, but it also whispered a kingdom to come in which order, sanity, health, and decency dwell under the safe shadow of Christ's scepter. Jesus' second coming will usher in a world in which children can't be sold for sex or shot in their schoolrooms.

○ Name something else you'll be deeply thankful to find missing in Christ's coming kingdom.

Jesus is the cure for a sick earth. The irony is that accepting His remedy is the wisest thing a person can do to serve his own best interests. I'm not advocating selfishness. We find our lives when we lose them for Christ's sake (Matt. 16:25).

I'm just pointing out a sliver of irony. The young ruler who wouldn't leave his riches to follow Christ fled the very concept Christ stated in the wake of their encounter. "There is no one who has left a house, wife or brothers, parents or children because of the kingdom of God, who will not receive many times more at this time, and eternal life in the age to come" (Luke 18:29-30).

Even in the face of death, not one of Christ's disciples went on record wishing he'd stuck with his old life. Now glance back at 2 Thessalonians 2:3. What other title is attributed to the man of lawlessness? Son of destruction

God creates. Satan destroys.

God builds. Satan dismantles.

The caption oozes the infection of an unholy antithesis. God creates. Satan destroys. God builds. Satan dismantles. God covenants with life. Satan contracts with death. God loves with a pure, white-hot affection we cannot fathom. Satan's hatred pants with a bloodlust still left unappeased by the combined horrors of history.

Reflect back on 2 Thessalonians 1:8-9. How exactly does verse 9 characterize "eternal destruction"?

away from the presence of the Lord and from the glory of his might.

The ESV describes the destruction as "away from the presence of the Lord." In the end, the hellishness of hell will be the absence of God. Through the exaltation of the son of destruction, hell will boil over like a cauldron of flaming lava onto the cold banks of earth. The son of destruction will not just deflect culture from God. He will infect culture with the Devil. He won't just snuff out the wick of public worship of God. He will demand all public worship for himself.

What will he proclaim according to 2 Thessalonians 2:4?

to be God.

The wording of the HCSB is particularly powerful: "He opposes and exalts himself above every so-called god or object of worship, so that he sits in God's sanctuary, publicizing that he himself is God."

It will be the ultimate publicity stunt. If you are using the NKJV, your Bible employs the title "son of perdition" rather than "son of destruction" in verse 3. The terms are synonyms, both translating the Greek *apóleia*, but perdition hastens to mind the final destination of this man of evil rather than his modus operandi.[6] He who will sow unprecedented destruction will likewise reap it himself.

While I was with them in the world, I kept them in Your name. Those whom You gave Me I have kept; and none of them is lost except the son of perdition, that the Scripture might be fulfilled.
JOHN 17:12, NKJV

Read John 17:12 (NKJV) in the margin and compare it to Luke 22:3-6. Luke 22:3 identifies the original son of perdition. Who was he?

Satan

What was Satan's involvement with him?

he entered Judas.

The phrase "son of perdition/destruction" appears only twice in Scripture. Tying a knot between the two occasions will help us trace the silhouette described in today's text. Wearing the name first in John 17:12, Judas is a prototype of the one in 2 Thessalonians. Satan is the infiltrating force in each "son" and each is a master of betrayal. Judas betrayed Christ. The coming son of perdition will betray every person who will follow him to hell. Don't imagine for a moment that the Devil looks out for the best interests of his followers. He's selling one-way tickets to a destination disguised mostly by mirrors. The travel brochure pictures a happy buyer, baiting her with vanity.

As tempting as it is to say we're living in the rebellion, we in the West still have too much freedom for public worship to fully qualify. Christians in America are on a fast track, however, to the fulfillment of at least one prophecy of Christ concerning His followers.

Read Matthew 10:22 and John 15:18-20. What is the prophecy and why will it happen?

you will be hated by all for my name's sake. the world hates you, because you are not of the world

Being hated is no small thing. Being stereotyped into a one-dimensional caricature is embarrassing. Never underestimate the power of ridicule.

Not every apostate will flee from faith over arrogance. Some will flee for the convenience of social acceptance. When it gets too hard to be hated, many will be too weak to stand the heat.

"But the one who endures to the end will be delivered" (Matt. 10:22).

Endure. Our Deliverer is coming.

Day Three

Faces of Evil

FLASH-FORWARD: False messiahs and false prophets will arise and perform great signs and wonders to lead astray, if possible, even the elect. Take note: I have told you in advance. *Matthew 24:24-25*

I met Houston at her worst. Her introduction rose with the sun on an early morning in late August 1972 with these words blaring from the car radio: "Good morning, Houston! The biggest city in the South!" I could have thrown up. My little brother and I had cried ourselves to sleep in the backseat of our parents' car on the overnight trek from the only town we'd ever called home.

We'd have all agreed that our family needed a fresh start, and none of us would ultimately regret the relocation. The culture shock, however, was brutal. I'd left a high school with a total attendance of around 1,200 and would enroll in one bursting with 4,600.

I sat straight up in the backseat and stared at the enormous city emerging along the interstate. "Why do those windows have boards on them?"

Dad replied that Houston had prepared for a Gulf Coast hurricane that had made a turn toward Florida.

Hurricane? It was only the first indication to me that we'd clearly moved to the wet side of Hades.

Less than a year later, headlines hit the Houston news with the force of a category 5 hurricane. Only this was the kind of hurricane you couldn't board your windows against, and it baptized our city in terror for months.

They called them the Houston Mass Murders. With the help of two teenage accomplices, an electrician by the name of Dean Corll tortured and murdered at least 28 boys ranging in age from 13 to 20. Bodies were discovered in four different locations following the confession of accomplice Elmer Wayne Henley, who ended the killing spree by shooting the ringleader.[7]

Details and descriptions surfaced that exceeded the bounds of my vilest imaginations. Houston had lost her innocence and we with her.

A teenage boy who lived in a neighborhood not far from mine stood transfixed in front of the television, his jaw dropped to the floor over Corll's depiction on the screen. He'd seen that guy before when he was walking home from the bus stop. The man had pulled over beside him in a van, rolled down the window, and cheerfully asked if he'd wanted a ride.

A murderer had been in our midst for three years, and we'd gone on our merry way like life was normal. That boy was too shy to say yes. Six years later I'd marry that boy.

By the time the man of lawlessness, "the son of destruction" (2 Thess. 2:3), is revealed, he will have seduced an unprepared world into a murderous ride. Our two-fold objective today is to compile a list of titles under the "aka" (also known as) heading to dig around for keys unlocking the success of his coming seduction. Read each segment with a biographer's eye, attentive to each detail, so that your imagination can shape a wanted poster of this individual and the captions underneath that describe his power.

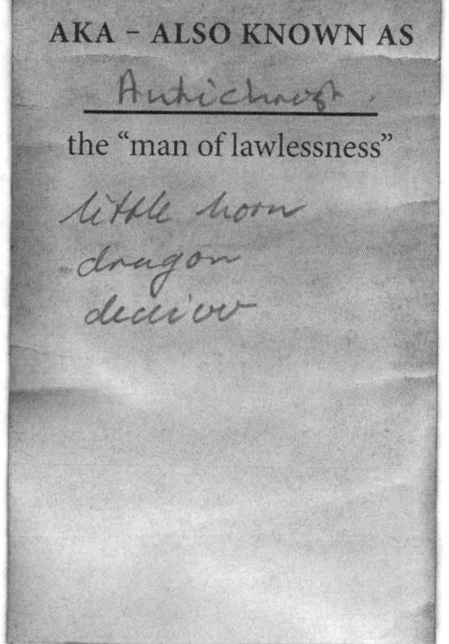

AKA – ALSO KNOWN AS
the “man of lawlessness”

Begin with 1 John 2:18-19. Who is coming, according to verse 18? Write the name here ____________ and also in the blank on the poster in the margin.

Can you think of any way to explain that one is coming, but many have already come?

○ Which historical rulers might qualify as types (pictures or examples) of antichrists who have already come? Explain your reasoning.

As foreshadowing as they may have been, none yet has fulfilled the prophecies Paul penned in 2 Thessalonians 2. "The spirit of the antichrist" (1 John 4:3) will be alive and active in the world through numerous individuals, doctrines, and atrocities long before the final, most lethal Antichrist emerges.

As we're shaping a prophetic biography of the man of lawlessness who is also called Antichrist, let's take special note of descriptions intimating that he will at first seem like a believer. Closer to the wording in 1 John 2:19, he may seem to be one of us.

According to the apostle John, this initial commonality is characteristic of antichrist figures and doubtless one key to the success of their seductions. The I'm-just-one-of-you approach can be authentic but, to the devious, it's a great cover for I-need-to-use-you.

First John 2:19 expresses a reality of vital theological importance. What did John state as proof that they did not belong to us?

Let this last portion of 1 John 2:19 adhere to your memory in boldest letters because it will be significant to us on day 4: "However, they went out so that it might be made clear that none of them belongs to us."

- Glance several chapters further to 1 John 4:2-3. What is another characteristic of "the spirit of the antichrist"?

The Book of Daniel speaks of a malevolent one to come who will surpass all others in boasts, blasphemies, and victories. Our time and space limit us to two sections, but they are tremendously informative.

Read each and record any information crucial to our biographical sketch of this man of lawlessness:

Daniel 7:7-8

Daniel 7:19-22

Add "little horn" to your "aka" list on the poster. The little horn of Daniel's vision (7:8) will burgeon into a power that makes the fourth beast "different from all the others, extremely terrifying" (7:19). He will wage war against the holy ones and will prevail "over them until the Ancient of Days" arrives and brings a judgment "in favor of the holy ones of the Most High" (7:21-22). Why then? Because the time will have come for the saints to possess the kingdom. Surer than our past, our future awaits in glorious custody, held tightly in the fist of God Most High.

Add "little horn" to your "aka" list on the poster.

No book of the Bible says more about the embodiment of evil in the final days than the Book of Revelation. The concentration is thickest in chapter 13 so, with patience and attention to detail, let's read it in several portions.

Read Revelation 13:1-4. According to verse 2, who gave this beast its power, throne, and authority? The ______________________.

Add this title to your "aka" poster.

So we have no doubt whom the revelator was implying in this depiction, check Revelation 12:9, in which the dragon is identified by name. Who is he? ______________________

What counterfeit of Christ is implied in Revelation 13:3-4?

The question in Revelation 13:4 is meant to send chills up our spines: "'Who is like the beast?'" We need look no further for the summit of blasphemy than these verses in Revelation 13. The question is meant to echo, bait, and switch the divine preeminence found in places like Psalm 113:5-6, "Who is like Yahweh our God—the One enthroned on high, who stoops down to look on the heavens and the earth?"

To catch the toxic flavor of the counterfeit in Revelation 13, all we have to do is diametrically oppose the sentiment that follows in Psalm 113. Our God, "raises the poor from the dust and lifts the needy from the garbage pile in order to seat them with nobles—with the nobles of His people. He gives the childless woman a household, making her the joyful mother of children" (Ps. 113:7-9).

So, who is like the beast? No one but the Devil himself. Ice-cold compulsion will replace compassion. Burying will replace raising. Nobles will dangle from puppet strings held in the claws of evil.

Nobles will dangle from puppet strings held in the claws of evil.

Now read Revelation 13:5-10. How long will the beast be allowed to exercise authority? 42 months

Calculate the number of months in years: 3½

Scholars throughout the centuries have argued over what this segment of time refers to and whether it should be taken literally or figuratively. I was mentored by a Bible teacher who stood firmly on this principle of interpretation: if plain sense makes common sense, seek no other sense. Therefore, I lean toward the expectation that this unsurpassed season of blasphemy and atrocity will be 3½ literal years, but we'll only know for certain once it is fulfilled.

While it is true that the Book of Revelation is highly symbolic, it is not exclusively symbolic. Where God has purposely retained a measure of mystery, we're better off treading lightly about claiming to have certainty.

Many believe the madness described in Revelation 13 coincides with the period of time Christ prophesied in Matthew 24:21-22. What words did Jesus use to describe it?

great tribulation

Press on for a few more minutes to view the most famous segment in Revelation regarding the beast.

Read Revelation 13:11-18. Reduce the job of the second beast into one basic sentence:

v14 It deceives those who dwell on earth.

How is the second beast able to deceive people? (vv. 13-14)

performs great signs, even make fire come down from heaven,

Give Christ's own words quoted in today's "Flash-Forward" another glance. Over and over Scripture warns that demonic power is capable of performing wonders. I once thought that any legitimate display of supernatural power could only come from God and that Satan was simply adept at faking magic tricks and spinning optical illusions. I was wrong. Demonic signs and wonders are at times described as false (2 Thess. 2:9) not because they are fake, but because they point to something false. They declare the glory of a grand deception.

Reread Revelation 13:15. What will the image of the beast be enabled to do and what will he, then, cause?

How will the economy be manipulated to bring honor and obedience to the beast (Rev. 13:16-17)?

Fast-forward three chapters to Revelation 16:13, and you'll see the second beast referenced as the "false prophet." It also puts the counterfeit triumvirate on blatant exhibition.

Read the verse and record the identification of the three in order:

It seemed fitting to wait until this concluding point to read and handwrite 2 Thessalonians 2:8-10. Please do so now.

Review today's material and add any details to the "aka" poster.

The glowing embers of Scripture kindle our hopes for rising heroes among the world's horrors. For every cruel Pharaoh, we can hope for a Moses. For every Nebuchadnezzar, a Daniel can emerge. For every maniacal Herod, a Joseph can flee with the infant Jesus. In the living night-terror of Hitler, faces of men like Dietrich Bonhoeffer and women like Irena Sendler lit candles in the darkness.

The capacity for good and evil in both the world and the human heart cannot be adequately measured by philosophy or science. Neither good nor evil can be defined without the other. To measure distance we must stretch a tape measure between two points.

Antichrist will meet the only Christ.

The end of times will not be left to hopes of a flickering candle. The thick, smothering blackness will break open to the all-consuming Light of the World. Antichrist will meet the only Christ. And then the fields that have, for centuries, been white for harvest will burn red with Armageddon.

Don't lose heart in our journey together, Sister. The week will get easier, the future brighter.

Day Four

A Strong Delusion

FLASH-FORWARD: For this reason God sends them a strong delusion so that they will believe what is false, so that all will be condemned—those who did not believe the truth but enjoyed unrighteousness. ***2 Thessalonians 2:11-12***

God is wholly secure in His sinless character. He doesn't feel a compulsion to protect Himself from misunderstandings by threading disclaimers on every sacred page. He doesn't have to take up for Himself because nothing can bring Him down. He doesn't incessantly qualify Himself because He is already qualified. He is God Almighty, enthroned in splendor, incapable of wrongdoing, unable to lie (Num. 23:19), and absent of all darkness (1 John 1:5).

God doesn't take up for Himself. Nothing can bring Him down.

Let there be no misunderstanding: for those who continue to refuse the light, God can put the darkness to use. If His ultimate purposes can be served, God can shift His hand and permit the darkness to do what it is dying to do. In case we jump to the conclusion that this process costs God nothing and us dearly, remember—He permitted the Devil to enter Judas Iscariot, a willing and open candidate, so that His own Son would be betrayed, arrested, and crucified.

Please read 2 Thessalonians 2:9-12 and write the segment in the back.

Does any part of it seem a little disturbing? Why or why not?

God sends the strong delusion to those who refused to love the truth & had pleasure in unrighteousness.

As pervasive as evil seems in our world, the power of darkness is being restrained until the time comes for the man of lawlessness to be revealed (2 Thess. 2:6-7). We will discuss that restraining force in our next video session.

Today we'll study New Testament occasions when God extends His leash on Satan and the power of darkness to serve divine purposes. Note that the Old Testament gives place to more examples than we have time and space to consider. The most prominent example is God's beloved servant, Job. God permitted Satan to test him to prove the man's faith genuine. The final result was a double portion of divine blessing (Job 42:10).

Leave the blank preceding each of the four numbered reading assignments in this lesson empty until you're asked to go back and fill it in at the end of that group of learning activities.

1. ______________________________

Read Luke 22:31-32.

Many Bible versions don't translate the switch from the plural usage of the word "you" to the singular but you can see it beautifully in the NET:

> *"Simon, Simon, pay attention! Satan has demanded to have you all, to sift you like wheat, but I have prayed for you, Simon, that your faith may not fail. When you have turned back, strengthen your brothers."*

Circle the words "you all" and draw a rectangle around all remaining appearances of "you" and "your" in the above segment.

If Jesus had been a Texan instead of a Galilean, He might've opted for, "Simon, Simon, Satan has demanded to sift y'all like wheat." In Luke 22:32 the remaining references to "you" and "your" are singular. Note that Satan wanted to sift all the disciples but the text specifies access to Simon Peter alone. But why him? He loved Jesus passionately and was among His closest cohorts. He'd walked on water and shown brilliance only God could have given him (Matt. 16:17).

○ The answer to *why Peter?* is found in *why a sifting?* What do you think any process of sifting can be meant to accomplish?

Satan salivates to sift all of us who follow Christ, but he seems to only be permitted divine access to those who need a serious sifting to fulfill their calling. Those who retain destructive or ungodly mind-sets and patterns despite divine rebukes (Matt. 16:23) are at greatest risk of a sieving. It's pure practicality. Something in Peter had to come out. Satan's intent is to sift us of our faith and leave the leaven; God hijacks the sifting to strain the leaven and unleash our faith. (For an example of leaven representing sin that is particularly invasive and prone to spread, see 1 Corinthians 5:6-7).

A sifting doesn't make you perfect. It makes you less prone to defeat.

I experienced a sifting in my thirties that is still, to date, the most terrifying season of my life. That time of unparalleled satanic seduction surfaced dark capabilities and deep injuries in me that I didn't even know existed. Satan wanted to sift me of any shred of godly character. God wanted to sift me of a dangerous victim mentality that would have kept me in a disastrous cycle all my life. A sifting doesn't make you perfect; it makes you less prone to defeat. If you've been sifted, you probably know it. It is a season in a believer's life blatantly characterized by the words "before" and "after."

Have you been through such a season? If so, describe it at least in generalities of your "before" and "after":

My before:

My after:

Now go back to the blank beside #1 and fill in these words: "God can allow Satan to sift someone like wheat."

2. God sometimes allows ______________________________
Read 2 Corinthians 12:7 and fill in blank #2 for yourself.

This point is too vital to leave out of our list, but we'll be brief because it is clearer than those we have ahead. Do you have something that you believe qualifies as a thorn in the flesh? If so, what it is?

3. ______________________________
Read 1 Corinthians 5:1-5.

What is the stated purpose for delivering this man over to Satan for the destruction of the flesh?

Eye-opening, isn't it? If the only way a person's soul can be saved is by handing him over to the Enemy of God for a time, God is fully capable of doing it.

A gift of bright grace wrapped in black paper

Sometimes we have to experience an onslaught of the Enemy to realize we want God. The mask of Satan peels back enough for us to realize we have been flirting with a monster, snuggling with a murderer, and dancing with a devil. God can allow someone to go through hell on earth to keep from going to hell for eternity. It's a gift of bright grace wrapped in black paper.

Whether the offender in 1 Corinthians 5:1 had professed faith in Christ or not is unclear. He is simply described as one among them. Either way, the goal of this severe mercy is salvation in the day of the Lord.

Please fill in the blank beside #3 with a heading in your own words.

4. ____

We finally circle back to our text for today. In #1 through #3 we sought to see that even in the leash He extends Satan, God's overwhelming priority is salvation and deliverance.

- Please view 2 Thessalonians 2:9-12 again. Based on these verses alone, why are people perishing?

Why exactly does God send them a strong delusion?

According to verse 12, who falls into this category?

I don't know of a more terrifying concept in Scripture than the comparable text in Romans 1:18-28. Please read these verses carefully and let's allow them to stir up a little fresh fear of God. Healthy fear of God saves lives.

Focus on Romans 1:24. What did God, therefore, do?

According to Romans 1:25, what had they done?

Does the thought that you could be handed over to your own cravings horrify you as much as it does me? When I think about how far I went and how justified God would have been to hand me over to my own foolish desires, I'm astonished by His mercy.

I'm astonished by His mercy.

Why not me? My sin plunged deep. What is the difference? God's ways are higher than ours and much exceed our understanding, but we can know from Scripture that God looks upon the heart, that He knows the end from the beginning, that His eyes cut like lasers through flesh and blood into attitudes and motives. He tests and tries. He reveals and He appeals. He wills for all to come to repentance. But if they refuse to love the truth, He can hand them right over to themselves for the condemnation that accompanies life without Him.

Maybe the concept of God handing a determined rebel over to herself seems one thing to us, but Him actually sending a strong delusion seems another. How do we grapple with that? The Greek translated "strong delusion" is *energeian planēs,* meaning "work of error." "The phrase is reminiscent of the earlier comment that the coming of the lawless one will be according to an *energeian tou satana,* 'work of Satan'" (v. 9).[8] A head buried in lies leaves a body open to an avalanche of deception. "Strong delusion" may suggest the man of lawlessness himself since only with God's sovereign release can Satan activate his ambassador.

They went out from us, but they did not belong to us; for if they had belonged to us, they would have remained with us. However, they went out so that it might be made clear that none of them belongs to us.
1 JOHN 2:19

Do you remember in our previous lesson when I told you to keep 1 John 2:19 close by? Glance at it again in the margin.

God sending a strong delusion to someone who refuses to love the truth sheds a glaring light on the grounds of his or her impending condemnation. God owes us no explanation for His righteous judgments—and clearly the text ties the purpose of the delusion to condemnation—but consider this question: *Could clarity be the irony of the delusion?*

I have a loved one that I knew was careless toward Christ, but I still wanted to believe he'd professed Him as Savior in childhood and was in temporary rebellion. He'd say some alarming things but, because I couldn't bear the thought of us not sharing the same eternal destiny, I'd still reason that his fusion of beliefs had not ruled out salvation. Over the course of several years, carelessness toward Christ morphed into resistance, and resistance morphed into full-fledged renouncement. He is now a devoted adherent to an opposing world religion. I love him deeply and continue to intercede but, if he doesn't end up in heaven, though I'll be heartbroken, I'll know why. A strong delusion surfaces a hidden devotion to deceit. The delusion clarifies the condemnation.

Notice with great care the ordering of events in 2 Thessalonians 2:10-11. They are already perishing because they refused to love the truth. Therefore "God sends them a strong delusion."

Paul would have been the last person on earth to charge God with giving up on somebody while there was still hope. Behold the job description Jesus Himself gave Paul at his conversion.

I now send you to them to open their eyes so they may turn from darkness to light and from the power of Satan to God, that by faith in Me they may receive forgiveness of sins.
ACTS 26:17-18

Before God sends a delusion, He sends a disciple. We must go.

Day Five

Obtaining the Glory

FLASH-FORWARD: He called you to this through our gospel, so that you might obtain the glory of our Lord Jesus Christ. *2 Thessalonians 2:14*

I was poring over commentaries for this lesson when I got the news that a dear friend's husband had suddenly died. She and I had exchanged texts 45 minutes earlier when he'd gotten to the ER. My friend is hard to scare, so I knew to pray with urgency. He'd caught a nasty flu that was flying around Houston, and he developed pneumonia. When she checked on him first thing that morning, she knew something was off. He wasn't himself. Then he was gone.

Just like that.

They fell in love at the ripe old age of 15. He was the first guy she ever dated and the last. I left my house to head to hers with my laptop and commentaries still open on the kitchen table. As it turned out, this was a lesson that books alone wouldn't teach.

Please read 2 Thessalonians 2:13-17 and handwrite it in the back.

Second Thessalonians 2:13 breaks the page with the transitional words "But we." The preceding part of the letter regarding delusion and condemnation is so weighty and woeful, the Holy Spirit dispatched a ray of sunshine to pierce the ominous cloud.

What phrase does Paul use to describe the Thessalonian recipients in verse 13? "Brothers beloved by the Lord"

That lifesaving identity should ring a bell from our journey's embarkation in 1 Thessalonians 1:4. He began addressing them as "brothers loved by God."

When I saw my friend later that day, she and I did the same thing we'd done on the phone soon after he died. We bawled. And with considerable volume. Her house was already crawling with family and close friends, but we stole a few minutes in the nook of her den. As she recounted what happened, we wept and shook our heads with disbelief. We did, however, have one well-timed laugh. While we were sitting together, a thoughtful text came in on her phone to this effect: "Heaven has gained an angel." He was godly and loving, but an angel? Well, no, and not only on the basis of technicalities like being two separate species of creation. Her husband was mischievous and, right about then, we were glad because recalling it was pure respite.

Ecclesiastes 3:4 says there is "a time to weep and a time to laugh." One of my favorite things about women is that we can manage to do both of those things in the space of five minutes.

You and I are something more endearing than angels. We're daughters. My friend's husband stood on the real estate of heaven that day, welcomed as a son of the living God. I wasn't favorably inclined toward Amanda and Melissa because they were angelic. I loved them voraciously because they were mine, born of my heart, and entrusted to my arms.

In the same way, you are a daughter loved by God, reborn of His heart and set apart by His Spirit. You are held in the crook of His arms.

Turn to the one-chapter Book of Jude and compare verses 1 and 21. What do they say concerning the love of God?

○ What do you think it means to keep yourself in the love of God? Respond in the margin.

Christ urged His followers to the same mindset in John 15:9: "As the Father has loved Me, I have also loved you. Remain in My love." Live in it. Breathe it. Constantly remind yourself of it. We'll know this journey invaded our hearts if, long after it ends, we see one another chiefly as sisters loved by the Lord. Any description detracting from that identity is fraudulent.

Any description detracting from "loved by God" is fraudulent.

Lock down tightly on 2 Thessalonians 2:14. Exactly why were we called through the gospel?

What we're about to learn is one reason why I love good commentaries. I might have tumbled past the immensity of these words: "so that you might obtain the glory of our Lord Jesus Christ" (2 Thess. 2:14).

What seems like bad news in Romans 3:23 is actually the golden key that unlocks this vault of pearls. What does it say?

Read the commentary excerpt by Charles Wanamaker. Then we'll boil it down.

> According to Rom. 3:23, "All have sinned and lack the glory of God." This idea derived from the Jewish belief that Adam had lost his luster when he sinned, and that eschatological salvation would therefore include the return of the divine glory, that is, God's outward appearance of brilliance, to saved humanity ... Thus when Paul talks about obtaining the glory of Christ he has in mind the eschatological transformation of the people of God into the form of Christ's divine existence. In an ultimate sense this was associated with the resurrection for Paul, as 1 Cor. 15:43 and Phil. 3:21 demonstrate.[9]

Think of it as Paradise Lost and Paradise Regained with a switch of terms to glory. Romans 3:23 tells us what our sin lost for us. Second Thessalonians 2:14 tells us what we'll ultimately gain. We know the name for it: glory.

We know adjectives that describe it, but we can no more define it than we can draw God with a pencil. Our finite minds possess insufficient creativity to picture the boundless, brilliant reflection of our Creator.

Our new bodies will bear the full measure of His image without breaking. We will be who God foresaw when He dusted His hands with this orb and formed the human frame. To reflect the very glory of Christ is to finally become who we were made to be. Romans 8:19-23 says that even the earth beneath our feet groans and aches, longing for the full revelation of the children of God bearing His gorgeous glory. First John 3:1-2 spins with marvelous mystery: "Look at how great a love the Father has given us that we should be called God's children. And we are! The reason the world does not know us is that it didn't know Him. Dear friends, we are God's children now, and what we will be has not yet been revealed. We know that when He appears, we will be like Him because we will see Him as He is."

This is glory: We will be like Jesus.

This is glory: We will be like Jesus. We will reflect the One curtained by clouds and crowned in holiness.

Romans 3:23 and 2 Thessalonians 2:14 set side-by-side comprise the saga of human existence in shorthand. They are the two constants in the equation of the great story.

Romans 3:23 + 2 Thessalonians 2:14 = the Redemption Story

Turn that "+" sign into a cross, and you'll supply the means to that redemptive end. Until Jesus appears and we are made like Him, the map spread over earth is like a rug that can be jerked from under our feet. With the soles of our shoes glued to the Rock of our Salvation, we can stand firm. "The Rock—His work is perfect; all His ways are entirely just. A faithful God, without prejudice, He is righteous and true" (Deut. 32:4).

- Look carefully at 2 Thessalonians 2:15. What did Paul tell the Thessalonians to stand firm and hold onto?

to the traditions that you were taught by us.

The NIV translates the Greek word *paradoseis* as "teachings" but many other translations render the word "traditions." Note the HCSB: "hold to the traditions you were taught." D.M. Martin wrote:

> Used in this context "tradition" (*paradoseis*) does not refer to mere human teachings or to the traditions of Judaism to which Paul previously devoted himself ... Rather, it refers to apostolic tradition delivered in the name of Christ (see also 3:6; 1 Cor. 11:2,23).[10]

In the Gospels when Christ criticized the traditions of the Pharisees and scribes, He pointed toward religious practices they prioritized over the Scriptures. In Mark 7:8-9, for instance, Jesus said, "'Disregarding the command of God, you keep the tradition of men ... You completely invalidate God's command in order to maintain your tradition!'"

Paul's reference in 2 Thessalonians 2:15 was to the apostolic tradition. The Holy Spirit Himself transmitted to apostles like John, Peter, and Paul the teachings that we see in Scripture. In the words of Dr. Leon Morris, "For us these traditions are preserved in the New Testament. But for Paul's readers there was no such volume. For them the Christian traditions were principally those which they had received 'by word of mouth.'"[11]

As several of us were setting out food for the grief-stricken family, a young woman we dearly love wept tenderly for the wife left behind. She said, "I know she [our widowed friend] can make it. She is strong." We all nodded because she is. As long as I live, I'll never forget how, Carol, a long-time friend, responded: "No, she's not just strong. She's faithful." Carol was exactly right.

What can be the difference between strong and faithful?

I'm not sure we do a woman justice when she endures something brutal, and we chalk it up to strength. Sometimes people with no strength at all emerge from a horrifying season. They used all the might they had just to hold on to Jesus. And He was enough. In their weakness, He was strong.

As we close, read the last two verses of 2 Thessalonians 2 in the margin. The ESV translates the word "comfort" rather than "encouragement." Either is beautiful, but my friend's tragedy has comfort on my mind. That's what I'm praying for her.

May our Lord Jesus Christ Himself and God our Father, who has loved us and given us eternal encouragement and good hope by grace, encourage your hearts and strengthen you in every good work and word.
2 THESSALONIANS 2:16-17

As I drove down the freeway from my house to hers, I said aloud to God, *Please don't let me say anything stupid.* She and I have been friends for decades, so she would've forgiven me but, still, I wanted to spare her. She loves Jesus. She holds firmly to His Word. She didn't need a Scripture from me. She needed a cup of coffee. So I fixed a nice strong one, heavy on the cream with two packets of raw sugar because that's how she likes it. When I handed it to her, I kissed her on the cheek. I love her so.

Coffee is a temporary comfort. It soon wears off. God's comfort is eternal. I don't know what heaven will be like, but I know this: we will bid this suffering good riddance and be forever comforted.

That is our good hope. There will be touch. There will be food. There will be conversation. There will be laughter. Surely there will be kisses.

And I, for one, hope there will be coffee.

Group Session Eight

REVIEW THE WEEK

Use these questions to guide your discussion of last week's homework.

● Principal Questions

DAY 1: What three sources of potential alarm did Paul list in 2 Thess. 2:2? (p. 166)
DAY 2: What specific events occur before the Day of the Lord (2 Thess. 2:1-7)? (p. 171)
DAY 3: What characteristic of the spirit of the antichrist is in 1 John 4:2-3? (p. 176)
DAY 4: Based on 2 Thessalonians 2:9-12 alone, why are people perishing? (p. 182)
DAY 5: What did Paul tell the Thessalonians to stand firm and hold onto? (p. 186)

○ Personal Discussion Questions

DAY 1: Have you ever been duped by someone who proved to be an imposter? (p. 168)
DAY 2: What will you be thankful to find missing in Christ's coming kingdom? (p. 172)
DAY 3: Which historical rulers might qualify as types of antichrists? (p. 175)
DAY 4: What do you think any process of sifting can be meant to accomplish? (p. 180)
DAY 5: What do you think it means to keep yourself in the love of God? (p. 185)

VIEW THE VIDEO

Introduction

As we approach our final week in our study of 1 and 2 Thessalonians, we come to one of the most mysterious portions in the letters combined. We will discuss what we can know clearly and what we can at least know more about.

What was happening at their present time and is still happening in ours:

1. The working of the ______________ of ______________. The NIV translates the phrase "the ______________ ______________ of lawlessness."

2. The ______________ ______________ over the mystery of ______________. Consider this quote from Dr. John Stott: "The restraint is both neuter and masculine, ______________ and ______________, a ______________ and a ______________."[1]

The three most plausible identities of the restrainer:

- The ____________ ____________ (He) and the work of the ____________ (it).
- ____________ (he) and the preaching of the ____________ (it).
- ____________ (he) and the ____________/power of the ____________ (it).[2]

What will happen before the Day of the Lord:

1. The ____________ will be ____________ of the ____________ (v. 7b).
2. The ____________ will ____________ (v. 3).
3. The ____________ of ____________ will be revealed. (v. 3) The word translated "revealed" is the lexical Greek ____________. Compare v. 9 where the word translated "coming" is ____________. According to Dr. C. A. Wanamaker, "That person's manifestation is a deceptive ____________ or '____________' of Jesus' future coming."[3]

- Mark 16:15: "____________ into all the world and ____________ the ____________ to the whole creation."
- 2 John 1:7 (ESV): "For many ____________ have ____________ out into the ____________ ... Such a one is the deceiver and the antichrist."

AND THEN ...

1. The Day of the Lord will ____________ with the ____________ of Christ.
2. The Lord Jesus will ____________ the ____________ one with His ____________ and bring him to ____________.

1. John Stott, *The Message of 1 & 2 Thessalonians* (Downers Grove, IL: InterVarsity Press, 1991), 168.
2. Ibid., 169–170.
3. Charles A. Wanamaker, *The Epistles to the Thessalonians: A Commentary on the Greek Text* (Grand Rapids, MI: Wm. B. Eerdmans Publishing Co., 1990), 245.

Week Eight

The Lord of Peace

Day One

Pray for Us

FLASH-FORWARD: Finally, brothers, pray for us that the Lord's message may spread rapidly and be honored, just as it was with you. ***2 Thessalonians 3:1***

About two weeks ago, I almost had an anxiety attack. Only once before have I come that close. It was after the moving van drove away from my home of 27 years with all our memories sealed up in cardboard boxes. Under those circumstances, at least I could've panicked with a measure of dignity. For the one two weeks ago, I was propped on a cushiony black chair in a nail salon. I'd been neck-deep in commentaries about apostasies and antichrists, when I got a calendar alert on my cell phone for a mani-pedi. The absurdity makes me want to stub my big toe on a doorjamb. I blame my mentor. She told me to make sure my nails were done—that I was not just a woman in ministry. I was a lady.

You'd think a person could sit back and enjoy some pampering but, of course, I could make a bubble bath stressful. That particular day I was at fever pitch with work stress. Always in a rush, I need to get both a manicure and a pedicure done simultaneously. The time-saving usually works well enough, but this particular day, something about them holding my hands and feet down while I had forty jillion things to do incited an acute compulsion to scream maniacally and flail my limbs. I had the psychosomatic symptoms of someone held hostage, her feet and hands tethered to a chair, being tortured with an hour-long foot-tickling by someone wearing a mask. It was awful. I stumbled numbly out of the salon in blue paper flip-flops and realized an hour later in the driveway that I'd left my boots by the cushiony chair. Wearing sunglasses, I retrieved them from the salon the next day.

Please read 2 Thessalonians 3:1-5 and handwrite it in the back.

- What do 1 Thessalonians 5:25 to 2 Thessalonians 3:1 have in common?

Brothers, pray for us.

Today we are studying the unstoppable privilege and power of prayer. No one can keep us from praying. People can tie up our hands and feet, but they cannot keep us from praying. They can cover our mouths with duct tape, but they cannot keep us from praying. They can arm-wrestle our wrists to the table, but they cannot keep us from praying. They can remove every public prayer from every civil institution, but they cannot keep us from praying. They can beat us, imprison us, and confiscate our belongings, but they cannot keep us from praying. They could pluck out our eyes and jerk out our tongues, but they still couldn't make us quit praying. Only one person on earth can stop my prayers: me. Only one person on earth can stop your prayers.

Put her signature here: ____.

But what if we stopped stopping our prayers?

Then let a devil shiver.

I counted 26 times in the HCSB that Paul wrote the word "pray" in his letters and 27 additional occasions where he used other forms of the word—like, "prays," "praying," "prayer," and "prayers." Add to these numbers the times Paul used synonyms like "supplication" and "intercession," and you have a man absolutely obsessed with prayer.

So, what's the point? Paul had been struck to the ground and temporarily blinded by a saving encounter with Jesus. He'd been divinely commissioned with as much detail and as clear an objective as any apostle in the New Testament. He'd had visions and dreams given to him by the Holy Spirit. He'd been raised to the third heaven and heard unutterable things. He'd survived beatings that should have killed him. He'd had prison chains snapped by an earthquake. His hands had been the gloves of God in countless wonders.

Paul pressed in and prayed hard.

Not one inspired writer of the New Testament letters had more to say about prayer. He did not sit smugly back, presuming that Jesus would fulfill His purpose through him with little proactive effort on his part. He pressed in and prayed hard. To Paul, prayer was part of the necessary means even to a divinely foreordained end.

Read the following segments and categorize the kinds of things for which Paul requested prayer:

Romans 15:30-32 to be delivered from the unbelievers in Judea, that his service to Jerusalem may be acceptable, so that he may, by God's will, visit Romans.

2 Corinthians 1:8-11
so that many will give thanks on our behalf for the blessing granted us through the prayers of many

Ephesians 6:18-19
for all the saints, for Paul, that words may be given to me to proclaim boldly the mystery of the gospel

Philippians 1:19-20
his deliverance, that with full courage Christ will be honored in his body, alive or dead.

Philippians 4:6 says, "Don't worry about anything; instead, pray about everything" (NLT). That means everything can be affected by prayer. Prayer is not an art we can master, because we can't master the Artist we approach.

Evolving in effectual prayer remains a lifelong quest, but quests are good. They keep us from getting stale and bored and arrogant. Over the last year, God has challenged me to bring Him my personal requests with an emphasis on *receiving* rather than *achieving*. I mentioned these two words to you on week 6, day 4, but let's slow down and take some time with them now.

The idea of shifting the approach of our prayer requests from achieving to receiving is not an original concept, but it's a fresh perspective for me.

When I use the word "achieving" in this context, I'm not talking about gains pursued by personal ambition for self-glorification. Think more in terms of seeking God to achieve nobler things like love for someone hateful, clarity for mind-tangling scenarios, and divine energy to leap over obstacles.

In this context, achieving is not a bad thing. The headwaters of every stream of provision are cupped in God's hands. I'm just learning that approaching Him with an emphasis on achieving is a pale second to an outlook of receiving.

What difference might the shift make?

I resist saying "always" or "never" in methods of prayer since pouring concrete on something alive and organic tends to smother it to death. At the same time, this shift has awakened me to the legion of things I request from God that He's already availed. My part in prayer is to actively acknowledge and embrace them.

For instance, instead of clamoring for a message I'm scheduled to give, I'm trying to ask Him for it with a calm and trusting heart. I proceed with Bible study, thanking Him in advance, and believing that I'll receive. Bless His merciful name, I do and with far less angst. The process rescues me from feeling the constant pressure to achieve. It takes more trust but offers less stress.

The long-term difference is huge. We shrink with stress. We grow with trust.

How could each of the verses in the margin support a receiving approach over an achieving approach to requests in prayer?

Jesus said, "Everyone who asks receives" (Matt. 7:8)—not "Everyone who asks achieves." The more we claw and clamor in prayer, the less we'll sense the peace of Christ. If going to our knees is our form of knee-jerking, that's a sacred instant reaction. Let's go right ahead. We're welcomed by God to cry out in a panic.

I'm just suggesting that we're never more anxious to receive from God than He is willing to provide. Let's quit acting like we're bothering God. When we pray, we're not standing at a counter, making an order with a free coupon to a cashier tired of cheapskates. Prayer is accepting a royal summons to the throne room of the king for breakfast with your dad. He says, "Come here, Child. I've got something to give you today." It's just what you needed and sought and you're so relieved. You don't have to do a tap dance to achieve it. You just hold out your hands to your Father and jubilantly receive it.

Because of our Lord Jesus Christ, we can pray with confidence as deeply loved and highly favored children of God who've been urged to ask. We do not know what the direction will be, but we know our Father will give it. We do not know what the provision will be, but we know our Father will make it. Living

Luke 11:13

Ephesians 1:3

2 Peter 1:3

2 Corinthians 9:8

our lives in achieve mode inadvertently places us on the defensive, feeling as if we're constantly harassing God for something He's reluctant to give.

"It's me again, God. I realize I begged You for stuff yesterday, but I need stuff today too. Just give me this one thing today, and I'd get out of Your hair."

Nothing is more appropriate than going to God to get what we lack. But, oh, the relief of realizing what bounty He's already spread before us on the banqueting table. His joy is to activate the needed resource in our current situation. No need to approach God like we're making a sales call. In the words of Romans 8:32, "He did not even spare His own Son but offered Him up for us all; how will He not also with Him grant us everything?"

Receiving is our active participation in what Jesus already does.

Receiving is our active participation in what Jesus already does. It is our verbal nod of agreement, saying yes to His best. A receiver gets to welcome what Jesus already wants.

○ Is any of this a shift for you or have you practiced this approach for years? Explain.

A new method can be a beautiful thing, but don't make what we've discussed today another rule to follow. We don't have to act quite that grown up. Prayer is more than a means to an end. It's the communion of a Father and child.

Something has reared up in my life again lately that tends to drive me crazy. It's wrapped up in a long-term relational challenge that I sometimes handle better than others. The other night after the lights were off and my man was snoring, it loomed large over me again and felt overwhelming. I pushed the covers back and slid down the side of the bed to my knees. I squeezed my eyes tightly, cupped my hands together just like a little kid, and whispered, "Help me."

And He did. And for some reason I have a lump in my throat. Oh, by all means, let's do grow up and mature in our believing lives and develop in the spiritual disciplines of our faith. But let's never get so old or sophisticated that we forget to come as little children. God loves you. He loves your company. He loves to search the depths of your soul and hear the dreams of your heart. He knows what troubles you when you crawl into bed and what awaits when you crawl out. He knows why you're scared and where you're unprepared. Somebody needs to hear this today: God does not resent you.

He protects His flock like a shepherd; He gathers the lambs in His arms and carries them in the fold of His garment.

ISAIAH 40:11

Don't be afraid, little flock, because your Father delights to give you the kingdom.

LUKE 12:32

Day Two

Abiding Words and Arriving Answers

FLASH-FORWARD: **How beautiful on the mountains are the feet of the herald, who proclaims peace, who brings news of good things, who proclaims salvation, who says to Zion, "Your God reigns!" The voices of your watchmen—they lift up their voices, shouting for joy together; for every eye will see when the LORD returns to Zion.** ***Isaiah 52:7-8***

When my man and I moved to the country, we moved his parents with us. We never had any question about it. They go where we go. They were in their late 70s when Keith and I came up with the harebrained idea to move lock, stock, and barrel to the sticks.

The timing was terrible because they'd barely gotten settled next to us in town. We braced ourselves for the dread on their faces when we presented the prospect. They had their bags packed before a soul could say "John Deere."

A vegetable garden leapt from the ground before a slab was poured for their house. The four of us city folks would sit in lawn chairs on its fair, brown edge, fanning ourselves, staring at the melons and cucumbers.

We'd gaze and sigh and after a while one of us would say, "We grow our own food." Then all four of us would split our sides laughing. It was perfectly and delightfully preposterous. We were posers and we knew it.

We quartered the first remotely ripe tomato, raised our four pieces like glasses clinking, and proposed a toast. "To country life! Hear, hear!" And we gulped down our firstfruits like people who meant it.

A few months ago we got four young chickens and a rooster. Papaw reasoned that he couldn't sleep past 5:00 a.m. anyway. He might as well hear a rooster crow. A few weeks later, that bad boy found his larynx and crowed all night long to beat the dawn. Then last week, enough commotion erupted from the chicken coup to send feathers flying when Memaw discovered our first egg. This time we responded, "Somebody empty a carton! We're laying our own eggs!"

Memaw fried that little dome of yellow sunshine in a skillet and, with a slice of crispy bacon, she fed it to Papaw like he was the king of the country. Sure enough, we had two eggs the next day.

It's like that in the believing life, isn't it? We wait and wait for fruit of our prayers and hopes and, just about the time we decide we're posers, a green tomato starts blushing and an egg pops up in the chicken coup. We turn out to be the real thing one inch at a time, and nobody's more surprised than we.

Today we're circling around some mathematics. We're going to continue drawing concepts out of the opening verse of 2 Thessalonians 3, but I don't want you to get behind on handwriting your verses in the back of the book.

Go ahead and write 2 Thessalonians 3:6-8 on the appropriate page, and we'll land on them in day 3.

Our previous lesson targeted prayer based on Paul's request in 2 Thessalonians 3:1. Reread this verse and record what he specifically asked the Thessalonians to pray:

We'll respond to this verse corporately for a few minutes in our final video session, but let's shift our chairs to a personal angle today. The ESV translates 2 Thessalonians 3:1 like this: "Finally, brothers, pray for us, that the word of the Lord may speed ahead and be honored, as happened among you."

Circle the word "us" in the verse.

The word implies that the way the Word of the Lord was going to speed ahead was atop the feet of Paul, Silvanus, and Timothy as they ran it forward. The Word wasn't going FedEx. It was going feetfirst and, when not by those three pairs, by the feet of the messengers who hand-carried their letters. Dusty, blistered, calloused, beautiful feet.

Please read Romans 10:14-17. Write the basic point of this segment in one sentence.

According to Romans 10:17, how does faith come?

According to the same verse, how does hearing come?

Whether or not we feel adequate for the task, we are the carriers now. We have vehicles for spreading the Word of God that our predecessors in the faith even a century ago couldn't have imagined. We each hold keys in our hands to the ignition of the gospel in our generation and sphere of influence.

Each day the sun comes up closer to the dawn of Christ's coming. If the Word of the Lord needed to speed ahead in Paul's generation, how expeditious should it be in ours? These are days for deliberate acceleration. We have wheels. We have wings. We have ways. We have means. At least for now, many of us also have freedom of speech. Should that freedom be withdrawn, we have an assurance tucked into the folds of 2 Timothy that is worthy of a standing ovation.

Read 2 Timothy 2:8-10. Finish this sentence based on the last statement in verse 9: "but

Feet can be chained, but God's Word cannot. Believers can be bound, but God's Word cannot. In 1573 a mother by the name of Maeyken Wens was arrested in Antwerp with other believers who refused to silence their declarations of Scripture. After she was burned at the stake, her son Adriaen, about 15 years old at the time, rummaged through the ashes that were left of his mother. There he found a telling keepsake. It was the screw they'd used to bolt her mouth shut.[1]

> O for a thousand tongues to sing
> My great Redeemer's praise,
> The glories of my God and King,
> The triumphs of His grace!
> My gracious Master and my God,
> Assist me to proclaim,
> To spread through all the earth abroad
> The honors of Thy name.
> Jesus! the name that charms our fears,
> That bids our sorrows cease;
> 'Tis music in the sinner's ears,
> 'Tis life, and health, and peace.
> He breaks the power of canceled sin,
> He sets the prisoner free;
> His blood can make the foulest clean,
> His blood availed for me.[2]

Gospel math prefers multiplication over addition.

For every messenger silenced, another messenger spoke. In the words of Acts 12:24, "Then God's message flourished and multiplied." That's the beauty of gospel math. It prefers multiplication over addition.

One tongue turned into a thousand. The word rang like a church bell from prison cells. It climbed the steepest mountaintops and crawled on bellies underground. It seeped beneath bolt-locked doors and bore holes through cement walls. It made its way to cotton fields, rice fields, and killing fields and to TV screens, laptop screens, and cell phone screens. We are the circuit runners now with a 25,000-mile marathon before us, wrapped like a belt around the bulging waistline of this planet. The job is not yet done because Christ is not yet back.

Many have not yet heard.

Many are not yet His.

We get to drive where our predecessors walked. It's time to stomp the accelerator. We don't have to be teachers, speakers, preachers, or communicators to become runners of the Word. We can take it with us in our bones. "For the word of God is living and effective and sharper than any double-edged sword, penetrating as far as the separation of soul and spirit, joints and marrow" (Heb. 4:12). Wherever we go, every word that abides in us arrives with us.

○ In the margin, name a few specific places you desire for the words of Christ that abide in you to arrive with you over the next month.

We don't need all the answers to share the hope. We don't need a class in methods to give a message. We don't have to earn degrees in apologetics to evangelize. Filled with the ink of the Holy Spirit, the apostle Paul did us an enormous favor. He put into words the things "of first importance" (v. 3, ESV) in 1 Corinthians 15:1-4.

● What things are of most importance (1 Cor. 15:1-4)?

Read Romans 10:8-13 with equal care. Record in the margin how any person on this broad earth can be saved.

We want to spend our lives studying the Word of God. It is our daily bread. It is milk. It is meat. In the gorgeous words of Colossians 2:2-3, we want to pursue "all the riches of assured understanding and have the knowledge of God's mystery—Christ." All the treasures of wisdom and knowledge are hidden in Him. We learned in week 6 that we aren't thoroughly equipped for our God-ordained works with our Bibles closed (2 Tim. 3:16-17).

All we have to know to sprint off the starting block with the saving words of Christ is what you documented above. The thing of first importance is this: Christ, the divine Son of God, came to earth and gave His life for our sins. He was raised from the dead so that we could receive eternal life (1 Cor. 15:1-4). We hold fast to this testimony until our final breath. We invite others to come to know Him too through their confession of Jesus Christ as Lord and the belief in their heart that God raised Him from the dead. "For everyone who calls on the name of the Lord will be saved" (Rom. 10:13).

"Everyone." What a spectacular word.

Romans 10:13 lands us right back in the exact spot where we found ourselves early in today's lesson. I'll write the portion out for you this time:

> *But how can they call on Him they have not believed in? And how can they believe without hearing about Him? And how can they hear without a preacher? And how can they preach unless they are sent? As it is written: How beautiful are the feet of those who announce the gospel of good things!*
>
> ROMANS 10:14-15

Pretty feet are never beautiful feet.

Since the fall of man in the garden of Eden, this earth has been has been riddled with thorns and thistles. The pavement gets hot. The sand, waist deep. You can get hurt out there, but here's the thing: pretty feet are never beautiful feet.

Maybe we'll prop them up at some point in heaven and let the swelling go down. Between now and then, tie your shoes, stretch your calves, tuck your courage, and run your heart out with the news until the whole world knows.

Day Three

Community Responsibility

FLASH-FORWARD: For we hear that there are some among you who walk irresponsibly, not working at all, but interfering with the work of others. *2 Thessalonians 3:11*

Through the Letters to the Thessalonians, we've gotten to watch the New Testament church in its early formation, when commands for conduct in Christian community were just beginning to drip from the quills of the apostles. What we see in the completed canon, the earliest believers received letter by letter through the wonder of progressive revelation.

The whole concept of divine inspiration is fascinating. Don't you wonder if they felt "a burning fire shut up in [their] bones" like the prophet Jeremiah (20:9, ESV) when they received words that would end up etched on the eternal page? Or did the words come to them gently like a still, small voice that, at the time, felt more like the better part of wisdom than divine revelation?

We know that all Scripture is God-breathed, but it could be that sometimes He blew that breath with a gust that nearly swept their hair off, and other times He whispered truth that could only be heard in silence.

With regard to the question about people who have never married, I have no command from the Lord, but I give my opinion as one shown mercy by the Lord to be trustworthy.
1 CORINTHIANS 7:25, NET

How does 1 Corinthians 7:25 add to the intrigue of divine inspiration?

No need to waste time wondering if Paul was aware of the divine authority upon his tongue when he dictated the segment that begins with these words: "Now we command you, brothers, in the name of our Lord Jesus Christ." A divine command is entrusted to a careful hand.

Read 2 Thessalonians 3:6-15 to retain your context but only add verses 9-12 to your handwritten portion in the back of your book.

What specific command did Paul issue in this portion?

- What command had he and his coworkers given the Thessalonians when they were still with them? (See v. 10.)

We still must hold down our jobs and pay for our food.

Lean chapters two and three of 2 Thessalonians against one another like an A-frame, and you'll find the tension built into our believing lives right at their touch point. Here on a playing field where heaven collides with hell, where eternal destinies hang in the balance, where antichrists abide and reckonings are due, where callings are sacred and workers are few, we still must hold down our jobs and pay for our food. My grandmother would have said it like this: Here we are scrubbing floors while the world's going to hell in a handbasket. Find relief in knowing that, actually, it's not. The Lord Himself will descend from heaven to claim it.

Please note that the command in 2 Thessalonians 3:10 was given for those who were unwilling to work, not for those who were unable to work. The Christian community was obliged to care for those among them in legitimate need. The lines between those who lacked and those who slacked had to be drawn boldly or the latter could give the former a bad name.

The Scriptures never heap a hint of shame on the heads of those in need. Jesus identified so strongly with individuals who lacked food, water, shelter, and clothing that He said to those who'd offer aid, "Whatever you did for one of the least of these brothers of Mine, you did for Me" (Matt. 25:40).

Second Thessalonians 3:6-12 issued a release: the community would not be responsible for the irresponsible. Instead they were commanded to neither "subsidize [their] freeloading" (2 Thess. 3:14, The Message) nor fraternize so closely that they'd take up their ways or appear to approve.

Part of our human condition is the susceptibility to catch things from one another. A virus-prone lot, we don't have to be cognizant to catch it. We just inhale the same air until it spreads to our lungs. Not everything contagious is detrimental. Joy can be caught. Zeal for the lost can be caught. Faith can be caught. But irresponsibility can also be caught.

Because we were called as laborers to the harvest, idleness short-circuits the system. It spreads between hosts with symptoms of entitlement and blame. The irony is that inactive hands often spark overactive tongues. To Paul, those who talk too much need more to do. Nobody will interfere with your job like somebody talking at your desk, refusing to do theirs.

Paul's words are so strong, we'd need pepper sauce to water them down: "If anyone does not obey our instruction in this letter, take note of that person; don't associate with him, so that he may be ashamed" (2 Thess. 3:14).

The command is to guard us against co-hosting an idle host. Community is communicable, and what's bred can be spread.

Paul urged the Thessalonians to catch the good work ethic they'd toiled hard to give them. "For you yourselves know how you must imitate us: We were not irresponsible among you" (2 Thess. 3:7).

Christianity does not vaccinate us against irresponsibility. We can bring some of the same bad habits into our saved condition that we coddled when we were lost. And they can go viral in community.

Idleness (ESV) and irresponsibility (HCSB) are not the only toxic conditions that can spread like a virus. Cynicism is an infection so deadly that it can snuff out the Holy Spirit in an entire congregation one clique at a time.

Years ago I watched something happen in a church that left a deep impression on me. A spirit of mockery and ridicule invaded a segment of the ministerial staff toward the pastor and several of his like-minded leaders. Cynicism finally crept like poison ivy right up the stairs onto the Sunday platform.

Ministers who were involved in various aspects of the church service sat in chairs on the stage for the entire hour. I began to catch their eyes cutting at one another when certain people would come to the microphone. At first I thought it was my imagination, but then I'd see them grin at one another or roll their eyes. The sight was dumbfounding because they were fine people individually. Together, however, they'd fed a dangerous strain of carnality.

If I had to peg the root of their cynicism, I think they saw themselves as smarter, more sophisticated, and more educated than those outside their circle. When the pastor preached or when those with simpler faith stepped to the microphone, the mockers turned up their collective noses, making caricatures of fellow Christians. The pastor was not remotely uneducated in the Scriptures, but what if he had been? Perhaps only one thing is more dangerous in a pulpit than ignorance: arrogance. It is a dangerous thing to treat contemptuously those whom God has called.

Read 1 Corinthians 1:26-31. Why is contempt between Christians grossly misplaced?

No human being can boast in the presence of God.

All of a sudden God seemed to drop an invisible grenade into the middle of that ministerial staff, and each one went flying in a different direction. The timing was so uncanny that it left me bug-eyed and put a rabid fear of God in me.

Over the years I've come to believe that Jesus has a particular distaste for cynicism. Mind you, He's forgiven me for worse. I only raise the issue because, like irresponsibility, cynicism is wildly contagious. After all, if you don't join the cynics, you fear that one day you'll be the object of their jokes.

The story had a good ending. All of those ministers, to their credit and the tested mettle of their character, served God faithfully elsewhere. When the pack broke up, the power broke off. But I've never forgotten it.

Read the definition of a cynic in the margin.

Did you notice the link to the Greek word *kynikos* meaning "dog"? Our word "canine" is akin to it. People offer numerous explanations, but no one can say for certain why the link exists or whether it was meant positively or negatively.

CYNIC

[Middle French or Latin, Middle French *cynique*, from Latin *cynicus*, from Greek *kynikos*, literally, like a dog, from *kyn-*, *kyo- n* dog]

1: *capitalized:* an adherent of an ancient Greek school of philosophers who held the view that virtue is the only good and that its essence lies in self-control and independence

2: a faultfinding captious critic *especially:* one who believes that human conduct is motivated wholly by self-interest[3]

I have no idea why they're connected, but this I will say, based on an amateur observance of human behavior: cynics tend to run in packs.

Several nights a week Keith and I hear the hair-raising howls of a pack of coyotes not far from our house. Every now and then one will saunter up in our yard in broad daylight, but it soon wanders off without doing any harm. The pack, however, is far more intimidating. We pull our dogs in the house when the pack howls, because together those wild dogs are looking for blood.

I don't think people set out to become critical or cynical or irresponsible. I think more often than not, we catch it from somebody.

○ Without mentioning names, describe a destructive attitude you've seen go viral among believers.

That's the nature of a virus and, incidentally, even people you love can make you sick. Jackson and Annabeth spent the night with Keith and me recently. We had a great time, but Annabeth was a little more subdued than usual. She wanted to snuggle in my lap more than play with toys, and I gladly soaked her up. Just before bedtime, I kissed her darling face and knew right away she had a fever. We'd all looked forward to the sleepover, and their parents really needed a carefree night out. I let them know that she was a bit feverish but assured them that our plans were still on schedule. After all, grandmothers are perfectly capable of taking care of sick children.

I put Annabeth to bed right next to me, so that I could check on her during the night. About 1:00 a.m., she rolled over toward me and sat halfway up, pinning my hair down with her right elbow. With me held properly captive, she proceeded to throw up all over my head. Talk about a shock. Recounting it tickles me so much I can hardly type. I quickly tried to rinse my hair out in the sink, but tending to Annabeth was the obvious priority.

Suffice it to say, we had a rough night. The next morning, I beheld a strange sight in the bathroom mirror. A huge chunk of my hair was as stiff as a board and sticking straight up like a banty rooster.

Be careful what you catch out there. Somebody you love could be the one with the bug.

Day Four
At All Times

The dawn is breaking and Christ is coming to save the day.

FLASH-FORWARD: May the Lord of peace Himself give you peace always in every way. *2 Thessalonians 3:16*

Remember not long ago in our series when I told you that I'd had a routine mammogram that put me on the table for a biopsy? Three months of living, working, serving, and writing have come and gone since then. The results were benign, but the radiologist still felt uneasy about it. He didn't like the look of it and said that I'd need to have an MRI on both breasts in 90 days. Rule keeper that I am, I scheduled it almost to the day.

I put on a hospital gown yesterday morning that had all the expected immodesty but, thankfully, my dignity was salvaged when the technician handed me a pair of one-size-fits-all blue paper shorts and insisted I wear them. I need you to work with me on this picture. Imagine a burly man of considerable age raised on fine Southern fare of chicken fried steak and cream gravy for three meals a day. I wore his shorts. I took a picture for you because I love you and, well, because life is hard and sometimes we have big shorts to fill.

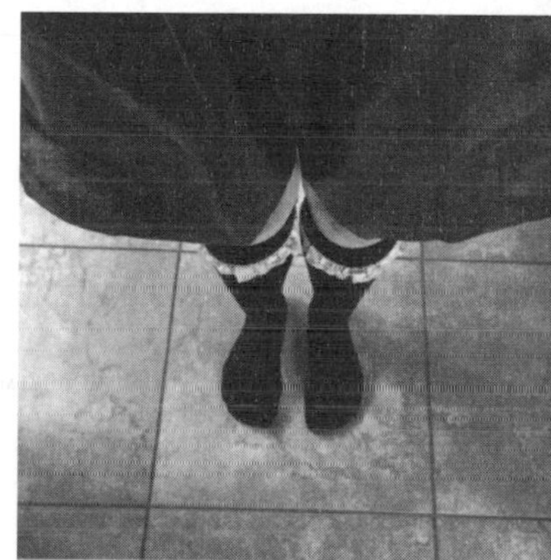

That's not all I failed to fill. I'll try not to cross the line here but, because of the location of the tissue abnormalities, I had to lie facedown in the MRI tube with two one-size-fits-all, gallon-sized cylindrical indentions made just for women. I wanted to know if I had to pay for the extra room or if they could discount my medical bill for requiring less space. While I learned that it doesn't work that way, I'd like to go on record suggesting that it should. If a bill gets passed to that effect, please don't hesitate to thank me.

When I begin a Bible study project like this one, I always wonder what life will bring. Not knowing is the hardest part of locking down a due date for the final manuscript. All the research, writing, rewriting, and videotaping takes 18 busy months. A lot of life happens in that length of time. As our journey together narrows to a close, I wonder what your last year and a half has been like and if you'd mind sharing a description.

So your answers will be less abstract, subtract 18 months from the present date and write the month and year of your calculation here: March 2013 __________. Between then and now, what kinds of things have come your way? Answer in phrases and make sure you list any positives alongside the negatives.

Keith Moore and I have had the best season of our married life. For any of you married women wondering when you might expect to get over the hump and onto your harmonious future, my man and I really hit our stride right about year 34. I know you are encouraged.

I write these words with a smile and a bit of a tease. This is no joke, however: sometimes a couple just needs to move and start over. I thought it would kill me to leave the house where I'd raised my babies, the tubs where I'd bathed them, the den where I'd rocked them, and the street where they'd ridden their bikes. We'd gone from high chairs to hair products in that house. Before I locked the front door for the last time, I stared at the tiny dining room where on innumerable early mornings I'd spread out my Bible, journaled, and prayed. I grew up in that little room. I learned the difference between the Books of Micah and Malachi there. I moved from my ridiculously idealistic expectations of family and ministry to deep, groaning prayers of desperation.

In that little space, I also documented seven years of ups and downs with a little boy entrusted to us. I prayed for every conceivable school need and athletic event for my daughters. I documented engagements, marriages, the deaths of both my parents, and the ecstasies of first holding my grandchildren. I wrote the first three in-depth Bible studies in that room with books stacked to the sky and supper burning on the stove. I was a mess. I'm still messy, but with considerably less darkness.

Life can grow dark though, can't it? As it all turned out, the last 18 months were much harder than I could have expected. I thank God for granting Keith and me such a good season because each of our girls endured devastating heartbreaks. Melissa went with me on the trip to Thessaloniki that officially launched this journey because we'd planned to partner again as we'd done in *Mercy Triumphs.* Soon after we returned, the bottom fell out of her marriage. The day-in, day-out pain she endured over the ensuing months nearly killed us to watch. Amanda, Curtis, Jackson, and Annabeth then suffered a very personal loss in their family that has caused tremendous grief.

We have cried hard this last year. We've fought depression and despair at times and asked God why certain events were permitted on our path.

○ I have a feeling you can relate and, if so, share how.

But, true to Moore form, we have also laughed. As my older brother often says, our family has a keen sense of the absurd and, of late, we've had no few absurdities for honing our comedic skills. God has been so faithful to us just as He has been faithful to you. In our darkest times, He'd light a candle in an unexpected corner to remind us He was there. Though we're still tiptoeing through a minefield, we're facing east, confident that the dawn is breaking and Christ is coming to save the day.

After withdrawing from all public writing for a full year, Melissa wrote her first official piece within the last few days. It was so beautiful that I sobbed. The article was too late for this project but right on time for whatever God has brewing in her heart. I'm simultaneously watching God raise up a warrior and leader in Amanda. The Enemy will not get the last word on either one of those young women. Or with you, my beloved Sister. Not if you don't let him.

Please read 2 Thessalonians 3:13-16 and handwrite the portion.

- Stare at that 16th verse. By what title is God called?

Lord of peace

Paul brought the first letter to the Thessalonians to conclusion with a similar title. Glance at 1 Thessalonians 5:23 and record the title here:

God of peace

The same divine designation is found in a tremendously powerful context in Romans 16:20. Please write the entire verse in this space:

The God of peace will soon crush Satan under your feet.
The grace of our Lord Jesus Christ be with you

Dissect the verse carefully. Under whose feet will Satan be crushed?

Most of us who know Christ have no doubt that Satan will be crushed under His feet. That victory is foretold in the first few pages of Scripture through God's curse upon the serpent in the garden after the fall of man. Genesis 3:14-15 says, "The LORD God said to the serpent … 'I will put enmity between you and the woman, and between your offspring and hers; he will crush your head, and you will strike his heel'" (NIV).

Jesus will never stop fighting for you.

I find the most stunning thing about Romans 16:20 is that Christ, in His majestic mercy, makes His victory ours. He will also crush Satan under our feet. All evil dominion and destruction will come to an end, and everlasting joy and triumph will be our spoils of war. It is enough that Jesus would win the victory for us, but He wants us to know the exhilaration of our own bruised feet on the neck of darkness.

Nothing is accidental about the divine title "God of peace" in Romans 16:20. The same is true of the "Lord of peace" (2 Thess. 3:16) at the conclusion of a letter foretelling bone-chilling events yet to take place. Peace never means more than in the context of war. Maybe one day in eternity God will let us see what was going on over our heads in the unseen realm while we were just trying to get through another day. Human vision captures a mere shadow of the true. At times we may wonder if the oppression we're sensing is a figment of our imaginations or if our feelings of warfare are just forms of religious psychosis.

Read Eugene Peterson's translation of Ephesians 6:10-13 below. Underline the words that speak to you loudly.

> *God is strong, and he wants you strong. So take everything the Master has set out for you, well-made weapons of the best materials. And put them to use so you will be able to stand up to everything the Devil throws your way. This is no afternoon athletic contest that we'll walk away from and forget about in a couple of hours. This is for keeps, a life-or-death fight to the finish against the Devil and all his angels. Be prepared. You're up against far more than you can handle on your own. Take all the help you can get, every weapon God has issued, so that when it's all over but the shouting you'll still be on your feet.*
>
> EPHESIANS 6:10-13, THE MESSAGE

So should we be relieved we're not imagining things or should we dart into paranoia and start slapping at the air like we're swatting invisible flies? Listen, people out there think we're weird enough. Let's try to keep the swatting to a minimum. It doesn't help anyway.

There's one enormous reason why we can have complete peace in the midst of an invisible war that results in such visible carnage. The reason is captured in black and white in all four of these verses: Deuteronomy 1:30; 3:22; 20:4, and Joshua 23:10.

Read each of those verses and document the concept they convey.

The LORD your God who goes out before you will himself fight for you ... before your eyes.

Several years ago I sat with a friend whose 20-year marriage had ended. She'd forced a crisis and threatened divorce in hopes of waking her husband up. Instead, he concurred and filed. Between broken sobs she said, "He didn't even fight for me." You will never, ever have to say that about Jesus. He will never stop fighting for you. He takes every assault on you personally. He goes before you onto every battlefield. He fights for you even when you're fighting yourself. As hated as you are by Satan, you never go head-to-head with him. Jesus does. And Jesus never loses a fight.

If your eyes could, for a moment, behold the battlefield around you, you'd be astonished by the sight. There you would see a thousand demons put to flight, because the Lord your God was fighting for you, as He promised.

"The LORD is a warrior" (Ex. 15:3). And "He is our peace" (Eph. 2:14).

Day Five

The Grace of Our Lord Jesus Christ

FLASH-FORWARD: The grace of our Lord Jesus Christ be with all of you. *2 Thessalonians 3:18*

Last week Jackson came home from his second-grade class and presented his mother with a folder chock-full of completed schoolwork. Stacked among the math assignments and spelling tests, she found a slice of pure gold: a stapled poetry book Jackson was required to fill with words from the wealth of his imagination. The second graders could write on any subject but write they must. Jackson's poetry book shot off to a great start with an inspiring but word-sparse piece entitled "Goblin Shark." His next entry was named "My Pants." And the next? "My Coat."

I'm always sad on the last day of a long Bible study journey. I feel a sense of loss with the final few sentences, knowing from experience how much I'll miss you and the intensity of our expedition through the Scriptures. We each have our own study lives, but there's something about staying the course and together poring over every word of a book of the Bible for weeks that demands a different discipline and forms a unique bond. I will miss it so much. Of course, I'm also elated that we made it to the end, but the beauty of being a woman is that I have no shame in feeling a dozen things at once.

○ What are some of the things going through your head on this final day? If you're glad it's over, own it!

There's also something to be said for quitting while we're ahead. After all, what if I'm right on the verge of writing about my pants or my coat? Next it could be my running shoes. Or, what if I looked down and saw my socks and settled into a lengthy diatribe on the benefits of dry feet? Let's enjoy our last few verses while we have the chance because, once we run out of sacred ink, it's a slippery slope from there.

Please read 2 Thessalonians 3:16-18 and, with the joy and satisfaction of knowing you've reached the final words, please handwrite the segment on the appropriate page.

This marked-up, gnarled-up workbook of yours represents no small accomplishment, my friend. Every coffee stain, tea stain, lunch stain, and tearstain on these pages represents a real-life straining, struggling, and striving to know the Immortal Invisible. It's easy to start something like this. It's another thing entirely to finish it. Maybe you completed it in eight weeks or maybe it's been eight months. Perhaps an earthquake has happened in your family too since you cracked open the cover. Maybe you've also cried a cradle of tears since jotting your name in that first lesson. Yet, here you are. You've made it. May God make such a ruckus of His delight in you that you're too red-faced to deny it.

We will save most of our discussions on the conclusion of 2 Thessalonians for our final session. One simple exercise for now: please compare the wording that Paul uses to begin and end both letters by reading 1 Thessalonians 1:1 and 5:28; 2 Thessalonians 1:1-2 and 3:18.

CHÁRIS

Grace, particularly that which causes joy, pleasure, gratification, favor, acceptance, for a kindness granted or desired, a benefit, thanks, gratitude. A favor done without expectation of return; the absolutely free expression of the loving kindness of God to men finding its only motive in the bounty and benevolence of the Giver; unearned and unmerited favor. *Cháris* stands in direct antithesis to *érga*, works, the two being mutually exclusive. God's grace affects man's sinfulness and not only forgives the repentant sinner, but brings joy and thankfulness to him. It changes the individual to a new creature without destroying his individuality (2 Cor. 5:17; Eph. 2:8,9).[4]

- What common thread embroiders together each greeting and benediction?

The grace of our Lord Jesus Christ.

Now reflect on the letters in their entirety. Without glancing at your Bible, what themes from these two letters are most memorable to you as we close?

God used Paul, Silas & Timothy to spread the gospel & to guide the new believers

What distinct metaphor does the apostle Paul use for believers in Christ in 2 Corinthians 3:2-3?

letter

We are letters "not written with ink but with the Spirit of the living God—not on stone tablets but on tablets that are hearts of flesh." Like 1 and 2 Thessalonians, the letters of our lives in Christ open with grace and close with grace. Each word of our testimony in between is glued to the page with grace.

Grace so floods the atmosphere of New Testament Scripture that defining it can be like lassoing the wind. "Unmerited favor" is the abbreviated definition we're often taught, but automatic answers—even beautiful ones—put our awe at risk. Something as glorious and divine as grace could take on all the routine of a "bless you" after a sneeze. Let's allow the longer definition in the margin to breathe some fresh life over us.

In regard to your current state of mind and circumstances, what stands out most to you in the definition?

unearned, unmerited favor.

Paul, Silvanus, and Timothy intended their readers to roll up both letters with hands sopping wet with grace. Like those original readers, we are saved by grace, chosen by grace, called by grace, and gifted by grace. Smugness and self-righteousness have no place in grace. Maybe a few word pictures could sketch illustrations for an encyclopedia of grace.

Grace is an inflated raft that can submerge to the floor of a sea to save you.
Grace is the silver thread that stitches up the shreds of mangled souls.
Grace calls the waitress to the table and sits her down to wash her feet.
Grace sees underneath the manhole on a street of self-destruction.
Grace is the air to draw a breath in the belly of a whale.
Grace is the courage to stand in the shamed wake of a frightful falling.
Grace is the only fire hot enough to burn down a living hell.
Grace waits with healing in His wings when we're too mad to pray.
Grace is the gravity that pulls us from depravity.
Grace races us to the Throne when we make haste to repent,
 and it always outruns us.
Grace treats us like we already are what we fear we'll never become.
Grace is the doorpost dripping red when the angel of death grips the knob.
Grace is the stamp that says "Ransomed" on a life that screams "Ruined."
Grace sets a table before me in the presence of my enemy, even when
 my enemy is me.
Grace is the cloak that covers the naked and the palm that drops the rock.
Grace is divine power burgeoning in the absence of all strength.
Grace proves God true and every self-made man a liar
 for the sake of his own soul.
Grace is the power to do what we cannot do
 for the name of Christ to go where it has not been.
Grace is a room of a thousand mirrors, all reflecting the face of Christ.

Write your own word picture if you have one.

Grace is saving a burning coal from the fire.

Grace is no simple greeting. It's a gift held out in nail-pierced hands. As we wave good-bye at the end of our trek through 1 and 2 Thessalonians, our hosts—Paul, Silvanus, and Timothy—flatly refuse to leave us the luxury of idealism. They offer help to a Christian culture prone to crave hype. We celebrate an accomplishment today but as those who are sober. The tips of our toes dance on troubled soil. The challenge before us is this: will the bad news surrounding us snuff out the good news entrusted to us?

Not long ago I had the privilege to serve at a large event down South. As we exited the freeway for our downtown destination, one place of business was so prominent and well lit that you couldn't miss it with an inch-thick blindfold. It was a high-dollar strip club with a giant marquee advertising in neon lights the names and showtimes of various dancers. I was in the car with several gentlemen, so we all felt a bit awkward when we pulled up to our hotel nearby.

"Wow," I said to break the tension. "That's an interesting view for the weekend." The words weren't cast like stones. With my background and former bondage, it's a miracle that I didn't end up somewhere worse. Still, the imposing structure was impossible to ignore. When I walked into my hotel room on the seventh floor, the picture window framed the marquee like it was custom-fit. The lights were so alive in my room late that night that I tightened the blinds together to darken the room so I could sleep.

My alarm went off well before daylight. Coming out of the bathroom to pour some coffee, I saw a long sliver of florescent orange light searing a laser beam across the bed through the thin gap between the curtains. The sight was so remarkable that I walked over to the window and threw open the blinds. An incandescent pumpkin-sun had set the horizon ablaze. I stood transfixed at the glass as it rose beside that club like an outdoor elevator ascending every floor. The sun then seemed to halt right on top of that marquee like it was momentarily hung on a nail. I stared at the sight with breathless wonder.

Still stirred by what I'd seen, I opened the conference that morning with the story and asked the attendees if they would pray with me compassionately for the women who worked there and for others employed in similar places. They welcomed the privilege and some eight thousand hearts raised the roof in unified rhythm. I had no idea until right after the session that 20 dancers from that very business were seated at the top of the arena. They were floored by the story and wept through the prayer, awed that Christ had pursued them with unabashed affection.

No door is so dark and scandalous that Jesus is unwilling to enter to make Himself one person's exit.

I could still sob over the gracious heart of God. He didn't bring the sun up over a steeple that day. He brought the sun up over a strip club. That is my Jesus. That is your Jesus. No door is so dark and scandalous that Jesus is unwilling to enter to make Himself one person's exit. For what good is light on this desolate sod if it refuses to show up in the darkness?

Thank you from the depths of my heart for the privilege to walk with you on this journey. I've put in a lot of miles with you over the last many months. In God's merciful timing, I write these final words just having heard from the radiologist. I'm clear for another six months.

We have our work cut out for us, you and I. We've been called to a hard world. If we turn our backs on it, we forfeit our assignments. Face out, Beloved. Be brave. Be bold. Love big. We won't be here long. Take the torch of the gospel to a land of souls and shadows.

For you are children of light, children of the day.

endnotes

WEEK 1

1. *Merriam-Webster's Collegiate Dictionary,* 10th ed, s.v. "we."
2. Charles A. Wanamaker, *The Epistles to the Thessalonians: A Commentary on the Greek Text* (Grand Rapids, MI: Wm. B. Eerdmans Publishing Co., 1990), 75.
3. *Merriam-Webster's Collegiate Dictionary,* s.v. "weird."
4. Curtis Jones, "Joy, Happiness, and Christmas" (sermon, Bayou City Fellowship, Houston, TX, December 9, 2012).
5. Spiros Zodhiates, *The Complete Word Study Dictionary: New Testament* (Iowa Falls, IA: World Bible Publishers Inc., 1992), s.v. "mimētēs."
6. Logos Bible Software. A. T. Robertson, *Word Pictures in the New Testament,* "1 Thessalonians 1:7." Bellingham, WA: Logos Research Systems, Inc.
7. The phrase "the word of the LORD came to" is found in the Old Testament 239 times in the NAS, 243 times in the ESV, 242 times in the KJV, and 209 times in the HCSB.
8. Charles Wesley, "Love Divine, All Loves Excelling."
9. John Stott, *The Message of Thessalonians* (Downers Grove, IL: InterVarsity Press, 1991), 36.
10. Gene L. Green, *The Letters to the Thessalonians* (Grand Rapids, MI: Wm. B. Eerdmans Publishing Co., 2002), 101.
11. Ibid, 102.
12. Stott, *Thessalonians,* 38.
13. Green, *Thessalonians,* 107.
14. Ibid, 35, 37, 38.

WEEK 2

1. If your NIV doesn't have "failure" (which some more recent copyrights do not include), try *biblegateway.com*'s New international Reader's Version at *www.biblegateway.com/passage/?search=1%20thes%202:1&version=NIRV.*
2. G. K. Beale, *1–2 Thessalonians* (Downers Grove, IL: InterVarsity Press, 2003), 65.
3. Zodhiates, *Dictionary,* s.v. "peripatéō."
4. Stott, *Thessalonians,* 57–58.
5. Ibid, 61.
6. Wanamaker, *Thessalonians,* 120.
7. Green, *Thessalonians,* 151.
8. F. F. Bruce, *1 and 2 Thessalonians,* Word Biblical Commentary, vol. 45 (Dallas: Nelson Reference and Electronic, 1982), 54.
9. Ibid.
10. Ibid, 53.

WEEK 3

1. *Merriam-Webster's Collegiate Dictionary,* s.v. "hinder."
2. Green, *Thessalonians,* 152.
3. Zodhiates, *Dictionary,* s.v. "ógkos."
4. Ibid, s.v. "hupérogkos."
5. R. C. H. Lenski, *Commentary on the New Testament: The Interpretation of the Acts of the Apostles* (Peabody, MA: Hendrickson Publishers, Inc., 2001), 705.
6. Gary S. Shogren, *1 & 2 Thessalonians,* Zondervan Exegetical Commentary on the New Testament (Grand Rapids, MI: Zondervan, 2012), 136.
7. Zodhiates, *Dictionary,* s.v. "thlíbō."
8. Wanamaker, *Thessalonians,* 141.
9. D. Michael Martin, *1, 2 Thessalonians,* The New American Commentary, vol. 33 (Nashville, TN: Broadman & Holman Publishers, 2001), 111.
10. Charles Wesley, "Come, Thou Long Expected Jesus."

WEEK 4

1. J. M. Barrie, *Peter Pan,* updated by John Caird and Trevor Nunn (New York: Dramatists Play Service, 1993), 93.
2. Bruce, *1 and 2 Thessalonians,* 77.
3. Martin, *1, 2 Thessalonians,* 134.
4. Wanamaker, *Thessalonians,* 163.
5. Leon Morris, *The First and Second Epistles to the Thessalonians,* The New International Commentary on the New Testament (Grand Rapids, MI: Wm. B. Eerdmans Publishing Co., 1991), 131.
6. Michael Holmes, *1 & 2 Thessalonians,* The NIV Application Commentary (Grand Rapids, MI: Zondervan, 1998), 140–141.
7. Morris, *Thessalonians,* 138.
8. Ibid, 142.
9. Ibid, 145.
10. "This term in Latin, *raptus,* is the source of the popular designation of this event as the 'rapture.'" R. L. Thomas, "1 Thessalonians," *Ephesians – Philemon,* The Expositor's Bible Commentary, vol. 11 (Grand Rapids, MI: Zondervan, 1981), 279.
11. Morris, *Thessalonians,* 140.

WEEK 5

1. Shogren, *1 & 2 Thessalonians,* 203.
2. J. R. R. Tolkien, *The Hobbit* (New York: Houghton Mifflin Company, 1997), 12.
3. "The Hobbit," directed by Peter Jackson, New Line Cinema, 2012.
4. Tolkien, 229.
5. Zodhiates, *Dictionary,* s.v. "orgé."
6. The Outline Bible Five Translation, "L–Z," Practical Word Studies in the New Testament, vol. 2 (Chattanooga, TN: Leadership Ministries Worldwide, 1998), s.v. "wrath."
7. Zodhiates, *Dictionary,* s.v. "nouthetéō."
8. R. C. H. Lenski, *The Interpretation of St. Paul's Epistles to the Colossians, to the Thessalonians, to Timothy, to Titus, and to Philemon* (Peabody, MA: Hendrickson Publishers, Inc., 2001), 356.

WEEK 6

1. John B. Polhill, *Acts,* The New American Commentary, vol. 26 (Nashville, TN: Broadman Press, 2001), 503.
2. David Teems, *Tyndale: The Man Who Gave God an English Voice* (Nashville, TN: Thomas Nelson, 2012), 259.
3. Ibid, 255.
4. Ibid.
5. Ibid, 262.
6. Ibid, xvii.
7. Zodhiates, *Dictionary,* s.v. "katartízō."

WEEK 7

1. Bruce, *1 and 2 Thessalonians,* 161.
2. Ibid, 163.
3. M. Scott Peck, *People of the Lie: The Hope for Healing Human Evil* (New York: Simon & Schuster, 1998), 65–66.
4. Ibid, 66.
5. Martin, *1, 2 Thessalonians,* 232.
6. Zodhiates, *Dictionary,* s.v. "apóleia," and Wanamaker, *Thessalonians,* 245.
7. "Dean Corll," *Wikipedia,* last modified February 16, 2014, *http://en.wikipedia.org/wiki/Dean_Corll.*
8. Martin, *1, 2 Thessalonians,* 249.
9. Wanamaker, *Thessalonians,* 267–68.
10. Martin, *1, 2 Thessalonians,* 255–56.
11. Morris, *Thessalonians,* 241.

WEEK 8

1. Michael Rusten and Sharon Rusten, *The One Year Book of Christian History* (Carol Stream, IL: Tyndale House Publishers, 2003), 558-59 .
2. Charles Wesley, "O for a Thousand Tongues to Sing."
3. *Merriam-Webster's Collegiate Dictionary,* s.v. "cynic."
4. Zodhiates, *Dictionary,* s.v. "cháris."

Group Session Nine

REVIEW THE WEEK

Use these questions to guide your discussion of last week's homework.

● Principal Questions

DAY 1: What do 1 Thessalonians 5:25 and 2 Thessalonians 3:1 have in common? (p. 191)
DAY 2: What things are of most importance (1 Cor. 15:1-4)? (p. 198)
DAY 3: What command had Paul and his coworkers given the Thessalonians when they were still with them? (p. 199)
DAY 4: By what title is God called in 2 Thessalonians 3:16? (p. 205)
DAY 5: What thread embroiders together each greeting and benediction? (p. 208)

○ Personal Discussion Questions

DAY 1: Is the idea of receiving rather than achieving a shift for you or have you practiced this approach for years? (p. 194)
DAY 2: What are a few specific places you desire for the words of Christ that abide in you to arrive with you over the next month? (p. 198)
DAY 3: What is a destructive attitude you've seen go viral among believers? (p. 202)
DAY 4: How can you relate to fighting despair and depression over events God has allowed in your path? (p. 204)
DAY 5: What are some of the things going through your head on this final day? (p. 207)

VIEW THE VIDEO

Introduction

In this final session, we will tie up our journey together with a string left dangling at the beginning of 2 Thessalonians 3, and the other left waiting at the end.

1. A ____________ ____________ request for ____________.

- That the word of the Lord may ____________ ____________ and be ____________. Compare Psalm 147:15.
- That we may be ____________ from ____________ and ____________ people.
- "Delivered"—Greek *rhúomai*: "from *rhúō*, to draw, ____________ ____________ the ground. To draw or snatch from danger, rescue, deliver. This is more with the meaning of ____________ to ____________ than merely ____________ from someone or something."[1]

Note the descriptions "wicked and evil." The Greek meaning of the first word is particularly interesting. Greek *átopos*—"from *a,* without, and *tópos,* ________. ________ ________ or ________ ________ ________. Inconvenient, prejudicial, hurtful, evil, improper (Acts 28:6). Of persons: ________, ________ (2 Thess. 3:2); of conduct: inconvenient, unsuitable, improper, wrong."[2]

Consider what could be a ________ Instant ________: "For ________ ________ have ________. But the ________ is ________." (ESV)

2. A significantly ________ ________. Imagine a handwritten version similar to this:

> Ὁ ἀσπασμὸς τῇ ἐμῇ χειρὶ Παύλου ... οὕτως γράφω
> Ἡ χάρις τοῦ κυρίου ἡμῶν Ἰησοῦ Χριστοῦ μετὰ πάντων ὑμῶν[3]

The benediction: The ________ of our Lord Jesus Christ be ________ ________ ________.

1. S. Zodhiates, *The Complete Word Study Dictionary: New Testament,* s.v. "rhúomai."
2. Ibid, "átopos."
3. F. F. Bruce, *1 and 2 Thessalonians,* Word Biblical Commentary, vol. 45 (Dallas: Nelson Reference and Electronic, 1982), 215–16.

Handwrite 1 & 2 Thessalonians

ESV

1 Thessalonians 1

:1 Paul, Silvanus & Timothy. To the church of the Thessalonians
in God the Father and the Lord Jesus Christ: Grace to you + peace
:2,3 WE always thank God for all of you mentioning you in our prayers.
WE continually remember before our God & Father your work produced by
faith, your labor prompted by love, and your endurance inspired
by hope in our Lord Jesus Christ.
:4,5 For we know, brothers loved by God, that he has chosen you, because
our gospel came to you not simply w. words, but also w. power, w. the
H.S. & w. deep conviction. You know how we lived among you for
your sake.
:6,7 You became imitators of us & of the Lord; in spite of severe
suffering, you welcomed the message w. the joy given by the H.S.
And so you became a model to all the believers in
Macedonia & Achaia.
:8-10 The Lord's message rang out from you not only in Macedonia &
Achaia - your faith in God has become known everywhere.
Therefore we do not need to say anything about it, for
they themselves report what kind of reception you gave us.
They tell how you turned to God from idols to serve
the living & true God, and to wait for his Son from
heaven, whom he raised from the dead - Jesus,
who rescues us from the coming wrath.

2:17-20. But since we were torn away from you, brothers,
for a short time, in person not in heart, we endeavored
the more eagerly & w. great desire to see you face to face,
because we wanted to come to you - I, Paul, again
& again - but Satan hindered us. For what is our
hope or joy or crown of boasting before our Lord Jesus
at his coming? Is it not you? For you are our
glory & joy.

1 Thessalonians 2

-4 For you yourselves know, brothers, that our coming to you
was not in vain. But though we had already suffered
and been shamefully treated at Philippi, as you know,
we had boldness in our God to declare to you the gospel
of God in the midst of much conflict. For our appeal does
not spring from error or impurity or any attempt to
deceive, but just as we have been approved by God
to be entrusted with the gospel, so we speak, not to
please man, but to please God who tests our hearts.
5-8 For we never came with words of flattery, as you know, nor with
a pretext for greed - God is witness. Nor did we seek glory
from people, whether from you or from others, though we
could have made demands as apostles of Christ. But
we were gentle among you, like a nursing mother taking
care of her own children. So, being affectionately desirous
of you, we were ready to share with you not only the gospel
of God but also our own selves, because you had
become very dear to us.
9-12 For you remember, brothers, our labor & toil: we worked night & day,
that we might not be a burden to any of you, while we proclaimed
to you the gospel of God. You are witnesses, and God also, how holy &
righteous & blameless was our conduct toward you believers. For
you know how, like a father with his children, we exhorted each one
of you & encouraged you & charged you to walk in a manner
worthy of God, who calls you into his own kingdom & glory.
3-16 And we also thank God constantly for this, that when you
received the word of God, which you heard from us, you accepted
it not as the word of men but as what it really is, the word of
God, which is at work in you believers. For you, brothers,
became the imitators of the churches of God in Christ Jesus
that are in Judea. For you suffered the same things from
your own countrymen as they did from the Jews, who killed
both the Lord Jesus & the prophets, and drove us out, and
displease God & oppose all mankind by hindering us from
speaking to the Gentiles that they may be saved - so as always to fill up the measure of their sins. But wrath
has come upon them at last!

1 Thessalonians 3

-3, Therefore when we could bear it no longer, we were willing to be left
behind at Athens alone, and we sent Timothy, our brother & God's coworker
in the gospel of Christ, to establish & exhort you in your faith, that no
one be moved by these afflictions. For you yourselves know that
we are destined for this.
-5 For when we were w. you, we kept telling you beforehand that
we were to suffer affliction, just as it has come to pass, and just
as you know. For this reason, when I could bear it no longer,
I sent to learn about your faith, for fear that somehow the
tempter had tempted you & our labor would be in vain.
-8 But now that Timothy has come to us from you, and has
brought us the good news of your faith & love, and reported that
you always remember us kindly & long to see us, as we long to
see you — for this reason, brothers, in all our distress & affliction
we have been comforted about you through your faith.
-10 For what thanksgiving can we return to God for you, for all the
joy that we feel for your sake before our God, as we pray most earnestly
night & day that we may see you face to face & supply what is lacking
in your faith?
11-13 Now may our God & Father himself, and our Lord Jesus, direct
our way to you, and may the Lord make you increase &
abound in love for one another and for all, as we do
for you, so that he may establish your hearts blameless
in holiness before our God & Father, at the coming of
our Lord Jesus with all his saints.

1 Thessalonians 4.

1-6 Finally, brothers, we instructed you how to live in order to
please God, as in fact you are living. Now we ask you &
urge you in the Lord Jesus to do this more & more.
For you know what instructions we gave you by the
authority of the Lord Jesus. It is God's will that you
should be sanctified; that you should avoid sexual
immorality; that each of you should learn to control
his own body in a way that is holy & honorable,

not in passionate lust like the heathen, who
do not know God; and that in this matter no one
should wrong his brother or take advantage of him.
The Lord will punish men for all such sins, as we
have already told you & warned you.
7-10 For God did not call us to be impure, but to
live a holy life. Therefore, he who rejects this
instruction does not reject man but God, who gives
you his Holy Spirit. Now about brotherly love we
do not need to write to you, for you yourselves
have been taught by God to love each other. And
in fact, you do love all the brothers throughout
Macedonia. Yet we urge you brothers to do so more & more
11+12 Make it your ambition to lead a quiet life, to
mind your own business & to work with your own
hands, just as we told you, so that your daily
life may win the respect of outsiders, and so that
you will not be dependent on anybody.
13-15 Brothers, we do not want you to be ignorant about those
who fall asleep, or to grieve like the rest of men, who
have no hope. We believe that Jesus died and rose again
an so we believe that God will bring with Jesus those
who have fallen asleep in him. According to the Lord's
own word, we tell you that we who are still alive
who are left till the coming of the Lord, will certainly
not precede those who have fallen asleep.
16-18 For the Lord himself will come down from heaven, with

a loud command, with the voice of the archangel
and w. the trumpet call of God, and the dead
in Christ will rise first. After that, we who are
still alive and are left will be caught up together
w. them in the clouds to meet the Lord in the
air. And so we will be w. the Lord forever.
Therefore, encourage each other w. these words.

1 Thessalonians 5

1-3 Now concerning the times & the seasons, brothers,
you have no need to have anything written to you.
For you yourselves are fully aware that the day of
the Lord will come like a thief in the night. While
people are saying, "There is peace & security," then
sudden destruction will come upon them as labor
pains come upon a pregnant woman, and they
will not escape.
4-8 But you are not in darkness, brothers, for that day to
surprise you like a thief. For you are all children
of light, children of the day. We are not of the night
or of the darkness. So then let us not sleep, as others do,
but let us keep awake & be sober. For those who sleep,
sleep at night, and those who get drunk, are drunk at
night. But since we belong to the day, let us be
sober, having put on the breastplate of faith & love,
and for a helmet the hope of salvation.
9-11 For God has not destined us for wrath, but to obtain
salvation through our Lord Jesus Christ, who died
for us so that whether we are awake or asleep we
might live w/ him. Therefore encourage one another &
build one another up, just as you are doing.
12-15. We ask you, brothers, to respect those who labor among
you and are over you in the Lord & admonish you, and
to esteem them very highly in love because of their
work. Be at peace among yourselves. And we urge
you, brothers, admonish the idle, encourage the faint-
hearted, help the weak, be patient w/ them all. See
that no one repays anyone evil for evil, but always
seek to do good to one another & to everyone.
16-28 Rejoice always, pray without ceasing, give thanks in all
circumstances; for this is the will of God in Christ
Jesus for you. Do not quench the Spirit. Do not
despise prophecies, but test everything; hold fast

what is good. Abstain from every form of evil.
Now may the God of peace sanctify you
completely, and may your whole spirit and
soul & body be kept blameless at the coming
of our Lord Jesus Christ. He who calls you is
faithful; he will surely do it.
Brothers, pray for us. Greet all the brothers w.
a holy kiss. I put you under oath before the
Lord to have this letter read to all the brothers.
The grace of our Lord Jesus Christ be with you.

2 Thessalonians 1

1-4 Paul, Sylvanus & Timothy, To the church of the Thessalonians
in God our Father & the Lord Jesus Christ. Grace to you & peace
from God our Father & the Lord Jesus Christ. We ought always
to give thanks to God for you, brothers, as is right, because
your faith is growing abundantly, and the love of everyone
of you for one another is increasing. Therefore we ourselves
boast about you in the churches of God for your
steadfastness & faith in all your persecutions and in
the afflictions you are enduring.
5-8 This is evidence of the righteous judgement of God,
that you may be considered worthy of the kingdom of
God, for which you are also suffering - since indeed God
considers it just to repay w. affliction those who afflict
you, and to grant relief to you who are afflicted as well
as to us, when the Lord Jesus is revealed from heaven
with his mighty angels in flaming fire, inflicting vengeance
on those who do not know God and on those who do
not obey the gospel of our Lord Jesus:
9-10 Who shall be punished w. everlasting destruction from
the presence of the Lord, and from the glory of
his power; When he shall come to be glorified in
his saints, and to be admired in all them that
believe (because our testimony among you was
believed) in that day.
11 To this end we always pray for you, that our God
may make you worthy of his calling and may fulfill
every resolve for good and every work of faith by his power,
12 so that the name of our Lord Jesus may be glorified
in you, and you in him, according to the grace of
our God and the Lord Jesus Christ.

2 Thessalonians 2

1-3 Now concerning the coming of our Lord Jesus Christ +
our being gathered together w. him, we ask you, brothers,
not to be quickly shaken in mind or alarmed, either
by a spirit or a spoken word, or a letter seeming to be
from us, to the effect that the day of the Lord has come.
Let no one deceive you in any way. For that day
will not come, unless the rebellion comes first, and
the man of lawlessness is revealed, the son of destruction,
4-7 who opposes and exalts himself against any so-called
god or object of worship, so that he takes his seat in the
temple of God, proclaiming himself to be God. Do you
not remember when I was still w. you I told you
these things? And you know what is restraining him
now so that he may be revealed in his time. For
the mystery of lawlessness is already at work. Only
he who now restrains it will do so until he is
out of the way.
8-10 And then the lawless one will be revealed, whom
the Lord Jesus will kill w. the breath of his mouth and
bring to nothing by the appearance of his coming.
The coming of the lawless one is by the activity of
Satan with all power and false signs + wonders,
and w. all wicked deception for those who are
perishing, because they refused to love the truth
+ so be saved.
11-12 Therefore God sends them a strong delusion, so that they
may believe what is false, in order that all may
be condemned who did not believe the truth but
had pleasure in unrighteousness.
13-17 But we ought always to give thanks to God for you,
brothers beloved by the Lord, because God chose you as the
firstfruits to be saved, through sanctification by the
Spirit and belief in the truth. To this he called you
through our gospel, so that you may obtain the

glory of our Lord Jesus Christ. So then, brothers,
stand firm and hold to the traditions that you
were taught by us, either by our spoken word or
by our letter. Now may our Lord Jesus Christ
himself, and God our Father, who loved us and
gave us eternal comfort and good hope through
grace, comfort your hearts and establish them
in every good work & word.

2 Thessalonians 3

1-5 Finally, brothers, pray for us, that the word of the Lord
may speed ahead & be honored, as happened among
you, and that we may be delivered from wicked & evil
men. For not all have your faith. But the Lord is
faithful. He will establish you and guard you against
the evil one. And we have confidence in the Lord
about you, that you are doing and will do the things
that we command. May the Lord direct your hearts
to the love of God and to the steadfastness of
Christ.

6-8 Now we command you, brothers, in the name of our
Lord Jesus Christ, that you keep away from any
brother who is walking in idleness and not in accord
w. the tradition that you received from us. For you
yourselves know how you ought to imitate us,
because we were not idle when we were w. you, nor
did we eat anyone's bread without paying for it,
but w. toil & labor we worked night & day, that

we may not be a burden to any of you.
-12 It was not because we do not have that right, but
to give you in ourselves an example to imitate.
For even when we were w. you, we would give you
this command: If anyone is not willing to work, let
him not eat. For we hear that some among you
walk in idleness, not busy at work, but busybodies.
Now such persons we command and encourage in the
Lord Jesus Christ to do their work quietly & to earn
their own living.
13-16. As for you, brothers, do not grow weary in doing
good. If anyone does not obey what we say in this
letter, take note of that person, and have nothing to do
w. him, that he may be ashamed. Do not regard
him as an enemy, but warn him as a brother.
Now may the Lord of Peace himself give you peace
at all times in every way. The Lord be w. you all.
17-18. I, Paul, write this greeting w. my own hand. This
is the sign of genuineness in every letter of mine;
it is the way I write.
The grace of our Lord Jesus Christ be w. you all.

CHILDREN OF THE DAY

The 28-Day Challenge

DAY 1: *Christ Jesus, Our Lord and Savior*

Before we proceed to our Scripture-prayers for overcoming sexual strongholds, please understand that all of us are utterly powerless to overcome strongholds until we've accepted Jesus Christ as our Lord and Savior. If you have never actually received Christ for yourself, I would be honored beyond measure to lead you through this simple transforming prayer:

Lord Jesus, I, ________________________, have realized I am hopelessly enslaved to sin and that I am powerless to save myself. I acknowledge that You are the Son of God and You have already paid the debt for my sin. All I need to do is claim it personally. I realize now that You died for me. You bore every single one of my sins, past, present, and future, when You hung upon the cross. I accept the gift of grace offered to me through Your sacrificial death. I cannot be good enough to work my way into heaven and eternal life with You. You paved the way for me through Your perfect, sinless sacrifice, and I gladly accept Your gift. Come and dwell in me, Jesus, through Your Holy Spirit and set me free to live in Your resurrection life. Thank You, God, in advance that You will never leave me or forsake me.

Without a doubt, all people who have never accepted Christ as Savior are held captive by the enemy, their primary stronghold being unbelief. These prayers, however, are primarily for the believer ...

DAY 2: *Enslaved*

Sexual sin is highly habitual and addictive, so it has the long-term effects Satan prefers. He is many things, but he's not very creative. He much prefers a long-lasting yoke to the flimsier brand. Satan uses the same thing over and over as long as he's getting results.

PRAY: How I thank you, God, that You will heal my waywardness. You love me freely (Hos.14:4). You will set me free! My faithful God, help me to call this to mind and therefore always have hope: Because of Your great love, I am not consumed, for Your compassions never fail. They are new toward me every morning; great is Your faithfulness. I will say to myself, "The Lord is my portion; therefore I will wait for Him" (Lam. 3:22-23). Yes YOU Jesus are my portion and I will trust You and receive Your love. My Father, I am unspeakably grateful that You have demonstrated Your own love for me in this: while I was still a sinner, Christ died for me (Rom. 5:8). You, God, loved me so much that You have given Your one and only Son, and since I believe in Him, I shall not perish but have eternal life. For You, God did not send Your Son into the world to condemn me but to save me through Him (John 3:16-17). When I'm feeling enslaved by my sin and shame, Jesus, please remind me again that You have set me free and help me fight the enemy today.

For more information about the 28-Day Challenge, go to *www.lifeway.com/28daychallenge*

DAY 3: *A Prisoner of Sin*

The moment the Enemy sees that you are becoming serious about being delivered from strongholds and being freed to pursue holiness, he will turn up the heat of temptation. Be alert and stand against him; however, if you happen to fall at times in your journey toward freedom, do not quit. Stand up, seek forgiveness, and get back on the freedom trail.

PRAY: My wonderful Savior, Jesus, as hard as this is for me to fathom, Your Word says that as Your Father has loved You, so You love me! You love me so much that You want me to remain in Your love. If I obey Your commands, I will remain in Your love, just as You have obeyed Your Father's commands and remain in His love. You told me this so that Your joy may be in me and that my joy may be complete (John 15:9-11). I want that complete joy free from sin! O, God, please help me to live obediently and have the joy of seeing You revealed in all sorts of marvelous ways. Lord God, I praise You and thank You for not treating me as my sins deserve. For as high as the heavens are above the earth, so great is Your love for those who fear You; as far as the east is from the west, so far have You removed my transgressions from me (Ps. 103:10-12). Set me free to new life in You, Lord. I do not have to be a prisoner to sin. Please help me to surrender my heart and mind to You and Your truth.

DAY 4: *Seeking Truth*

When we are challenged to repent of cherished sin, all God is waiting for us to do is invite Him to change our hearts and bring about the supernatural work of true repentance. He is looking for our willingness to let go of the sin, both physically and emotionally. God will not let the issue rest until repentance takes up full residency in the heart. Why? Because until the heart change comes, we will continue to be at an overwhelming risk of returning to sinful actions.

PRAY: Lord God, if I claim to be without sin, I deceive myself, and the truth is not in me. If I confess my sins, You are faithful and just and will forgive my sins and purify me from all unrighteousness. (1 John 1:8-9) Help me, Lord! I need Your truth in me! Lord, I confess that I have been living in the flesh, and therefore, ignoring You. Lord, I want to be pleasing to You. (Rom. 8:7-8) Father, please help me to accept the fact that I have not outsinned Your ability to forgive me! I am still forgivable as I come to You in sincere repentance. Lord God, cause my heart, soul, and mind to be so overtaken by Your grace that I share the testimony of the sinful woman who anointed Your feet. You said of her, "I tell you, her many sins have been forgiven—for she loved much. But he who has been forgiven little loves little." (Luke 7:47) Lord Jesus, make our story a love story.

DAY 5: *Renewed Focus*

God desires to renew our thinking and change our habits. It's a process that takes time. God is not expecting totally unblemished earthly perfection. His Son alone filled that requirement. He is looking for hearts in constant pursuit of Him and His righteousness.

PRAY: O Lord, You have searched me and You know me. You know when I sit and when I rise; You perceive my thoughts from afar. You discern my going out and my lying down; You are familiar with all my ways. Even before I speak, Lord, You know what I am going to say. Where can I go to escape Your Spirit? Whether I am focused on You or the Devil himself, Lord You are there (Ps. 139:1-4,7-8). Father, I thank You that while You love me completely, You know everything about me. Help me to be completely truthful with You. I don't need to hide anymore. This then is how I know that I belong to the truth, and how I set my heart at rest in Your presence whenever my heart condemns me. For You, God, are greater than my heart, and You know everything. Lord, help me to abide in You by keeping Your commands (1 John 3:19-20,24). God, help me to move beyond all my past failures to focus on pressing forward with You now. Lord, no matter what kind of sufferings my decisions have caused me, I thank You that my present sufferings are not worth comparing with the glory that will be revealed in me (Rom. 8:18).

DAY 6: *Soul Ties*

Sexual engagement forms a soul tie that was meant for marriage alone. Scripture tells us that when we engage in any realm of sexual intimacy with someone besides our marriage partner, we are tying ourselves to them. It can form a soul tie that is absolutely out of the will of God and must be renounced severely so we can reclaim such surrendered ground. A soul tie to anyone besides our spouse is outside the will of God and becomes an open target for the continuing, destroying schemes of the Devil. Someone who has had many sexual partners may be thinking, I don't have soul ties to any of them. I don't give them a second thought. Please understand that you may be in one of the most binding sexual strongholds of all because you have completely segregated your emotions. You are being terribly but successfully deceived.

PRAY: Lord God, I acknowledge to You that my body was not meant for sexual immorality, but for You, Lord. You were meant to take authority over this body and bring it sanctification and meaning. I know that my body is a member of Christ, Himself. I shall not then take the members of Christ and unite them in an ungodly relationship (1 Cor. 6:13-15). I have been foolish, disobedient, deceived, and enslaved by all kinds of passions and pleasures (Titus 3:3). I acknowledge the misery of living outside of You, Lord. Father, I thank You in advance that I am going to be set free from this sin and I can become a slave to You, reaping glorious benefits that lead to holiness (Rom. 6:22).

DAY 7: *Sins Against the Body*

Satan knows that sexual sin is unique in its attack and overwhelming impact on the body of the individual believer. Since the Spirit of Christ dwells in the temple of believers' bodies, getting a Christian engaged in sexual sin is the closest Satan can come to personally assaulting Christ. That ought to make us mad enough to be determined to live victoriously. Sins against the body also have a way of sticking to us and making us feel like we are that sin rather than the fact that we've committed that sin.

PRAY: Lord, help me to flee from sexual immorality. I long to escape sinning against my own body. Help me to truly embrace the fact that my body is a temple of the Holy Spirit, who is in me, whom I have received from You. I am not my own (1 Cor. 6:19). Thank You, Father! I am so much better off belonging to You than belonging to myself! Father, You found my life worth buying at a tremendously high price. Therefore I desire to honor You, God, with my body (1 Cor. 6:18-20). Lord, cause Your glory to fill this temple of God like You did in the days of old (2 Chron. 5:14).

DAY 8: *Stop Doing Wrong*

Ceasing outward behavior is a huge step in the right direction, but we can't stop there. Isaiah 1:16-17 says, "Stop doing wrong, learn to do right." In other words, God's Word tells us to follow up the cessation of sinful actions by learning how to live righteously. Our strongholds are certainly not limited to external behaviors; in fact, our unhealthy actions are simply more obvious indicators of an internal problem.

PRAY: Lord God, I desire to bow down to You in worship. I want to kneel before the Lord my Maker; for You are my God, and I am among the sheep of Your pasture, the flock under Your care (Ps. 95:6-7). When I said, "My foot is slipping," Your love, O Lord, supported me! When anxiety was great within me, Your consolation brought joy to my soul (Ps. 94:18-19). Even if I cry out in distress evening, morning, and noon, You will never fail to hear my voice (Ps. 55:6-17). O Lord, because You are my help, I sing in the shadow of Your wings. My soul clings to You; Your right hand upholds me (Ps. 63:7-8). Lord, I acknowledge to You that I have been led astray. However, today and everyday, Jesus, help me to reach for You and cling to You alone. Change me from the inside out.

DAY 9: *A New Beginning*

PRAY: You, God, created my inmost being; You knit me together in my mother's womb. I praise You because I am fearfully and wonderfully made; Your works are wonderful. I know that full well. You saw me when I didn't yet have form, Lord. You planned out my days before I was born (Ps. 139:13-14,16). Lord, help me to remember that You have so much more planned for me. Father, my body is not horrible. I have simply misused it. Please sanctify it and take it over completely. Help me to draw near to You, God, with a sincere heart in full assurance of faith, having my heart sprinkled to cleanse me from a guilty conscience and having my body washed with pure water. Help me to hold unswervingly to the hope I profess, for He who promises is faithful (Heb. 10:21-23). Lord, even if I were the very worst of sinners as sometimes I feel I am, You still forgive and are willing to use those who put their trust in You! Thank You, God!

DAY 10: *Turning to God*

PRAY: Father, according to Your Word, a person can be handed over to Satan, so that the sinful nature may be destroyed and her spirit saved on the day of the Lord (1 Cor. 5:5). O, God, please help me not to continue to resist repentance and be handed over to Satan for a season. Please help me to turn my life over to You now. Lord, I long to be one with Your Spirit again. Dear God, no matter what I once was, I have been washed, I have been sanctified, and I have been justified in the name of the Lord Jesus Christ and by the Spirit of our God (1 Cor. 6:11). O Christ, cause Your love to absolutely compel me to do what is right in this challenging situation. Help me to be convinced that because One died for all, therefore all died. Help me to realize and fully appreciate the fact that because You died for all, we who live should no longer live for ourselves but for You who died for us and was raised again (2 Cor. 5:14-15). Please don't let me miss the joy and fulfillment of living my life for You. Please don't let my own mistakes stand in the way of fulfilling Your plan for my life.

DAY 11: *Taking Responsibility*

All we have to do to remain bound in any area is to refuse to take responsibility for our strongholds and repent of the sin involved. Friend, you wouldn't be holding this book in your hands if you didn't have enough humility to admit to the threat of a stronghold or two.

PRAY: O Christ, cause Your love to absolutely compel me. Help me to realize and fully appreciate the fact that because You died for all, we who live should no longer live for ourselves but for You who died for us and was raised again (2 Cor. 5:14-15). Please don't let me miss the joy and fulfillment of living my life for You. Please don't let my own stubbornness of heart stand in the way of fulfilling Your plan for my life. Lord God, help me to see that the "good" You want me to do in response to my sin is to repent and receive Your help and turn my life entirely over to You. I do not have to settle for a life hopelessly entangled in sin. Set me free, Lord. You demonstrated Your love for me in that while I was still a sinner, You died for me (Rom. 5:8).

DAY 12: *Deliver Me, Lord*

PRAY: Father, this process of breaking free is hard work! Please remind me often that it is also a very good work. Help me to know without a doubt that any effort You require of me will have effect. Please help me never to give up, no matter how long it takes. Lord, I admit that I reaped absolutely no benefit from the things I am now ashamed of. Those things result in death. But now that I have been set free, the benefit I am reaping leads to holiness and the result is eternal life. Lord God, I desire to claim the words Moses delivered to Your ancient people: Help me not to be afraid. Enable me to stand firm so I will see the deliverance that You, the Lord, will bring me today. You, Lord, will fight for me; help me only to be still (Exod. 14:13-14). Father God, make me strong and courageous. Help me not to be afraid or terrified because of anyone else or because of anything I've done in the past. You, the Lord my God, go with me; You will never leave me or forsake me (Deut. 31:6). Lord, how I thank you for the assurance that You will not reject Your people; You will never forsake Your inheritance (Ps. 94:14).

DAY 13: *From Darkness to Light*

PRAY: Lord God, I was once darkness, but now I am light in You. Help me to live now as a child of light for the fruit of the light consists in all goodness, righteousness, and truth. Help me to see You and find out what pleases You (Eph. 5:8-10). Lord, I remember the height from which I have fallen. Father, when I sin against You and choose to walk in deception rather than truth, please send others to gently instruct and confront me. Grant me repentance leading me to knowledge of the truth (2 Tim. 2:25). Father God, continue to teach me. Help me to recognize what is in accordance with the truth that is in Jesus (Eph. 4:21). O Merciful Father, please help me never to exchange the truth of God for a lie (Rom. 1:25). If any area remains in my life where I have made such a tragic exchange, reveal it and set me free.

DAY 14: *Cleanse My Body*

PRAY: Lord, I willingly admit that I am weak in my natural self. I used to offer the parts of my body in slavery to impurity and to ever-increasing wickedness. I now offer them in slavery to righteousness leading to holiness (Rom. 6:19). Christ Jesus, I count myself dead to sin but alive to God in You. Therefore I will not let sin reign in my mortal body so that I obey its evil desires. I choose not to offer the parts of my body to sin, as instruments of wickedness, but rather I offer myself to God, as one who has been brought from death to life. I offer the parts of my body to You as instruments of righteousness. Sin shall not be my master, because I am not under the law but under grace (Rom. 6:11-14). Lord God, help me draw near to You with a sincere heart in full assurance of faith, having my heart sprinkled to cleanse me from a guilty conscience and having my body washed with pure water (Heb. 10:22). Father, I thank You that You've had mercy on me according to Your unfailing love; according to Your great compassion You blot out my transgressions. You can wash away all my iniquity and cleanse me from my sin ... You can create in me a pure heart, O God, and renew a steadfast spirit within me. (Ps. 51:1,2,10)

DAY 15: *Holy Refuge*

Remember, friend: Long-term victory results from many short-term victories that finally collide, forming new habits.

PRAY: Father God, according to Your Word, if I'm really going to be one of Your disciples, I must hold to Your teaching. Then I will know the truth, and the truth will set me free (John 8:31-32). Help me to see the vital link between Your truth and my liberty. Father God, help me, enable me, strengthen me to put to death whatever belongs to my earthly nature: sexual immorality, impurity, lust, evil desires and greed, which is idolatry. Teach me Your way, O Lord, and I will walk in Your truth; give me an undivided heart, that I may fear Your name (Ps. 86:11). Redeem me, O Lord, the God of truth (Ps. 31:5). Help me to remember that nothing and no one can be redeemed without truth: The God of truth! Do not withhold Your mercy from me, O Lord; may Your love and Your truth always protect me (Ps. 40:11). Father, please help me learn how much Your truth protects me. Without it, I am vulnerable to the enemy and to my own flesh. O God, send forth Your light and Your truth to my life. Let them guide me; let them bring me to Your holy mountain, to the place where You dwell (Ps. 43:3).

DAY 16: *Pure Obedience*

In 2 Corinthians 11:2-3, the apostle Paul expressed the heart of God in his desire that the Church be presented to Christ as a "pure virgin to Him." He went on to say, "But I am afraid that just as Eve was deceived by the serpent's cunning, your minds may somehow be led astray from your sincere and pure devotion to Christ." What better way to get to people who are supposed to be presented as pure virgins to Christ?

PRAY: Father, this moment I am choosing the way of truth. I want to set my heart on Your laws (Ps. 119:30). Help me to choose the way of truth the rest of my days. Please help me always to be aware that the enemy will be up to his old tricks. Even the devout believer can be led astray if not held continually on the path by Your Word and keenly aware of Satan's schemes. Help me not to be deceived by the serpent's cunning. Father God, You have adamantly warned Your children not to be deceived (James 1:16). Am I presently being deceived in any way? If I am, please reveal it to me and give me the courage to cease cooperating with deceptive schemes. Help me to live in pure obedience to You, full of grace and truth.

DAY 17: *Set Apart*

Only in Christ Jesus, our Merciful Redeemer and Blessed Hope, can we regain our virginity. No, not physically, but emotionally, mentally, and spiritually. We can also allow Him to set apart these bodies that He has chosen to be the temple of His Holy Spirit henceforth to be sanctified, clean vessels. Not only is this possible, this is God's will!

PRAY: Lord God, You have promised me to one husband, Jesus Christ, and You want to present me as a pure virgin to Him. Please remake me into a pure virgin emotionally, mentally, and spiritually, and even set this body apart to be used as an instrument of righteousness from now on. Please help me not to be deceived by the serpent's cunning and allow my mind to be led astray from my new commitment of sincere and pure devotion to Christ (2 Cor. 11:2-3). Thank You, God, for promising that no temptation has seized me except what is common to man. And You, God, are faithful; You will not let me be tempted beyond what I can bear. But when I am tempted You will also provide a way out so that I can stand up under it (1 Cor. 10:13).

DAY 18: *Set Free*

Many men and women are engaged in binding, nonsexual affairs. The cure takes place in the inmost places of the heart and mind. More than anything, the key to deliverance is not just being delivered from but being delivered to. The reason we keep going back to our old strongholds is that we have temporarily been delivered from the sin practice, but we did not follow through with deliverance straight to the healthy heart of God.

PRAY: God, please don't give me over in the sinful desires of my heart to sexual impurity for the degrading of my body with someone else. I admit that I have exchanged the truth of You, God, for a lie (Rom. 1:24-25). Lord, Your Word is clear: wickedness suppresses truth (Rom. 1:18). Father God, when I've offered myself to sexual sin, I have offered myself as a slave to it. I am a slave to the one whom I obey whether I am a slave to sin, which leads to death, or to obedience, which leads to righteousness (Rom. 6:16). Thanks be to You, my God, that, though I used to be a slave to sin, I am wholeheartedly choosing to obey the form of teaching to which I was entrusted. I am being set free from sin and am becoming a slave to righteousness (Rom. 6:17-19).

DAY 19: *Loving Discipline*

The believer in Christ always has hope for recovery, but God means for hope to become a vivid reality through complete restoration. We must repent wholeheartedly, receive the Lord's loving discipline, and cooperate fully with His plan for recovery. The process can be hard, painful, and somewhat lengthy because we have to allow God to remove all the broken remnants of the ties to the ungodly relationship and fill in the holes with His loving Spirit until we are smooth and whole. No matter how hard, the resulting freedom will be worth it.

PRAY: According to Your Word, a man's ways are in full view of the Lord, and You examine all our paths. The evil deeds of a wicked man ensnare him; the cord of his sin holds him fast. He will die for a lack of discipline, led astray by his own great folly (Prov. 5:21-23). You are the Lord my God, who brought me out of slavery; You broke the bars of my yoke and enabled me to walk with my head held high (Lev. 26:13). How I thank You for this, O Lord. Help me to keep my eyes looking straight ahead and fix my gaze directly before me. Make level paths for my feet and strengthen me to take only the ways that are firm. Help me not to swerve to the right or the left; keep my feet from evil (Prov. 4:25-27). Lord, self-discipline is a fruit of the Spirit. Please fill me with Your Spirit and empower me with a self-discipline only You can give (Gal. 5:22-23). God, thank You for discipling me for my good, that I may share in Your holiness (Heb. 12:10).

DAY 20: *Guarding Against Adultery*

Not only are extramarital affairs rampant, but couples who are physically monogamous may be far from emotionally and mentally monogamous. Christ blew the door off marriage as an assumed impenetrable fortress against sexual immorality with Matthew 5:27: "You have heard that it was said, 'Do not commit adultery.' But I tell you that anyone who looks at a woman lustfully has already committed adultery with her in his heart." Alarming numbers of believing couples have unhealthy marriages because sexual perversion and pornography entered the home under the guise of "spicing things up." God can spice things up. And His choice of spice brings edification, healing, and the kind of romance that lasts. When a marriage is wholeheartedly surrendered to Jesus Christ's authority by both a husband and a wife, sooner or later, that marriage is going to spice up! If you think God is stuffy, you might want to take another look at the Song of Songs!

PRAY: Lord God, Your Word says that You bless the home of the righteous but Your curse is on the house of the wicked (Prov. 3:33). Lord, please help me cleanse my home of any kind of materials that support or fuel wickedness. Make this the kind of home You can fully bless. Lord, You detest perversity, but You take the upright into Your confidence (Prov. 3:32). Please make me a person You can take into Your confidence.

DAY 21: *Restoration*

God deeply desires for us to grant Him total access to set apart every single part of our lives—body, soul, and spirit—to His glorious work. Yet, Satan desires to undermine the sanctifying work of Christ. He knows that all believers have been "set apart" from the unclean to the clean, and from the unholy to the holy. He also knows that when believers act like the sanctified people they are, God is released to do powerful wonders among them (Josh. 3:5).

PRAY: Father God, Your Word says that I have been made holy through the sacrifice of the body of Jesus Christ. Being holy means that I have been set apart for sacred use rather than common use. I will be tempted at times to think like the unholy person I used to be (Heb. 10:10). Keep me on track. Help me not to call anything impure that You have made clean (Acts 10:15). Lord, who can say, "I have kept my heart pure; I am clean and without sin"? (Prov. 20:9). Lord, I am powerless to possess a pure and clean heart on my own. Only You can do it for me. Create in me a pure heart, O God, and renew a steadfast spirit within me. . . . Restore to me the joy of Your salvation and grant me a willing spirit to sustain me (Ps. 51:10,12).

DAY 22: *Living Out Godly Faith*

PRAY: Lord God, since I have a great high priest who has gone through the heavens, Jesus Your Son, help me hold firmly to the faith I profess. For I do not have a high priest who is unable to sympathize with my weaknesses, but I have one who has been tempted in every way, just as I am, yet was without sin. Help me then to approach the throne of grace with confidence, so that I may receive mercy and find grace to help me in my time of need (Heb. 4:14-16). My justification is found in Your Son and my Savior, Jesus Christ (Rom. 8:30). He is faithful even when I am not (2 Tim. 2:13). Thank You, Father, that I can be absolutely sure You will never leave me or forsake me because I am in Jesus (Heb. 13:5). Father God, through constant use of the solid food of Your Word, help me to train myself to distinguish good from evil (Heb. 5:14).

DAY 23: *Guarding My Heart*

PRAY: Lord, I have come to understand that my heart is deceitful above all things (Jer. 17:9). Please help me recognize ways my heart and my feelings are deceiving me. Lord God, help me to guard my heart above all else, for it is the wellspring of life. Help me to put away perversity from my mouth and keep corrupt talk far from my lips (Prov. 4:23-24). My merciful God, since I have been raised with Christ, set my heart on things above, where Christ is seated at the right hand of God. Help me set my mind on things above, not on earthly things (Col. 3:1). Lord, please take my passions and redirect them first and foremost toward You. Be the chief focus of all my passions and create a new heart within me with healthy emotions. Dear Jesus, You told Your close followers, who were taught how to seek the Father's heart, that whatever they asked for in prayer they were to believe they received it and it would be theirs (Mark 11:24). O, Father, help me to know Your heart intimately so that I'll know how to pray, what to pray, and believe in advance that I will receive it!

DAY 24: *A Renewed Mind*

PRAY: God, please help me to love You with my whole heart, soul, mind, and strength, for this is Your priority for my life (Mark 12:30). Help me also to love others so that I will not want to engage them in any kind of dishonoring activity (Mark 12:31). Lord, I ask You now to let Your peace, God, which transcends all understanding, guard my heart and my mind in Christ Jesus (Phil. 4:7). Break my heart when I even think of doing what is dishonorable, Lord. Jesus, whatever is true, whatever is noble, whatever is right, whatever is pure, whatever is lovely, whatever is admirable—if anything is excellent or praiseworthy—help me to think about such things (Phil. 4:8-9). When Your words come to me, help me to eat them; make them my joy and my heart's delight, for I bear Your name, O Lord God Almighty (Jer. 15:16). Increase my appetite for Your Word, my Sufficiency! Lord, please help me not to merely listen to the Word, and so deceive myself. Please help me to do what it says (James 1:22). Your Word works, but if I am to experience it personally, I must be obedient. I need Your help, Lord. Above all else, help me to love You, the Lord my God, with all my heart and with all my soul and with all my strength (Deut. 6:5).

DAY 25: *Merciful Healing*

PRAY: Lord, help me to rid myself of all malice and all deceit, hypocrisy, envy, and slander of every kind. Like a newborn baby, help me to crave pure spiritual milk, so that by it I may grow up in my salvation, now that I have tasted that the Lord is good (1 Pet. 2:1-2). For I am one of Your chosen people, O God, part of a royal priesthood, a holy nation, a people belonging to God, that I may declare the praises of You who called me out of darkness into Your wonderful light. I have now received mercy. You urge me as a stranger in this world to abstain from sinful desires, which war against my soul (1 Pet. 2:9-11). Lord Jesus, You Yourself bore my sins in Your body on the tree, so that I might die to sins and live for righteousness; by Your wounds I have been healed. For I was like a sheep going astray, but now I have returned to the Shepherd and Overseer of my soul (1 Pet. 2:24-25). Because of Your great love for me, You, God, who are rich in mercy, made me alive with Christ even when I was dead in transgressions—it is by Your grace that I have been saved (Eph. 2:4-5). Father God, how great is the love You have lavished on me, that I should be called a child of God! And that is what I am! (1 John 3:1).

DAY 26: *Pursuing Righteousness*

PRAY: Lord, Your Word says how I can keep my way pure: by living according to Your Word. I will seek You with all my heart; help me not to stray from Your commands. Help me to hide Your Word in my heart that I might not sin against You (Ps. 119:9-11). Because I know Your name, Lord, I will trust in You, for You, Lord, have never forsaken those who seek You (Ps. 9:10). Holy God, turn my eyes away from worthless things; preserve my life according to Your Word. Take away the disgrace I dread, for Your laws are good (Ps. 119:37,39). Lord God, teach me knowledge and good judgment, for I believe in Your commands. Before I was afflicted I went astray, but now I obey Your Word. You are good, and what You do is good; teach me Your decrees (Ps. 119:66-68). Lord God, guard my course and protect my way as I pursue a righteous, victorious life in You (Prov. 2:8). Lord, help me not to despise Your discipline and not to resent Your rebuke, because You discipline those You love (Prov. 3:11-12). Glorious God, how I celebrate the fact that my eyes have never seen, my ears have never heard, and my mind has never conceived what You have prepared for me and all others who truly love You.